미술로, 세계로
TO THE WORLD THROUGH ART

MMCA 국제미술 소장품 기획전 《미술로, 세계로》
2022. 1. 20. – 2022. 6. 12.
국립현대미술관 청주 기획전시실

Highlights of MMCA Global Art Collection from the 1980s–1990s: To the World through Art
January 20 – June 12, 2022
MMCA Cheongju Special Exhibition Gallery

관장
윤범모

학예연구실장
김준기

미술품수장센터운영과장
임대근

학예연구관
김경운

전시기획
이효진

전시보조
허동희

전시운영
장수경

그래픽디자인
1-2-3-4-5, 박현진

전시조성
이지혜

교육
이승린, 박소현

홍보
정원채, 진승민, 홍보고객과

고객지원
연상흠, 이소연

행정지원
미술품수장센터관리팀

작품출납
권성오, 김진숙

보존수복
권희홍, 김미나, 김영목, 김태휘, 김해빛나, 신정아,
차순민, 최남선, 한예빈

공간디자인
스튜디오 프래그먼트

조성공사
화성 테크윈

운송설치
솔로몬아트

영상설치
올미디어

사진
이현무

영상
차동훈, 강지영, 엽태준, 정지웅

도움을 주신 분들
(사)현대미술관회, 소마미술관, KBS 미디어, 경향신문,
동아일보, 매일경제, 조선일보, 강윤주, 김유진, 김익환,
김효영, 류지연, 명이식, 문정숙, 임히주, 이소영, 이영주,
최현아, 팽미화, 황지영, 황채금

Director
Youn Bummo

Chief Curator
Gim Jungi

Head of Curatorial Department
of National Art Storage Center
Lim Dae-geun

Senior Curator
Kim Kyoungwoon

Curator
Lee Hyojin

Curatorial Assistant
Huh Donghee

Technical Coordination
Jang Soogyeong

Graphic Design
1-2-3-4-5, Park Hyunjin

Space Construction
Lee Jihye

Education
Lee Seungrin, Park Sohyeon

Public Relations
Jung Wonchae, Jin Seungmin,
Communications and Audience
Department

Customer Service
Yeon Sang-heum, Lee Soyeon

Administrative Support
MMCA Cheongju Administration Team

Collection Management
Kwon Sungoh, Kim Jinsook

Conservation
Kwon Heehong, Kim Mina, Kim Youngmok,
Kim Taehwi, Kim Haebichna, Shin Jeongah, Cha Sunmin,
Choi Namseon, Han Yebin

Space Design
Studio Fragment

Space Construction
Hwa Sung Techwin

Shipping and Installation
Solomon Art

Equipment Installation
All-Media

Photography
Lee Hyunmoo

Film
Cha Donghoon, Kang Jiyoung, Yeop Taejoon,
Jeong Jiwoong

Special thanks to
Membership Society for MMCA, SOMA (Seoul Olympic
Museum of Art), KBS Media, Kyunghyang Shinmun,
Donga Ilbo, Maeil Business Newspaper, Chosun Ilbo,
Kang Yoonju, Kim Yoojin, Kim Ikhwan, Kim Hyoyoung,
Liu Jienne, Myeong Yishik, Moon Jungsook, Limb
Hijoo, Lee Soyoung, Lee Youngjoo, Choi Hyuna, Paeng
Mihwa, Hwang Jiyoung, Hwang Chaegeum

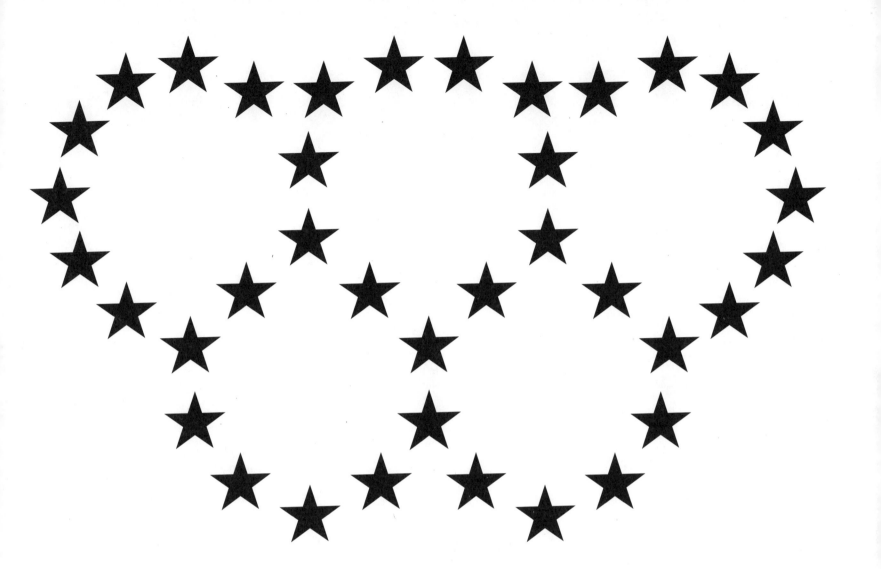

Highlights of MMCA Global Art Collection from the 1980s–1990s:
To the World through Art

* This book is a catalog of *To the World through Art*, the exhibition for MMCA Global Art Collection
  curated by MMCA, Cheongju.
* In this catalog, English name of National Museum of Modern and Contemporary Art,
  Korea is marked 'MMCA', the abbreviation for it.
* The titles of artworks and archives included in this catalog follow the publishing guidelines of MMCA.
* For newspaper articles, the notation of the original text was followed.
* We did not find copyright holders for some artworks. As soon as the copyright holder is confirmed,
  we will go through the formal consent confirmation process.

MMCA 국제미술 소장품 기획전
《미술로, 세계로》

일러두기
* 이 책은 국립현대미술관 청주에서 개최하는 국제미술 소장품 기획전 《미술로, 세계로》의 전시 도록입니다.
* 이 도록에서 국립현대미술관의 영문 명칭은 MMCA(National Museum of Modern and Contemporay Art)로 표기했습니다.
* 본 책자에 수록된 작품과 자료의 명제는 국립현대미술관의 표기법을 따랐습니다.
* 신문 기사의 경우, 원문의 표기법을 따랐습니다.
* 이 책의 일부 작품은 저작권자를 찾지 못했습니다. 저작권자가 확인되는 대로 정식 동의 확인 절차를 밟겠습니다.

Highlights of MMCA Global Art Collection from the 1980s–1990s: To the World through Art

Youn Bummo
Director, National Museum of Modern and Contemporay Art, Korea

MMCA has collected 8,785 pieces of artwork from its opening until 2020. Among them, 925 works are in the international art collection; however, they have received relatively little attention as research subjects. *Highlights of MMCA Global Art Collection from the 1980s–1990s: To the World through Art* is dedicated to examining the background and opportunity of collecting international art and reminding the significance and their value in the context of art history.

This exhibition focuses on MMCA's international art collection from 1978 to 2000 and shows its development from the 1980s to the 1990s. As the intercontinental tension of the Cold War was unwinding, hopes for the developing information and communication technology to connect the world as one grew stronger. South Korea, in particular, aspired to strengthen its national competitiveness by hosting the 1988 Summer Olympics Games in Seoul. Regardless of public or private sectors, there was a growing interest in globalizing all aspects of the country, and its art scene was no exception. In 1986, the MMCA completed a new building in Gwacheon. In 1988, South Korea successfully hosted the Summer Olympics. As a result, entering the global art scene grew more robust while the inflow of art from other countries began to expand in various ways. It is notable that the number of international artworks collected during this period was 668 in total, which is double the size of its collection over the next 20 years. Moreover, the donation of 101 pieces of sculpture and painting after *Olympiad of the Art*, a satellite event for the 1988 Summer Olympics, served as a momentum to MMCA's building of international art collection. Until the early 1980s, the collections had no choice but to rely on donations from a number of patrons or visiting artists from other countries.

Nevertheless, amid the growing trend of globalization in the 1990s, MMCA actively began to take part in global exchanges. As a result, the museum had collected artworks by internationally renowned artists from other countries with increased budgets.

This exhibition showcases 104 pieces of sculpture, painting, print, and drawing by 96 artists from Americas, Europe, Asia, Africa, and Oceania that had not been on public display for a long time, including Robert Rauschenberg, A.R. Penck, Claude Viallat. We hope that the exhibition will serve as a foundation for rediscovery and further research of the international art collection of MMCA. Furthermore, it will be a starting point for in-depth, interdisciplinary research that approaches the collection from not only a regional and periodical perspective but also a political and economic one.

We want to express our profound gratitude to the cooperating organizations, media companies, and researchers for their contribution in *Highlights of MMCA Global Art Collection from the 1980s–1990s: To the World through Art* and each of our museum members' efforts to realize this exhibition.

국립현대미술관 국제미술 소장품 기획전
《미술로, 세계로》를 열면서

윤범모
국립현대미술관 관장

국립현대미술관은 개관 이래 2020년까지 8,785점의 소장품을 수집했습니다. 이 가운데 국제미술 소장품은 925점으로 한국 근현대미술 작품과 비교하여 상대적으로 조사연구의 대상으로 덜 주목받아온 것이 사실입니다. 이러한 상황에서 이번에 개최하는 《미술로, 세계로》전시는 국제미술 소장품의 수집 배경과 계기를 살피고, 그 미술사적 의의와 가치를 환기시키게 하여 의의가 새롭습니다.

전시는 해외미술품 수집의 시점인 1978년부터 2000년까지, 1980-90년대에 수집된 국제미술 소장품의 수집활동과 전개에 초점을 맞췄습니다. 당시 세계는 20세기 전반의 동서 냉전시대가 끝나고, 정보통신과 교통기술의 발달로 자유로운 이동과 통합을 통해 전세계가 하나로 연결될 것이라는 기대에 차 있었습니다. 특히 우리나라는 제24회 서울 올림픽 개최지로 선정된 이후, 민관 구분 없이 국가경쟁력 강화를 향한 열망으로 휩싸였고, 사회 전반에 걸친 '국제화' 분위기가 고조되었습니다. 미술계 또한 예외가 아니어서 한국미술의 해외진출에 대한 관심이 뜨거워지는 한편, 1986년 국립현대미술관 과천 신축과 88 서울 올림픽을 기점으로 해외미술의 국내 유입도 보다 다양화되기 시작했습니다. 이 시기 수집된 국제미술 소장품은 668점으로, 이후 20년간 수집된 작품 수의 2배가 넘는 양을 차지하는 것도 특기할 만합니다. 더구나 올림픽 부대행사였던 세계현대미술제(서울올림픽 조직위원회 주최)를 통해 101점의 조각과 회화를 기증받은 것은 국제미술 소장품 수집의 획기적인 계기가 되었습니다.

1980년대 초까지 국립현대미술관의 국제미술 소장품은 한국을 방문한 소수의 해외미술 작가나 일부 미술계 인사의 기증에 의존할 수밖에 없었습니다. 그러나 1990년대의 '세계화' 기류 속에서 소장품 구입예산 증액과 적극적인 교류를 통해 국제적 명성의 해외작가 작품을 적극적으로 수집할 수 있었습니다.

이번 전시는 미주, 유럽, 아시아, 아프리카, 오세아니아 등 세계 전역을 아우르는 해외 작가 96명의 조각, 회화, 판화, 드로잉 등 104점을 선보입니다. 전시를 통해 로버트 라우센버그(Robert Rauschenberg), A. R. 펭크(A. R. Penck), 클로드 비알라(Claude Viallat) 등 장기간 공개되지 않았던 다수의 국제미술 소장품을 소개하고, 미술사적 연구가치를 환기하며, 이후 국제미술 소장품의 심화 연구를 위한 밑거름을 마련하고자 했습니다. 이 전시를 시작으로 국립현대미술관 국제미술 소장품에 대한 지역·시대별 연구뿐만 아니라 사회문화와 정치외교, 경제 등 다학문적 접근을 통한 심도 있는 연구가 실천될 수 있기를 희망합니다.

《미술로, 세계로》를 위해 도움을 주신 협력기관과 언론사, 연구자들께 깊은 감사를 드리며, 아울러 전시의 진행과 마무리를 위해 힘써준 미술관 가족들에게도 고마움을 전합니다.

To the World Through Art: the First Step in the Global Art Collection of MMCA

Curatorial Essay

Lee Hyojin
Curator, National Museum of Modern and Contemporay Art, Korea

1. The number of collections is 10,919, including 2,134 pieces from the Lee Kun-hee Collection, received in 2021. As this count was released very recently, the number of additions was not included in the data used for this exhibition. In the case of international art collections, it is continuously in the process of checking the status of artists to confirm if the nationality of the artist is unclear or has changed, as well as the Korean artists with foreign nationality.

2. Choi Noh-suk, "The National Museum of Modern and Contemporary Art where has nothing to see," *Kyunghyang Shinmun*, March 28, 1979.

By 2020, the number of collections at MMCA reached 8,785. Among them, the number of works by foreign nationals, that is, the international art collection, is about 925 pieces, which account for a little more than one-tenth of the total collection.[1] As already mentioned in several previous studies, the MMCA was opened in 1969, while having no single piece of collection of its own, in accordance with the Ministry of Culture and Information's judgment that the Korean Art Exhibition needed a space to host. In 1973, as the MMCA moved from Gyeongbokgung Palace to the current location at Deoksugung Museum of Art, although it was in the form of contracted workers, curatorial experts were appointed and gradually began to take the form of an art museum rather than an administrative institution. However, the number of collections was only 291, and 132 pieces, the 45% of total were donated at the 10th anniversary of the MMCA's opening, As revealing the situation and problems of the museum, it showed that the 'donation' was a way fill in poor collections while comparing then-current status of art museums in overseas.[2] Fortunately, major artworks of Korean modern and contemporary art were discovered and steadily collected starting with the exhibition called *60 Years of Korean Modern Art* in 1972, but information on trends in the international art scene was still limited, and acquiring international art collections were too early for a discussion.

In the 1960s and 1970s, in a social atmosphere that wanted to overcome the wounds of war and to use it as a stepping stone for the national economy to take off by encouraging international exports, artists were also eager to promote Korean art abroad through participation in international art events such as the São Paulo Biennial and the Paris Youth Biennale. It was a time when the activeness of Korean artists in overseas also emerged as an action state leading the internationalization of Korean art. Since then, through government-led cultural events such as the opening of the MMCA in Gwacheon in 1986, the 1988 Seoul Olympics, and the 1-993 The Taejeon EXPO (International Exposition, Korea, 1993), President Kim Young-sam's declaration of globalization in 1994, 'globalization' had naturally been set as a common goal and value for the whole nation. While paying attention to the 'globalization' phenomenon that penetrated Korean society until the 1990s, this exhibition aimed to contain information that needs to be reminded or is newly discovered in the process of examining the context in which international artworks of the MMCA were collected.

1. Overseas Artists Visiting Korea

Belgian Contemporary Art Show, which was held at Deoksugung in 1952, even before the roar of the Korean War stopped, was the first international art exhibition held in Korea after the liberation. In fact, this exhibition was not planned to be in Korea, but it stopped by Korea on the way back from the exhibition in Tokyo. In addition, a Chinese-American watercolor artist Dongkingman's exhibition, which was held at the American Cultural Center in 1954 as Korea's first foreign artist's solo exhibition, led to his visit to Korea on his world tour with the help of the United States Department of State. This could be an example of what level and ways in international cultural exchange had to remain at the time in the process of reorganizing the domestic social order through the liberation and the Korean War. Subsequently, international art exhibitions introduced in Korea were part of cultural exchanges through governments' diplomatic agencies such as the USIS, the French Arts Exchange Association, Goethe-Institut (the German cultural institution), and UNESCO, or they were events hosted by media companies. Even in the 70s, when the MMCA opened, the aspect did not change much. Among the international art collections of the MMCA, the first work that could accurately identify the collecting route would be *Vacant Mountain* (p. 88) by Liu Ye Zhao, an American-Chinese painter. Richard Franklin and Adrienne Walker Hoard, collected one after another, were American artists who visited Korea through the Fulbright Scholarship Program and both worked as exchange professors at Seoul National University, Hongik University, and Ewha Womans University, respectively. During his two years as an exchange professor at Seoul National University since 1977, Richard Franklin was immersed in Korean customs and materials. He continued his research on techniques using bamboo and Hanji, the Korean paper; he held a solo exhibition at MMCA recapitulating his research and works. Adrienne Walker Hoard had participated in an exhibition of paintings and photographs at the Cultural Exchange Center of the US Embassy in Korea in 1981 under the title of *USA–Korean Impression*; she donated two of her exhibited works *Temple of Clouds* and *Garden of Jeju* (pp. 92–93). The solo exhibition of Filipino artist Manuel Baldemor, held at the Philippine Embassy in Korea and at the Greenhills Art Center in Manila in the same year, were also titled as *Korean Impressions*.

8

미술로, 세계로: 국립현대미술관 국제미술 소장품 수집의 첫걸음

이효진
국립현대미술관 학예연구사

1. 2021년 수증된 이건희컬렉션 2,134점까지 포함한 소장품 수가 10,919점이나, 최근에 집계된 자료여서, 이 전시에는 적용시키지 않았다. 국제미술 소장품의 경우, 작가의 국적이 불명확하거나 달라진 경우, 해외 국적의 한국 작가 등 그간의 변동 상황을 확인하는 작업이 지속적으로 진행 중이다.

2.「볼 작품 없는 국립현대미술관」,『경향신문』, 1979년 3월 28일 자.

로잡습니다.

효진,「미술로, 세계로: 국립현대미술관 제미술 소장품 수집의 첫걸음」

8, footnote 1.
e number of Collections is 10,919, luding 2,134 pieces from the Lee n-hee Collection, received in 2021 evision)
number of Collections is 10,919, luding 2,134 pieces received 2021

정)
현대미술관의 소장품 수는 919점으로, 이 글에서는 2021년 수집된 품 2,134점은 포함하지 않았다.

정)
7, 24줄
아운데 1990년《국제현대회화전》은 를 소재로 한

정)
아운데 1990년《서울국제미술제》는 를 소재로 한

2020년까지 수집된 국립현대미술관의 소장품 수가 8,785점에 달한다. 그 가운데 해외 국적의 작가 작품, 즉 국제미술 소장품은 약 925점으로 전체 소장품의 10분의 1이 조금 넘는 양이다.[1] 이미 앞선 여러 연구에서 언급했듯이 국립현대미술관은 1969년 대한민국미술 전람회의 전시장소가 필요하다는 문공부의 판단에 따라 단 한 점의 소장품도 없이 개관하였다. 1973년 국립현대미술관이 경복궁에서 덕수궁 석조전으로 옮겨가면서, 계약직 형태이긴 했지만 학예 전문위원이 위촉되고 차츰 행정기관이 아닌 미술관의 형태를 갖추기 시작한다. 그러나 개관10주년이었던 1979년 국립현대미술관 소장품의 수는 291점에 불과했는데 이마저도 전체작품의 45%인 132점이 기증작이었다. 국립미술관의 실태와 문제점을 밝히며, 해외미술관의 현황과 비교하며 부실한 소장품을 채울 수 있는 방안으로 독려했던 것이 '기증'이었다.[2] 다행히 한국 근현대미술은 1972년 《한국근대미술60년전》 전시를 시작으로 주요 미술품이 발굴되고 꾸준히 수집되었지만, 해외 미술의 동향에 대한 정보는 제한적일 수밖에 없었고 국제미술 소장품 수집에 대한 논의는 시기상조였다.

1960, 70년대, 전쟁의 상흔을 극복하고 해외수출을 장려하여 국가 경제 도약의 발판으로 삼고자하는 사회 분위기 속에서, 미술가들도 상파울루비엔날레, 파리청년비엔날레 등 국제미술행사 참여를 통해 한국미술을 해외에 널리 알리겠다는 열의에 차 있었다. 재외 작가들의 활동도 한국미술의 국제화를 이끄는 활약상으로 대두되던 시기였다. 이후 1986년 국립현대미술관 과천 개관, 1988년 서울 올림픽, 1993년 대전 EXPO(세계박람회) 등 정부 주도의 굵직굵직한 문화행사를 치르고, 1994년 김영삼 대통령의 세계화 선언('세계 중심 국가를 이루기 위한 발전 전략은 모든 부문의 세계화')에 이르기까지, '세계화'는 자연스럽게 온 국민의 공동의 목표이자 가치로 새겨졌다. 이 전시는 1990년대까지 우리 사회를 관통했던 '세계화' 현상에 주목하면서, 국립현대미술관 국제미술이 수집된 맥락을 살펴보는 과정에서 새롭게 발견하거나, 되새겨야할 정보들을 담고자 했다.

1. 한국을 방문한 해외미술

한국전쟁의 포성이 채 가시기도 전인 1952년, 덕수궁에서 열렸던《벨기에 현대미술》전은 해방 후 국내에서 이루어진 첫 해외미술 전시였다. 사실 이 전시는 한국 전시로 기획되었던 것이 아니라 도쿄 전시를 마치고 돌아가는 길에 한국에 들른 것이었다. 또한 1954년 국내 첫 해외작가 개인전으로 기록된 중국계 미국 수채화가 동킹만(董景文)의《수채화작품전》도 세계여행 중 한국 방문을 계기로 미국 국무성의 도움을 받아 열리게 되었다. 이는 해방과 한국전쟁을 거치고 국내 사회질서가 재편되는 과정에서의 당시 국제 문화교류가 어떤 수준과 방식에 머무를 수밖에 없었는지를 보여주는 예라고 할 수 있겠다. 뒤이어 국내에서 선보인 해외미술 전시도 미국공보원(USIS), 프랑스예술교류협회, 독일문화원, 유네스코 등 정부 외교기관이나 국제협력기구를 통한 문화교류의 일환이거나 언론사 주최의 이벤트적인 성격이 강했다. 국립현대미술관이 개관한 1970년대에도 양상은 크게 달라지지 않았다. 국립현대미술관 국제미술 소장품 가운데 수집 경로를 정확히 확인할 수 있는 첫 번째 작품은, 미국계 중국화가인 류예자오(Liu Ye Zhao, 1910-2003)의〈공산불견인(空山不見人)〉(88쪽)이다. 뒤이어 풀브라이트(Fulbright) 장학 프로그램을 통해 한국을 방문해 각각 서울대, 홍익대와 이화여대 미술대학에서 교환교수로 활동했던 리처드 프랭클린(Richard Franklin, 1939-)과 에이드리언 워커 호워드(Adrienne Walker Hoard, 1946-)의 작품이 기증되었다. 프랭클린은 1977년부터 2년간의 서울대 미대 교환교수 기간 동안 한국의 풍속과 소재에 심취해 대나무, 한지를 이용한 기법 연구를 지속해 왔으며, 국립현대미술관에서 그 연구와 작업성과를 종합한 개인전을 열었다. 에이드리언 워커 호워드는 1981년 주한 미국대사관 문화교류처에서《미국-한국의 인상(USA-Korean Impressions)》이라는 주제로 회화와 사진전시를 열고 출품작 두 점,〈구름의 전당〉과〈제주의 정원〉(92-93쪽)을 기증했다. 같은 해 주한 필리핀 대사관과 마닐라 그린힐스 아트센터에서 열린 필리핀 작가 마누엘 발데모어(Manuel Baldemor, 1947-)의 개인전 제목도《한국의 인상(Korean Impressions)》이다. 그가 개인전을 마치고 미술관에 기증한 작품〈새마을 운동〉(90쪽)은 비단에 채색하고 인장까지 찍어 전통 한국화 기법의 특징을 살리고자 한 작가의 의도를 보여준다. 가지런하게 정리된 농지와 농가주택들, 노랗게 익은 들판과 흥에 넘친 사람들의 일상이 희망에 찬 필치로 표현되어, 마치 1970년대 한창이었던 새마을 운동 선전 포스터의 한 장면을 보는 듯한 인상을 준다. 한편 1981년은 우리 경제가 제2차 석유파동(1979)과 5·18 광주민주화운동 등 정국혼란과 사회적 불안을 딛고 경제가 다시 회복세로 돌아선 해이기도 했다.

3. Lee Yongwoo, "What Kind of Works Will the Museum of Modern and Contemporary Art fill?," *Dong-A Ilbo*, April 16, 1983., Chung Joong Heon, "The Gwacheon Museum of Modern and Contemporary Art Lack of Budget 'Worried about the exhibition room without works'," *Chosun Ilbo*, November 15, 1984.

4. Chung Joong Heon, "*Museum of Modern and Contemporary Art, Unexpected Popularity*," *Chosun Ilbo*, November 26, 1986.

5. According to the records left in *Contemporary Art News* (1978–2000) published by the Membership Society of MMCA, from the late 1970s to right after the Olympic in Seoul, the key figures and artists from overseas such as Pontus Hultén, Pierre Restany, Arman, Tadao Ando, Anthony Caro, Barbara London, and others continued to visit.

6. Chung Joong Heon, "Korean Contemporary Art in America," *Chosun Ilbo*, July 25, 1981.

7. Membership Society for MMCA, *Contemporary Art News*, June 30, 1989.

8. Conversation with Yoo Jun-sang (art critic), written by Lee Ji-hee, *MMCA 1986: Opening of the Gwacheon Pavilion.*, Chung Joong Heon, "*Worrying about the lack of budget for the Gwacheon Museum of Modern and Contemporary Art, Exhibition Room Without Works*," *Chosun Ilbo*, November 15, 1984.

The piece called the *Saemaeul Undong (The New Village Movement*, p. 90), which he donated to the museum after the end of his solo exhibition, showed the artist's intention to follow of the characteristics of traditional Korean techniques by coloring silk and stamping. The daily lives in the neatly arranged farmland, farmhouses, ripen fields in yellow, and excited people were expressed in hopeful strokes, giving the impression of seeing a scene of the *Saemaul Undong* propaganda poster in the 1970s. Meanwhile, 1981 was also the year when the Korean economy recovered from political turmoil and social unrest, including the Second Oil Crisis (1979) and the May 18 Gwangju Democratization Movement. On September 30, 1981, Seoul was designated as the venue for the 1988 Summer Olympics at the 84th International Olympic Committee General Assembly (Baden-baden, West Germany), inspiring our society as a whole, followed by the announcement of a detailed plan to build the MMCA in Gwacheon. In addition to the exhibition of Henry Moore, which was held to commemorate the opening of Ho-Am Gallery in 1982, the MMCA also hosted exhibitions of foreign artists with various nationalities, such as France, England, Mexico, and Senegal. However, since most of the exhibitions were still co-hosted by newspapers, broadcasters, and foreign embassies in Korea, it did not lead to the chances of acquisitions to the museum's collection. Yet, it was meaningful that the international art collections collected in the early days by the MMCA stemmed from foreign artists' interest in 'Korean things.' The MMCA did not have a system to implement organized international exchanges, but having works as a result of foreign artists' interest and expression in Korea would have been a clue to understanding the early international art exchanges in the Korean art scene.

2. Art Communication and Exchange at the Global Level.

From the beginning of the construction of the MMCA, the lack of collections and curatorial professionals had been frequent subject matters for the people from in and outside the art community who concerned about the status of the only national museum of art. The attention gathered on the announcement of the new building in Gwacheon was actually half-excited and half-concerned. In particular, several newspapers rushed to cover articles on the concerns of what to fill the 4,390 pyeong (14,512.4m²) exhibition area of Gwacheon Hall, which was nearly six times larger than the 740 pyeong (2,446.28m²) exhibition area in Deoksugung.[3] What was repeatedly mentioned in these articles was the weak collection of international artists.

It was reasonable to guess how much the concern was as it was even offered to lend artworks to be exhibited at free of charge by government agencies and art organizations in the United States and Europe. In an interview three months after the opening of MMCA Gwacheon in 1986, Director Lee Kyungsung also expressed his ambition to focus on purchasing arts from overseas, lamenting the lack of collection of foreign artists' works, highlighting that the special international art exhibition would continue throughout the following year.[4] The reason why foreign personnel's visit was considered important, because it was intended to be an opportunity to expand the horizon of international art exhibitions and collections.[5] The representative example would be that the Brooklyn Museum of Art's curator Gene Baro, who visited the MMCA in April 1981, saw the exhibition *Korean Drawing '81* and decided to tour to hold the exhibition at the Brooklyn Museum of Art in New York in June.[6] Dr. Alexander Tolnay, former directer of the Villa Merkel, Stadtmuseum Esslingen Galerie (a municipal art museum in Esslingen, Germany), co-curated an exhibition *Zeitgenossische Deutsche Malerei (German Contemporary Paintings* held at the MMCA in May 1989 under the auspices of the German Embassy in Korea and Membership Society for MMCA. He visited the museum and donated three prints including Sigmar Polke's works.[7] According to Yoo Joon-sang, head of the curatorial department at the time, Andy Warhol's self-portrait (two pieces), Robert Rauschenberg, and Christo's works (p. 108), which would be the museum's representative international art collections acquired in 1987, were also purchased in New York at a lower price than originally proposed with a help of arrangement by Nam June Paik.[8] Paik co-organized an exhibition called *Beuys Vox* with Jung Ki-yong, representative of Gallery Won, to commemorate the relationship with Joseph Beuys after his sudden death of from a heart attack in 1986. Many of the works exhibited in this exhibition were donated to the museum by Jung of Gallery Won. This includes works to reflect on the autobiographical stories of the two artists, including *Cards of Beuys and Paik* (pp. 110–111), which contain Joseph Beuys's recoded performance smashing Paik's piano with an ax at Paik's first video-art exhibition *Exposition of Music — Electronic Television* (Parnass Gallery in Wuppertal, Germany) in 1963.

3. 이용우, 「현대미술관 어떤 작품으로 채우나」, 『동아일보』, 1983년 4월 16일 자, 정중헌, 「과천 현대미술관 예산 부족 '작품 없는 전시실 우려'」, 『조선일보』, 1984년 11월 15일 자.

4. 정중헌, 「현대미술관, 예상 밖 인기」, 『조선일보』, 1986년 11월 26일 자.

5. (사)현대미술관회에서 발행했던 『현대의 미술』(1978-2000)의 기록에 따르면, 1970년대 후반부터 서울 올림픽 직후까지 퐁투스 훌텐, 피에르 레스타니, 아르망, 안도 타다오, 안소니 카로, 바바라 런던 등 해외 미술계 주요인사 및 작가들의 방문이 끊이지 않았다.

6. 정중헌, 「미국서 선보이는 한국현대미술」, 『조선일보』, 1981년 7월 25일 자.

7. (사)현대미술관회, 『현대의 미술』, 1989년 6월 30일 자.

8. 유준상(미술평론가) 대담, 이지희 기록, 『국립현대미술관 1986: 과천관의 개관』참고. 정중헌, 「과천 현대미술관 예산부족, '작품없는 전시실 우려'」, 『조선일보』, 1984년 11월 15일 자.

9. 1988년 세계현대미술제의 국외 운영위원이었던 피에르 레스타니(Pierre Restany)도 이미 1986년 2월 28일에 (사)현대미술관회를 방문하여 「프랑스 현대미술, 최근 10년의 경향」에 대해 강연한 바 있다. 『현대의 미술』 39호(1986).

10. 사단법인체로 발족하는 관회의 정관과 이사진 명단이 기록되어 있다. "본회는 국립현대미술관의 국가적 사회적 기능 및 발전을 돕고 현대미술에 대한 일반인의 인식과 이해를 증진함을 목적으로 하며, 이 목적을 달성하기 위하여 다음 각 호의 사업을 행한다. 1. 국립현대미술관 사업의 지원 2. 현대미술의 계몽 및 보급. 3. 우수 미술작품의 발굴을 위한 정보교환. 4. 현대미술의 국제 미술교류. 5. 정기 미술강좌를 통한 현대미술의 이해증진 외", 『현대의 미술』 13호(1981).

1981년 9월 30일, 서독 바덴바덴에서 열린 제84차 국제 올림픽 위원회 총회에서 서울이 1988년 하계올림픽 개최지로 지정되며 우리 사회 전반이 한껏 고무되었다. 이어 국립현대미술관 과천 신축 세부 계획이 발표되어 어느 때보다 미술에 대한 관심이 높아졌다. 1982년 호암갤러리 개관기념전이었던 《헨리 무어》 전시를 비롯하여, 국립현대미술관에서도 프랑스, 영국, 멕시코, 세네갈 등 다양한 국적의 해외미술 전시를 진행했으나 여전히 신문이나 방송사나 주한 외국대사관 공동주최의 전시가 대다수여서 미술관의 소장품 수집으로 이어질 만한 계기를 갖지 못했다. 다만 국립현대미술관이 초창기에 수집한 국제미술 소장품들이 해외작가들의 '한국적인 것'에 대한 관심에서 비롯된 것이라는 공통점은 의미가 있다. 국립미술관으로서 국제교류를 이행할만한 체계를 갖추고 있지 못했으나, 해외작가들의 '한국'에 대한 관심과 표현의 결과인 작품을 소장하고 있다는 것은 한국미술계의 초기 국제 미술교류의 단면을 이해하는 실마리라 할 수 있을 것이다.

2. 미술교유(交遊) 미술교류(交流)

국립현대미술관 건립 초기부터 소장품 부실, 전문 학예인력 부재는 단 하나뿐인 국립미술관의 위상을 염려하는 미술계 내외 인사들의 단골 소재였다. 과천관 신축 발표에 모아진 관심도 사실상 기대 반 우려 반이었다. 특히 이전에 덕수궁미술관의 전시면적 740평에 비해 6배 가까이 넓은 과천관의 전시 면적 4,390평은 무엇으로 채워야 할 것이냐는 고민을 여러 신문에서 앞다퉈 다루기도 했다.[3] 여러 기사에서 어김없이 언급한 것이 '외국작가 소장품'의 부실이었다. 미국과 유럽의 국가기관이나 미술단체에서 전시할 작품을 무료로 임대해주겠다는 제안을 받을 정도였으니 그 우려가 어느 정도였는지 짐작할 만하다. 1986년 과천관 개관 후 인터뷰에서, 이경성 관장은 외국작가 작품 수집이 미비한 실정을 개탄하며, 국제미술 특별전을 연중 계속해나가서 해외미술품 구입에 주력하겠다는 포부를 밝히기도 했다.[4] 해외인사의 미술관 방문이 중요하게 간주되었던 것도, 국제미술 전시와 소장품의 지평을 넓힐 수 있는 계기로 삼고자했기 때문이다.[5] 1981년 4월 미술관을 방문했던 브루클린 미술관의 큐레이터 진 바로(Gene Baro)가 《한국현대 드로잉 '81》 전시를 관람하고, 바로 6월의 브루클린 미술관 순회전시를 결정하고 추진했던 것이 그 대표적인 예다.[6]

독일 에슬링엔(Esslingen) 시립미술관장이었던 알렉산더 톨나이(Alexander Tolnay)박사는 주한독일대사관과 (사)현대미술관회의 후원으로 1989년 5월 국립현대 미술관에서 개최했던 《독일현대회화》전을 공동기획하고, 지그마르 폴케(Sigmar Polke, 1941-2010) 등 3점의 판화를 미술관에 기증했다.[7] 1987년 미술관의 대표적인 국제미술 컬렉션으로 손꼽히는 앤디 워홀(Andy Warhol, 1928-1987)의 자화상(2점), 로버트 라우센버그(Robert Rauschenberg, 1925-2008), 크리스토(Javacheff Christo, 1935-2020)의 작품(108쪽) 구입도 유준상 당시 학예실장의 회고에 따르면, 뉴욕에서 백남준이 만남을 주선하고 흥정을 통해 당초 제시한 가격보다 저렴하게 구할 수 있도록 도왔다고 한다.[8] 1986년 요제프 보이스(Joseph Beuys, 1921-1986)가 심장마비로 갑작스레 사망한 이후, 백남준은 원화랑 정기용 대표와 자신과 보이스의 관계를 추억하는 《보이스 복스(Beuys Vox)》라는 전시를 기획했다. 이 전시에 출품되었던 다수의 작품이 원화랑의 정기용 대표에 의해 미술관에 기증되었다. 여기에는 1963년 백남준의 첫 비디오아트 전시 《음악의 전시 — 전자 텔레비전》(파르나스 갤러리, 부퍼탈, 독일)에서 요제프 보이스가 백남준의 피아노를 도끼로 부수었던 퍼포먼스 기록을 담은 〈보이스, 백, 카드〉(110-111쪽) 등 두 작가의 자전적 이야기와 예술적 동지로서의 만남을 되짚어 볼 수 있는 작품들이 포함되어 있다.

한편 1978년 순수 미술애호가들의 자발적 모임이자 미술관 후원단체로 설립된 '현대미술관회'(이하 '관회')는 1990년대 초까지 국립현대미술관의 역할을 보완하였다. 1981년에는 사단법인 현대미술관회로 발족했다. 당시의 정관에는 관회의 역할로 '현대미술의 국제 미술교류'가 명시해두어 있는데, 국내외 경제, 문화계의 네트워크를 동원하여 국립현대미술관을 보좌하기 위한 국제교류의 지평을 넓히고자 했던 의도를 짐작케 한다. 1990년대 초까지 다수의 해외 미술계 인사와[9] 도널드 저드(Donald Judd, 1928-1994), 크리스토와 잔 클로드, 조나단 보로프스키(Jonathan Borofsky, 1942-), 앤서니 카로(Anthony Caro, 1924-2013) 등 20명 이상의 국립현대미술관 국제미술 컬렉션 주요 소장작가의 초청을 직접 주선했다.[10] 2000년까지 관회에서 기증한 작품 가운데는 데이비드 호크니(David Hockney, 1937-)의 포토콜라주 작업인 〈레일이 있는 그랜드캐년 남쪽 끝〉(100-101쪽), 로스 블렉크너(Ross Bleckner, 1949-)의 〈노란심장들〉(105쪽) 등 해외미술품 6점이 포함되어 있다.

9. In 1988, Pierre Restany, who was a member of the international managing committee of *Olympiad of the Art*, also visited Membership Society for MMCA on February 28, 1986 and delivered a lecture titled '*The Trend of the Last Decade in France.*' *Contemporary Art News*, No. 39 (1986).

10. The articles of incorporation and the list of directors of the association, which was established as an incorporated non-profit association then, were published in *Contemporary Art News* in the June 1981 issue. "The purpose of this association is to help the national social functioning and development of the National Museum of Modern and Contemporary Art, and to enhance the public's awareness and understanding of contemporary art."
1. Support for the National Museum of Modern and Contemporary Art's Projects
2. Enlightenment and dissemination of contemporary art 3. Exchange of information to discover excellent works of art
4. International exchange of contemporary art
5. Promotion of understanding of contemporary art. *Contemporary Art News*, No.13 (June, 1981).

11. "Message from Paris to the Seoul Exhibition of Modern French Masterpieces," *Chosun Ilbo*, March 6, 1970.

12. Art critic Oh Kwang-soo, who participated as a Korean commissioner at the *São Paulo Biennial* on the 30th anniversary of its foundation in 1979, remarkably mentioned the increasing number of prints and drawing entries in the world art scene. Oh Kwang-soo, "A Journal from the Sãao Paulo Biennial — a Laboratory for Comtemporary Art without the Mainstream," *Dong-A Ilbo* October, 19, 1979.

13. In 1970, 24 countries (82 people) participated in the first exhibition and in 1972, 31 countries (199 people) participated in the second exhibition, and it was held in the form of a contest. More than 200 people participated in the opening ceremony of the second exhibition, but it was later suspended due to circumstances of the organizers until the third exhibition resumed in 1981.

Meanwhile, 'Membership Society for MMCA', founded in 1978 as a voluntary group of pure art lovers and a museum sponsorship organization, complemented the museum's social education, international exchange, and publication of newsletters when the MMCA was functioning as an administrative entity for 'exhibition' until the early 1990s. Later in 1981, it was extablished as an incorporated non-profit organization. It was intended to expand the horizon of international exchanges to assist the MMCA by mobilizing networks of domestic and international economic and cultural circles; the articles of the association in 1981 even specified its mission as 'International Exchange of Contemporary Art.' In addition to their invitation to a number of art figures [9] in overseas, they also invited more than 20 major artists of collections of international art at the MMCA, including Donald Judd, Christo and Jeanne-Claude, Jonathan Borofsky, and Anthony Caro.[10] The Membership Society for MMCA took the lead in donating art works, starting with Kim Whanki's, bequeathing to the MMCA until 2000; its donation includes David Hockney's photomontage work *The Grand Canyon South Rim with Rail, Oct. 1982* (pp.100–101), Ross Bleckner's *Yellow Hearts* (p.105), and six other artworks from international artists.

3. The World gazing Through Art

Until the 1980s, nearly half of the domestic international exhibitions were on prints. Among the international exhibitions held in Korea until the 1970s, there were many exhibitions of replicas of famous Western paintings, or even art posters. The first exhibition of the National Museum of Korea was also *International Print Exhibition* (January 1 – 31. 1957), which was co-hosted by the Art Society of Korea. At a time, when logistics and transportation were not smooth, replicated prints of Western masterpieces were relatively easier to transport than sculptures and paintings; it had given opportunities to experience Western art for local art lovers, art students, and the general public. The MMCA's first international exhibition *Modern French Masterpieces* (1970) was co-organized to celebrate the 50th anniversary of The Chosunilbo's foundation, was also a exhibition of prints and tapestry works of masters such as Picasso, Rouault, and Matisse. Bernard Antonioz, director of Artistic Creation at the French Ministry of Cultural Affairs, who organized the exhibition at the time, explained how modern modern technology and origianl artistry were in printmaking, which were merely taken in the art scene in the past, as they were taking the majority of the exhibition, even by taking quotes from Renoir and Degas.[11] In fact, from 1960, prints began to be the spotlights internationally as a 'modern medium and technique,' and printmedia divisions were already independently recognized in the Venice Biennale and the São Paulo Biennial, emerging as a new genre for formative experiments, not just as printing techniques.[12] In Korea, new experiments and attempts had been made on printmaking, centering on artists who had studied abroad or visited international art events such as the São Paulo or the Venice Biennale. Founded in 1970 by *Dong-A Ilbo* and held at the MMCA, *the Dong-A International Print Biennale* showed the attempts of the Korean art community to expand international exchanges through 'prints.'[13] At *the 4th Seoul International Print Biennale* co-hosted with the MMCA, the museum purchased 10 works, including award-winning pieces, as collections. In addition to the international art collections of the MMCA, which were collected in the early to mid 1980s, prints accounted for the majority. In 1982, 17 prints by European and Asian artists, including Janos Ber, were donated by Gallery Du Haut Pavé in France; in 1986, a print researcher and critic Pierre Wicart donated lithographs by 26 French artists, including Paul Aïzpiri and Bernard Buffet.(p.127) Wicart's were works that expressed traditional subjects in lyrical landscape such as European gardens and harbors following traditional lithographic techniques, which created an exotic European atmosphere.

3. 그림으로 보는 세계

1980년대까지 국내에서 개최된 국제전시 가운데 거의
절반 가까이 판화 전시였다. 1970년대까지는 서양 유명
회화의 복제본, 즉 아트포스터를 전시한 것도 적지
않았다. 국립박물관의 첫 전시도 한국조형문화연구소와
공동주최했던 《국제판화전》(1957. 3. 1.–3. 10.)이었다.
물류와 운송이 원활하지 않았던 당시로서는 조각이나
회화에 비해 판화의 운송이 용이했던 측면도 있다. 서양
명화의 복제품이나 석판화류는 미술애호가, 전공자나
일반인들이 서양의 미술을 접할 수 있는 계기가 되기도 했다.
조선일보 창간 50주년기념으로 공동 기획했던 국립현대
미술관의 첫 해외전시 《루브르미술관소장 현대프랑스
명화전》(1970)도 피카소, 루오, 마티스 등 거장들의 판화와
태피스트리가 대다수였던 판화 전시였다. 당시 전시를
추진했던 프랑스 문화성예술국장 베르나르 안토니우스는
판화가 주를 이루는 이 전시에 대해 과거에 군소예술로
치부됐던 판화가 얼마나 현대적인 기술과 독창적인 예술성을
지녔는지 르누아르와 드가가 남긴 말을 언급하면서
설명하고 있다.[11] 실제로 1960년부터 판화는 국제적으로
'현대적인 매체와 기법'으로 각광받기 시작했고, 이미
베니스비엔날레, 상파울루비엔날레 등에 판화부가 독립되어
단순한 인쇄기법이 아니라 조형 실험을 위한 새로운
장르로 부상하기 시작했던 것이다.[12] 우리나라에서는 국외
유학을 다녀오거나 상파울루나 베니스비엔날레 같은
국제미술행사에 참석했던 예술가를 중심으로 판화에 대한
새로운 실험과 시도가 이루어졌다. 1970년 동아일보사가
창설하고 국립현대미술관에서 진행된 《동아 국제판화
비엔날레》는 '판화'를 매개로 국제교류를 확장하고자 한
국내 미술계의 시도를 보여준다.[13] 국립현대미술관과
공동개최했던 제4회 《국제판화비엔날레》에서 미술관은
수상작을 포함한 10점의 작품을 소장품으로 구입했다.
1980년대 초중반 수집된 국립현대미술관 국제미술 소장품은
이외에도 판화가 대다수를 차지한다. 1982년 프랑스의
오 파베 화랑(Galerie du Haut Pavé)에서 야노스
베르(Janos Ber) 등 유럽 및 아시아 작가들의 판화 17점,
1986년에는 판화 연구 및 평론가 피에르 위까르(Pierre
Wicart)가 폴 아이즈피리(Paul Aïzpiri, 1919–2016),
베르나르 뷔페(Bernard Buffet, 1928–1999) 등 26점의
프랑스 작가의 석판화를 기증했다.(127쪽) 피에르 위까르의
판화는 유럽의 정원이나 항구 등 서정적인 풍경화 등
전통적인 소재를 정통 석판화 기법으로 표현한 작품으로
이국적인 유럽의 정취를 자아낸다.

4. 서울은 세계로, 세계는 서울로

"서울은 세계로, 세계는 서울로"는 1988년 서울 올림픽
개막식에서 IOC(국제올림픽조직위원회) 사마란치 위원장이
올림픽 개회선언으로 외쳤던 구호이다. 88 서울 올림픽은
이전의 모스크바와 LA 올림픽에서 목격했던 냉전의 벽을
허물고 동서간의 화합을 일궈낸 것으로 전 세계인들의
이목을 집중시켰다. 정부는 대대적으로 '문화올림픽'를
표방하며 전후로 우리의 전통문화를 소개하고, 해외의
문화예술행사를 유치할 수 있는 계기로 삼고자 했다. 서울
올림픽의 기념 문화예술행사 가운데 하나인 세계현대
미술제는 90억원이라는 막대한 예산이 투입된 대대적인
행사였다. 본래 잠실 올림픽 주경기장 인근 공터(현재
올림픽공원 자리)에 올림픽 기념 조형물을 설치하기로 했던
것이 조각공원 건립을 위한 국제문화예술행사로
확대되었다. 당초 계획이 변경된지 한 달 만에 제5차
세계올림픽연합회(ANOC) 총회에 조각공원 건립계획안이
보고되고, 그로부터 10개월 후, 세계현대미술제
운영위원회의 국내외 운영위원이 확정되었다. 4개월 후인
1987년 7월 3일 첫 행사인 제1차 《국제야외조각전》이
개최되었다. 동구권을 포함한 16개국 17명의 작가가
참여하여, '돌'과 '콘크리트'를 재료로 한 조각 17점을 현장
제작 설치하였다. 이후 제2차 《국제야외조각전》에
17개국 19명의 작가들이 철, 브론즈, 합성수지, 목재를
재료로 한 작품 19점을 현장 제작하여 설치했다.
뒤이은 《국제야외조각초대전》에서는 64개국 158명의
작가들이 자국에서 제작한 야외 조각을 국내로 이송하여
올림픽공원에 기증, 영구 설치하였다. 회화 분야에서는
국립현대미술관이 64개국의 해외작가가 참여한 《국제현대
회화전》의 운영과 진행을 맡았다. 90억이라는 기록적
예산이 투입된 국제행사를 2년 미만의 기간 동안 기획에서
실행까지 완료했다는 사실은 가히 기록적이었으나
편파적인 기획과 운영에 대한 당시 미술계의 우려와 반발은
상당했다.[14]

11. 「《현대프랑스명화전》 서울 전시에 붙이는
파리에서 온 메시지」, 『조선일보』, 1970년
3월 6일 자.

12. 1979년 창립 30주년 상파울루비엔날레에
한국측 커미셔너로 참가했던 미술평론가 오광수는
판화, 드로잉의 출품작 수가 증가하고 있음을
세계미술계의 두드러진 변화로 언급하고 있다,
오광수, 「상파울루비엔날레 참가기, 주류 없는
현대미술 실험장」, 『동아일보』, 1979년 10월
19일 자 참고.

13. 1970년 제1회 전시에는 24개국(82명),
1972년 제2회 전시에는 31개국(199명)이
참가하여 공모전 형식으로 진행되었다. 제2회 전시
개막식에 200명 이상이 참여하는 등 관심을
모았으나 이후 1981년 제3회 전시가 재개될 때까지
주최 측의 사정으로 중단되었다.

14. 당시 국내 미술계의 반발과 타협, 조정의
과정은 『서울올림픽미술제 백서: 무엇을 남겼나』,
88 올림픽세계현대미술제 변칙운영저지를 위한
범미술인대책위원회 편집(서울: 도서출판 얼굴,
1989)에 상세히 기록되어 있다.

4. Seoul to the World, the World to Seoul

"Seoul to the World, the World to Seoul." This was the slogan that Juan Samaranch, the president of the International Olympic organizaing Committee (IOC), shouted out when he declared the opening at the opening ceremony of the 1988 Seoul Olympic. The 1988 Seoul Olympics drew attention from people around the world for breaking down the walls of the Cold War, as seen at the previous Moscow and LA Olympics, and for creating harmony between East and West. The government advocated 'the Cultural Olympics' on a large scale, introducing Korean traditional culture before and after, and using it as an opportunity to host more international cultural and artistic events. *Olympiad of the Art* one of the cultural and artistic events commemorating the Seoul Olympics, was also a big event with a huge budget of 9 million Dollars. Originally, a sculpture in part of a celebration of the Olympics was supposed to be installed on an empty site nearby the Jamsil Olympic Main Stadium (now the Olympics Park), but the plan was expanded to an international cultural and artistic event to build a sculpture park. Just within a month, a plan to build a sculpture park was reported to the 5th Association of National Olympic Committees (ANOC) General Assembly. Ten months later, domestic and international members of the Managing Committee of *Olympiad of the Art* were formed, and it led to *the 1st International Open-Air Sculpture Symposium* four months later. 17 artists from 16 countries, including the countries from the East-European bloc, participated in the on-site installation of 17 pieces made of 'stone' and 'concrete' as materials. After that, 19 artists from 17 countries have produced and installed 19 works made of iron, bronze, synthetic resin, and wood at *the 2nd International Open-Air Sculpture Symposium*. In the subsequent *International Outdoor Sculpture Exhibition*, 158 artists from 64 countries transferred their own outdoor sculptures to Korea and donated them to be permanently installed at the Olympic Park. In the field of painting, the MMCA was in charge of operating and hosting *International Contemporary Painting Exhibition*, which foreign artists from 64 countries join in. The fact that an international event with a budget of 9 billion won was executed from planning to completion in less than two years was record-breaking, but concerns and opposition from the art community at the time were considerable about the biased planning and hasty operation.[14]

Thus, the Managing Committee of *Olympiad of the Art* partially accepted the claims of the art community and concerns about damage to cultural properties (Mongchontoseong Fortress; the remains of an ancient earthen fortification), they decided to change the location of the outdoor sculpture installation. In the case of *International Contemporary Painting Exhibition*, the initial plan was revised more dramatically. The exhibition was divided into the originally planned international exhibition *International Contemporary Painting Exhibition* and the domestic exhibition *Korean Contemporary Art Festival* from the decision to include 21 Korean artists, including domestic Managing Committee members. After all, 158 artworks of 158 artists from 64 countries were displayed in the international exhibition, and 500 artists submitted 500 works in the domestic exhibition, displaying sculptures, installations, paintings, and crafts in the same place in the same size space at the same time as some art circle requested. Peter KNAPP, who participated in the painting exhibition, was also the one who designed the poster for *Olympiad of the Art*, and he actively reflected the slogan of the 1988 Seoul Olympics: "Seoul to the world, and the world to Seoul." Although the members of International Managing Committee were appointed from arbitrary nominations rather than a public competition, the selected members were quite famous and influential figures in the international art scene. The committee members were as following: Pierre Restany, the world-renowned critic who opened the beginning of French Nouveau Realism, Thomas Messer, director of the Solomon R. Guggenheim Museum in New York, Ante Glibota, director of Paris Art Center, Yusuke Nakahara, and Gerard Xuriguera. Despite the fuss happened during the planning stage, there was no doubt that this event served as an opportunity for Korean contemporary art to advance to the international art scene and introduce the international art to Korea. Meanwhile, in a guide for artists participating in *International Contemporary Painting Exhibition*, there was a phrase encouraging artists to display one piece and donate one piece to the MMCA. In fact, through this event, the museum received 62 paintings from artists from 42 countries (including eight communist countries) and 39 sculptures from sculptors who participated in *the 2nd International Open-Air Sculpture Symposium*. As a result, it was a fulgurous opportunity to acquire 101 artworks to the international art collection, which was more than a third of total, at once by 1987. (pp. 136–167)

14. The process of backlash, compromise, and mediation in the domestic art scene at that time is described . Art Criticism Research Group, "Olympiad of the Art, what did it leave behind?", *Whitepaper of Olympiad of the Art—What's left?*, edited by The antitrust committee of artists on 88 Olympics World Contemporary Art Festival, (Seoul: Ulgul publication, 1989).

이에 세계현대미술제 운영위원회는 미술계의 주장과 문화재(몽촌토성) 훼손 우려를 일부 수용하여 야외조각 설치장소를 변경하였다. 《국제현대회화전》의 경우는 최초 계획을 더욱 급격히 수정하였다. 회화전 출품작가로 당연직으로 국내 운영위원이었던 작가를 포함하여 21명의 국내 작가가 참여하기로 였던 것에서 아예 전시를 당초 계획했던 국제전시 《국제현대회화전》과 국내전시 《한국현대미술전》으로 분리시켰다. 최종적으로 국제전에는 64개국의 작가 160명의 160점이 전시되었고, 국내전에는 500명의 작가가 500점의 작품을 출품하여 일부 미술계의 요구대로 동시에 동일한 장소에서, 동일한 면적의 공간에 조각, 설치, 회화, 공예 한국현대미술 작품을 전시하였다. 회화 전시에 참여했던 피터 크나프(Peter Knapp, 1931-)는 세계현대미술제의 포스터를 디자인한 장본인이기도 했는데, 태극기의 팔괘를 적극 차용하여 '서울을 세계로, 세계를 서울로'라는 88 서울 올림픽의 기치를 적극 반영한 것으로 보인다. 세계현대미술제 국외 운영위원은 공모를 거치지 않은 독단적인 지명으로 지적받았지만, 프랑스 누보 레알리즘의 시초를 열었던 세계적인 평론가 피에르 레스타니(Pierre Restany), 뉴욕 구겐하임 관장이었던 토마스 메서(Thomas Messer), 파리아트센터 대표였던 안테 글리보타(Ante Glibota), 나카하라 유스케(Nakahara Yusuke), 제라르 슈리게라(Gerard Xuriguera)는 국제미술계에서 지명도나 영향력이 적지 않은 인물들이었다. 기획단계의 잡음에도 불구하고, 이 행사는 한국의 현대미술이 국제무대로 나아가고, 해외 미술계의 현장을 국내에 소개하는 계기가 되었음은 의심할 수 없는 사실이다.

한편 《국제현대회화전》참여 작가를 위한 안내문에 '1점을 전시하고, 1점을 국립현대미술관에 기증할 것을 독려'하는 문구가 있어 눈에 띈다. 실제로 국립현대미술관은 이 행사를 통해 42개국(공산권 8개국 포함)의 작가로부터 회화 62점, 2차 야외조각심포지엄에 참여했던 조각 작가로부터 39점의 조각을 기증받았다. 이로서 1987년까지 국제미술 소장품의 3분의 1이 넘는 101점의 작품을 일시에 수집하게 되는 국제미술 소장품 수집의 전격적인 계기를 맞았다.(136-167쪽)

15. Representative exhibitions related to this matter include 'Primitivism' in 20th Century Art: Affinity of the Tribal and the Modern of the Museum of Modern Art (MoMA) in 1984 and Magicians of the Earth (orig. Magiciens de la Terre) of the Pompidou Center in Paris in 1989. The former placed African tribal crafts in perfuctory interrelationships with Western Modernism; while the latter was evaluated as a 'global exhibition' by displaying the works of artists from Asia, Southern Europe, and Africa on the same line, it was criticized for intentionally removing the cultural specificity of individual countries. Paul O'Neil, The Culture of Curating and the Curating of Culture(s), (Cambridge: MIT Press Ltd, 2012), 69.

16. Kim Jung-Jee, "The History of the Venice Biennale (1895–2003) and its Relationship to the Art of that Time (Orig. Die Geschichte der Venice Biennale (1895–2003) und ihrer Beziehung zur Kunst jener Zeit (2005))", Journal of History of Modern Art, no. 17, (2005), 226.

17. "Art-Foreign Exchange Exhibition Active," Dong-A Ilbo, June 1, 1988., Refer to the timeline of group/ individual exhibitions "60 Years of Foreign Art Domestic Exhibition," Kimdaljin Art Archives and Museum, 236.

18. Pierre Restany of France, David Burden and George Sega of the U.S., and Bonito Oliva of Italy were internatioanl judges, while Lee Kyungsung (then-director of the MMCA) and Lee Il (art critic) were domestic judges.

19. The first exhibition, Capitalist Realism (Orig. Kapitalistischer Realismus; 1964), organized by René Block, featured Gerhard Richter, Zigmar Polke, Wolf Postel, and K. P. Bremer, which contained satire and humor about democratization of the market, multi-plexing of images, and no-relationship between art and politics. He was the person in the scene of contemporary art in the late 20th century, which became a hot issue with Fluxus and Neodada. In addition to the 8th Biennale of Sydney in 1990, he participated as a director of the SeOUL OF FLUXUS in 1993 in Korea, as a curator in Art Cologne, and as a director of the 4th International Istanbul Biennial, and an international judge and advisor to the 1995 Gwangju Biennale. "Interview — Renée Block, a judge and advisor of Gwangju Biennale," JoongAhng Ilbo, October 3, 1995., "Speculative Interview with Renée Block," ART FORUM, April, 2014, https://www.artforum.com/print/201404/speculative-realism-an-interview-with-rene-block-45758

5. Art, a Window to the World

It was relatively recent that contemporary art around the world introduced a pluralistic perspective that excludes the artist's nationality, ethnicity, and cultural characteristics and evaluates only based on the artist's work. Starting from the mid-1980s, attempts to escape Western-centered art history of Europe and the United States had emerged. However, such attempts were even led by Western artists and curators, which eventually untangled limited percep-tions of non-Western artists in different ways.[15] On the other hand, Olympiad of the Art was recog-nized as an event with a lot of conflict and distur-bance, but it was an international art event with the participation of artists from Africa, the Middle East, and Asia, as well as the East-European bloc, which was unusual participation for the communist coun-tries at the time. It was not until the 44th Venice Biennale in 1990 that African countries began to partake, starting with Nigeria and Zimbabwe.[16] The reason that the participating countries were able to be evenly distributed in the Western-centered international art scene even in the biasedly formed with the mostly-Western members in the International Management Committees seemed to be because of the Olympic spirit, which proclaims to be 'a place of harmony for people around the world,' preceded the realm of contemporary art. Despite discord and fuss, Olympiad of the Art had left a positive effect on international exchanges of Korean art. As the atmosphere of globalization intensified, along with the liberalization of imports of artworks and the 1994 declaration of globalization by the Kim Young-sam administration, international art events in various scales were hosted, and the number of internatioanl exhibitions flowing into Korea increased significantly.[17] Among them, the 1990 Seoul Interna-tional Art Festival attracted domestic and internatio-anl attention as a venue for passionate works and competition of artists from the West working on Hanji.[18] This international art event served as an opportunity to confirm the modernity of Korean art and secure various networks with the international art community. Among them was René Block, which had organized various international art events.[19] He donated two collaborated artworks of K. P. Brehmer, Gerhard Richter (p. 190), and Sigmar Polke from UMWANDLUNGEN: The Artistic Conversion of Technolo-gy, an exhibition on German contemporary art co-organized with the MMCA in 1991, and he also proposed to acquire the Readymade Boomerang Portfolio, a collection of entries from the 8th Biennale of Sydney in 1990. The establishment of the Korean Pavilion for the Venice Biennale in the same year as the founding of the Gwangju Biennale in 1995 showed the results of international art exchanges that have continued to expand since the Seoul Olympics.

The MMCA's international art collection had also seen a decrease in the number of donated works compared to before, but a variety of works that fill the contemporary art history had been collected through ambitious acquisitions. The collection of international artworks at the MMCA acquired in 1990 were significant in that it opened the door to view the world beyond the fence and the world beyond the window through 'art.'

The Global Village, mentioned in Marshall McLuhan's book Understanding Media: The Extensions of Man (1964), is a word that foreseen the world that would lead to one with the development of electronic communication media. With the end of the East-West Cold War with German Reunification, this meta-phorical expression has been more clearly imprinted on the minds of citizens around the world. Among them, Korea has been more emotionally enthusiastic about the banner of 'globalization,' especially with the successful hosting of the 1988 Seoul Olympics and the leap forward of the national economy. In such social atmosphere, the international expan-sion and globalization of Korean art had been merely a kind of motto until the founding of the Gwangju Biennale and the establishment of the Korean Pavil-ion at the Venice Biennale in 1995. It was common to see that the ideology and philosophy of contempo-rary modern art within the pluralism and cultural nomadism began to be accepted in earnest beyond the boundaries of region and state. Nevertheless, it is noteworthy that the number of acquisitions of international artworks by the MMCA after 2000 has been 296, less than half of the 629 works collect-ed until the 1990s. This exhibition is designed to look back at what occasion and path the MMCA had selected and collected for the international art collections before the map of globalism, with the full-scale globalization of Korean contemporary art, had been established. It is both strange yet pleasant to discuss about the era of art globalization again at a time when 'deglobalization' is resurfaced due to COVID-19. Many of the exhibition's entries have been dormant in storage for nearly 30 years. Looking at the works that have been held back for a long time, I hope that it will be a time to remember the memories of those days before the grand word Millennium appeared.

15. 이와 관련된 대표적인 전시로, 1984년 뉴욕현대미술관(MoMA)의 《20세기 예술의 원시주의》, 1989년 파리 퐁피두 센터의 《지구의 마술사들》전시를 들 수 있다. 전자는 아프리카 부족 공예품을 서구 모더니즘과 형식적 상호관계 속에 배치했다는 점, 후자는 아시아, 남미, 아프리카 출신 예술가들의 작업을 동일선 상에 전시하여 '전(全)지구적 전시'라 평가받았지만, 개별 국가의 문화적 특수성을 의도적으로 제거했다는 비난을 받았다. 폴 오닐(Paul O'Neil), 『동시대 큐레이팅의 역사: 큐레이팅의 문화, 문화의 큐레이팅(The Culture of Curationg and the Curationg of Culture)』, (서울: 더 플로어 플랜, 2019), 63.

16. 김정희, 「베니스비엔날레(1985-2003)의 역사와 당대 미술과의 관계」, 『현대미술사연구』 제17집(2005. 6.): 226.

17. 「미술-해외교류전 활발」, 『동아일보』, 1988년 6월 1일 자., 『외국미술 국내전시 60년』, 김달진자료박물관편, 236. 단체전/개인전 연표 참고.

18. 프랑스의 피에르 레스타니, 미국의 데이비드 버든(David Burden)과 조지 시걸(George Sega), 이탈리아의 보니토 올리바(Bonito Oliva)가 국외 심사위원, 국내 심사위원은 이경성(국립현대미술관장)과 이일(미술평론가)이 맡았다.

19. 르네 블록(René Block)이 기획했던 첫번째 전시 《자본주의적 사실주의자(Kapitalistischer Realismus)》(1964)는 시장의 민주화와 이미지의 다중화, 예술과 정치의 관계없음 등에 대한 풍자와 유머를 담은 것으로 게르하르트 리히터, 지그마르 폴케, 볼프 포스텔, K. P. 브레머 등이 참여하였다. 그는 이후로도 플럭서스, 네오다다와 같이 뜨거운 이슈가 되었던 20세기 후반 동시대 미술의 현장에 함께했던 인물이다. 1990년 시드니 비엔날레를 비롯하여, 1993년 국내의 플럭서스 페스티벌, 아트 퀼른 기획, 이스탄불 비엔날레 총감독, 1995년 광주 비엔날레 국외 심사위원이자 자문위원으로 참여했다. 「〈인터뷰〉 광주비엔날레 자문, 심사위원 르네 블록씨」, 『중앙일보』, 1995년 10월 3일 자. 「Speculative Interview with René Block」, 『ARTFORUM』, April, 2014. https://www.artforum.com/print/201404/ speculative-realism-an-interview-with-rene-block-45758

5. 미술, 세계를 보는 창

전 세계의 동시대 현대미술에서 작가의 국적이나 민족, 문화적 특성을 배제하고 작가의 작업만을 기준으로 평가하는 다원주의적 관점이 도입된 것은 비교적 최근의 일이다. 80년대 중반부터 유럽과 미국 등 서구 중심 미술사관에서 벗어나고자 하는 시도가 대두되었으나 그 역시 결국은 서구권 기획자의 입장에서 비서구권 작가들에 대한 제한된 인식을 각기 다른 방식으로 풀어낸 것에 지나지 않았다.[15] 베니스비엔날레 조차 1990년 제44회에 이르러서야 비로소 나이지리아와 짐바브웨를 시작으로 아프리카 국가들의 참여가 시작되었다.[16] 그에 반해 세계현대미술제는 당시로서는 이례적으로 공산국가였던 동구권은 물론 아프리카와 중동, 아시아권 작가들까지 고루 참여했던 국제미술행사였다. 서구권 중심의 국제미술계에서 대다수 국외 운영위원이 서구권 출신으로 구성된 편파적인 운영위원회에서도 참여국가가 골고루 안배될 수 있었던 것은, '세계인의 화합의 장'이라는 올림픽 정신이 현대미술의 영역에 앞섰기 때문으로 보인다. 과정 중의 갈등과 잡음에도 불구하고 세계현대미술제는 한국미술의 해외교류에 긍정적인 영향을 끼쳤다. 미술품 수입개방화 조치와 김영삼 정부의 1994년 세계화선언 등 세계화 분위기가 더욱 고조되면서 미술계에도 크고 작은 국제미술행사가 생겨나고, 국내로 유입되는 국제전시 개수도 큰 폭으로 증가하였다.[17] 이 가운데 1990년 《국제현대회화전》은 '한지'를 소재로 한 서구권 작가들의 열띤 작업과 경쟁의 장으로 국내외의 주목을 받았다.[18] 이러한 국제예술행사는 한국미술의 현대성을 확인하고, 해외 미술계와의 다양한 네트워크를 확보할 수 있는 계기가 되었다. 이 가운데는 다양한 국제미술행사를 조직해왔던 르네 블록(René Block)이 있었다.[19] 그는 1991년 국립현대미술관과 공동기획했던 독일 현대미술 전시인 《테크놀로지의 예술적 전환》(1991. 3. 1-4. 14.)를 통해 K. P. 브레머(K. P. Brehmer, 1938-1997), 게르하르트 리히터(Gerhard Richter, 1932-)와 지그마르 폴케의 합작품 2점을 기증하고(190쪽), 1990년 시드니비엔날레 출품작 모음인 『레디메이드 부메랑 포트폴리오』를 수집 제안했다(189쪽). 이어 1995년 광주비엔날레 창립과 같은 해 베니스비엔날레 한국관 신설은 서울 올림픽 이후 지속적으로 확장세를 지켜온 국제미술교류의 성과를 보여주는 것이었다. 국립현대미술관 국제미술 컬렉션도 이전에 비해 기증작의 수는 줄었지만, 의욕적인 수집활동을 통해 현대미술사의 면면을 채우는 다채로운 작품들이 수집되었다. 1990년에 수집된 국립현대미술관 국제미술 소장품은 '미술'을 통해 울타리 너머의 세상, 창문 너머의 세계를 조망할 수 있는 빗장을 열었다는 점에서 의의가 있다.

마셜 맥클루언이 저서 『미디어의 이해』(1977)에서 언급한 '지구촌'은 전자통신매체의 발달로 하나로 연결될 전 세계를 예언한 말이다. 1990년 독일 통일과 함께 동서 냉전시대가 종식되면서, 이 은유적인 표현은 세계 시민들의 뇌리에 더욱 확실히 각인되었다. 특히 우리나라는 88 서울 올림픽의 성공적 개최와 국가 경제의 도약의 한가운데서 '세계화'라는 기치에 더욱 감성적으로 열광했다. 이러한 사회적 분위기 속에서 '한국미술의 해외진출과 세계화'는 일종의 표어에 가까운 것이었다. 지역과 국가의 경계를 넘어 다원주의, 문화적 유목주의 등 동시대 현대미술의 이념과 철학을 본격적으로 수용하기 시작한 것을 2000년 이후로 보는 것이 일반적이다. 그럼에도 불구하고 2000년 이후에 수집된 국립현대미술관의 해외미술품의 수가 296점으로, 1990년대까지 수집된 작품 수 629점의 절반에도 못 미친다는 사실은 특기할 만하다. 이 전시는 한국현대미술의 본격적인 세계화, 글로벌리즘의 지형도가 안착되기 이전에 국립현대미술관은 어떤 계기와 경로로 국제미술 소장품을 선정하고 수집해 왔을지 그 배경을 살펴보기 위해 기획되었다. 코로나로 인해 '탈(脫)세계화'가 언급되는 시기에, 다시 미술의 세계화 시대를 이야기하는 것이 어색하기도 하고, 또한 반갑기도 하다. 이번 전시의 출품작 가운데 상당수는 30년 가까이 수장고에 잠들어 있던 것이다. 오랜 기간 숨죽이고 있던 작품들을 하나하나 살펴보면서, 밀레니엄이라는 거창한 단어가 등장하기 이전 그 시절 기억을 추억하는 시간이 되기를 희망한다.

The Globalisation of Korean Art through the 1980s-90s

Oh Kwang-su
Art critic and former director of MMCA

1.

If the '60s and '70s did not exist, the '80s and '90s wouldn't have influenced the Korean art world. That's not a simple statement but the reality of Korean art history.

In the '80s and '90s, Korean society looked outwards and internationally. However, in the '60s and '70s, it was closed and regional. Both periods are contrasting and reciprocal, forcing the Korean art world to make urgent and drastic changes looking towards the future. As a result, the '90s revitalised Korean art brought with it more affluent.

Until the '80s, the Korean art world struggled despite the liberation from the Japanese occupation, as did Korean society. Conflicts between generations, confrontations of aesthetic ideology, and opposition between Academicism and anti-Academicism were factors that constantly frustrated the achievement of art as the maturity of the zeitgeist. Nevertheless, in the 70s, it gradually entered the stage of loosening its shackles to the past. In the process, developing social awareness, economic vitality, and democratisation are due to rising national status. The national power, which grew suddenly from developing countries to middle-income countries, has added positive energy to society. Again, no one can dismiss that the national status of joining a large open international community served as the background for Korean art access into the international art community. The entrance of Korean art on the international scene also encouraged the overseas expansion of Korean artists.

Meanwhile, Korean artists participated in international exhibitions as individuals. Korean art tried to partake in a significant international event at the national level. The Biennale de Paris and the São Paulo Biennial in the early 60s gave a chance to advance Korean art. Participation in the global scale of events aroused explosive interest from the Korean art world. This enthusiasm had a tremendous impact on the development of art in the era. Attending the two consecutive biennales in the early 60s was a golden opportunity to measure Korean art globally. Since its second edition, the Biennale de Paris invited Korean artists, so expectations were higher than the other biennales. The biennale attempted to distinguish itself, as it was a latecomer compared to Venice and São Paulo. Only young artists, 35 or less, were allowed to their talents are by no means fully developed and are still experimenting; they do not get a chance to display their skills until they are more fully established. It was a very adventurous idea at that time. What young artists expect is that they are by no means complete but focused on experiments. Compared to the fact that Venice and São Paulo invited already established artists with guaranteed authority and stability, it is a reverse of the idea. It may be related to the pride of France, which claims to be the birthplace of Contemporary Art, following the existing biennales. However, contrary to many people's concerns, it caused considerable sensations. It seems that art sympathised with the challenge and creation for new things rather than completion and authority.

There were four Korean entries for the Paris Biennale in 1961, including Kim Tschang-yeul, Chung Chang-sup, Chang Seongsoun, and Cho Yongik. Park Seobo, Youn Myeongro, Choi Kiwon, and Kim Bongtae then submitted in the third round in 1963, and Lee Yangno, Chung Sanghwa, Jung Young-yeol, Ha Chonghyun, Park Chongbae, Choi Manlin, and Kim Chonghak in the fourth round in 1965. Most of the artists participating in the Paris Biennale were members of the Contemporary Artists Association, formed in 1957, and the 1960 Art Association. They were artists selected from a representative group of young Korean artists.

Of course, the subsequent participation at the Paris Biennale became a place to gauge the level of our young artists at the time. Sources from Paris at the time said they were surprised that the level of Korean artists was unexpectedly high. It can be said that the ideology they pursued was attributed to the sympathy of universal aesthetics that came as a result of the so-called Abstract and Abstract Expressionism. After the war, the country that went through another war was not inferior to any other European country.

1980, 90년대를 통한 한국현대미술의 국제화 양상

오광수
미술평론가, 국립현대미술관 전(前) 관장

1.

80, 90년대 이전에 60, 70년대가 있었다. 60, 70년대가 없었다면 80, 90년대는 없었을 것이다. 이는 단순한 숫자놀이가 아니라 우리 미술에 있어 80, 90년대는 60, 70년대의 준비기가 없었다면 불가능했을 것이란 이야기다. 80, 90년대를 열린 시대, 국제화 시대로 부른다면 60, 70년대는 닫힌 시대, 국내시대라 말할 수 있다. 그만큼 대비적이면서 상대성을 지닌다는 점에서 의미를 부여할 수 있을 것 같다. 준비 기간이 긴박하고 치열한 만큼 완성기는 더욱더 풍요로운 결실을 맺기 마련이다.

해방 후 80년대에 이르기까지 우리 사회가 질곡의 시대인 만큼 우리 미술계도 앞이 보이지 않는 어두운 긴 터널의 시대였다. 세대간의 갈등, 조형이념의 대립, 아카데미즘과 반 아카데미즘의 반목이 순수한 정신의 발효로서 예술의 성숙을 부단히 저해한 요인이었다. 그것이 70년대에 들어오면서 서서히 극복의 단계를 맞이하게 되었다고 할 수 있다. 사회, 경제적인 활성화와 민주화의 의식이 국가적 위상을 고양한 데 기인한 것임은 말할 나위도 없다. 개발도상국에서 중진국으로 숨가쁘게 끌어올린 국력이 사회 전반에 긍정적인 열기를 더해준 것이다. 열린 국제사회로 진입해간 국가적 위상이 미술의 국제사회 진입의 배경이 되었다는 점은 누구도 부정할 수 없을 것이다.

우리 미술의 국제사회로의 진입은 미술가 개인의 해외 진출도 한몫을 담당했지만, 국제전에서 국가 단위로 참여한 것이 결정적인 기여였다고 할 수 있다. 60년대 초의 파리비엔날레, 상파울루비엔날레의 참여가 한국미술의 국제진출 첫걸음이었다. 국제전의 참여는 국내에 폭발적인 관심을 불러일으켰다. 이 같은 열기는 한 시대 미술의 전개에 엄청난 영향을 주었음은 물론이다.

60년대 초반의 잇따른 두 국제전의 초대는 우리 미술을 국제적인 척도로 그 수준을 가늠하게 하는 절호의 기회였다고 할 수 있다. 파리비엔날레는 2회부터 초대되었기에 그 기대가 더욱 컸다. 베니스나 상파울루에 비해 창설이 늦은 후발주자였기 때문에 기존의 비엔날레와 차별화를 시도한 것을 엿볼 수 있다. 참여의 범주를 35세 미만의 청년작가들로 한정한 점이 그렇다. 상식적으로 본다면 대단히 모험적인 발상이 아닐 수 없다. 젊은 작가들에게 기대하는 것은 결코 완성에 있는 것이 아니라 실험에 중점을 두었다는 것이다. 베니스나 상파울루가 이미 완성된 작가, 권위와 안정이 보장된 작가 중심이란 사실에 비하면 역발상이 아닐 수 없다. 현대미술의 종주국을 자처하는 프랑스가 이미 존재해 있는 기존의 비엔날레를 따라간다는 것이 자존심에 관계된 것인지도 모른다. 그러나 많은 사람들의 우려와는 달리 상당한 반향을 불러일으켰다. 예술이란 완성과 권위보다는 새로운 것으로의 도전과 창조란 사실에 공감한 결과였지 않았나 싶다.

1961년 파리비엔날레 한국 측 출품작가는 김창열, 정창섭, 장성순, 조용익 등 4명이었다. 이어 1963년 3회에는 박서보, 윤명로, 최기원, 김봉태가, 1965년 4회에는 이양노, 정상화, 정영열, 하종현, 박종배, 최만린, 김종학이 출품하였다. 파리비엔날레 참가작가들 대부분이 1957년에 등장한 현대미술가협회와 1960년에 등장한 1960년 미술협회의 회원들이었다. 당시 한국의 젊은 미술가들의 대표적인 그룹에서 선정된 작가들이었다.

잇따른 파리비엔날레의 참여는 당시 우리의 젊은 미술의 수준을 가늠해 볼 수 있는 자리가 되었음은 물론이다. 당시 파리의 소식통에 의하면 한국 작가들의 수준이 예상외로 높았다는 데 놀랐다는 것이었다. 이들이 추구했던 이념이 이른바 앵포르멜로 불리는 뜨거운 추상, 표현적 추상으로 국제적으로 널리 파급되었던 경향에 상응됨으로써 오는 보편적 미의식의 공감에 기인된 것으로 볼 수 있는가 하면 전후 또 한 차례의 전쟁을 겪은 국가가 유럽의 어떤 국가와 비교해도 낙후되어 있지 않다는 점에 대한 경이로움의 반응이라고 할 수 있을 듯하다.

São Paulo Biennale, in which Korean artists participated, was an international biennale launched after World War II and ambitious to emerge South America as another international centre. Korea being invited here also suggests that Korea was gradually attracting attention from the international community. In 1963, Kim Whanki, Kim Kichang, Kim YoungJoo, Yoo Youngkuk, Suh Seok, Han Yongjin, and Yoo Kangyul participated, followed by Lee Ungno, Kwon Okyon, Kim Jong-young, Lee Seduk, Kim Tschang-yeul, Park Seobo, and Chung Changsup in 1965. In the first year, it was centred around older artists. Still, the second is that the ratio of older generations (pre-war generations) and new generations (post-war generations) is becoming equal. The desire to participate in international events is changing around the post-war era. As it was the first time participating in an international exhibition, the art community's response was inevitably hot. The selection process was a painful one. There was no specialised organisation for artist selection but was led by the Korean Fine Arts Association. There was extreme opposition from artists who were dissatisfied with the selection, which led to the so-called scandal of an open letter in solidarity. It has become an annual affair from artists discontented with the association's selection. It should be seen as nothing more than reflecting the low awareness of the international event. It reveals a lack of understanding of the global art world. The protestors were claimed it was restricted to abstract art and the selection process was not transparent.

2.

The unique phenomenon that appeared in the 70s can be the advancement of Korean art into Japan. It was possible to advance to Japan due to the normalisation of diplomatic relations between Korea and Japan in 1965. Amid active exchanges between Korea and Japan, the entry of Korean contemporary art into Japan is likely to be pointed out as the most noticeable phenomenon. The cultural interchange between the two countries should take place in an equal position. However, art exchanges between Korea and Japan give the impression that Korean contemporary art is entering Japan unilaterally.

The first exhibition in Japan was the Korean Contemporary Art Exhibition held at the National Museum of Modern Art in Tokyo, Japan, in 1968. It was centred on Korean painting as well as Western painting. The participating artists included Byun Chongha, Choi Youngrim, Kim Foon, Kim Youngjoo, Kwon Okyon, Lee Seduk, Nam Kwan, Yoo Youngkuk, Rhee Seundja, Yoo Kangyul, Chung Changsup, Chun Sungwoo, Ha Chonghyun, Park Seobo, Kim Chonghak, Kim Sangyu, Youn Myeongro, Quac Insik, and Lee Ufan. Of course, it was centred on abstract art, which became the mainstream of contemporary art, excluding the academic tendency. Compared to Japanese contemporary art, the geometric abstract or optical art that was at the centre at the time stood out. Although this exhibition happened as a ceremonial event, it seemed meaningful. It served as a bridgehead that caused the globalising of Korean art in the 70s.

Five Korean Artists and Five Kinds of White held at the Tokyo Gallery in 1975 was successful. The first one in the 70s was planned and selected by Japanese art critic Yusuke Nakahara. The selected artists are Kwon Youngwoo, Park Seobo, Lee Dongyoub, Suh Seungwon, and Her Hwang. Although it is a small-scale exhibition, it attracted attention in that it showed artists working only with white colour.

Given that white monochrome emerged as a new trend in the younger generation at the time, I think this exhibition may have catalysed the launch of monochromatic paintings later. The answer can be found in the question of 'why is it white', which was very relative compared to contemporary Japanese art. Nakahara said that white was not viewed as a colour due to Korea's achromatic aesthetic preference. Therefore, it does not deviate from the monochrome category from a universal point of view. Still, it differs from colour, so it is said to be nothing more than a uniquely Korean sentiment that cannot be seen anywhere else.

비슷한 시기에 참여한 상파울루비엔날레는 2차 세계대전 이후에 출범한 국제전으로 남미를 또 하나의 국제적 중심으로 부상시키려는 야심에 찬 것이었다. 여기에 한국이 초대되었다는 것도 국제사회에서 한국이 점차 관심을 받고 있었음을 말해준다. 처음 참가한 1963년도는 김환기, 김기창, 김영주, 유영국, 서세옥, 한용진, 유강열 등 7명이, 이어 1965년도에 이응노, 권옥연, 김종영, 이세득, 김창열, 박서보, 정창섭 등이 참여하였다. 첫해는 기성작가들 중심이었으나 두 번째는 기성세대(전전세대)와 신진세대(전후세대)의 비율이 대등해지고 있다. 국제전의 참여의 열망이 전후세대 중심으로 변화되어가고 있음을 엿볼 수 있다. 국제전 참여가 최초인만큼 미술계의 반응이 뜨거울 수밖에 없었다. 작가 선정에 진통을 겪었음은 말할 나위도 없다. 작가선정을 위한 기구가 따로 존재했던 것이 아니고 한국미술협회가 주도했기 때문에 인선에 불만을 품은 작가들의 반발이 극심했다. 작가선정에 불만을 품은 작가들이 연동하여 이른바 연서(連署) 소동(연대서명의 항의서)이 한동안 연례행사처럼 되었던 것은 잘 알려져 있는 일이다. 국제전에 대한 인식이 저급했음을 반영한 것에 지나지 않는다고 보아야 할 것이다. 왜 추상 일변도냐에서 작가선정을 공모형식을 통해 뽑아야 한다는 등 국제전에 대한 인식이 부족했음을 그대로 드러내고 있다.

2.

1970년대에 진입하면서 나타난 독특한 현상은 우리 미술의 일본 진출이라고 할 수 있다. 일본으로 진출이 가능했던 것은 1965년 한일국교 정상화가 이루어졌기 때문이다. 한국과 일본의 여러 부문에 걸친 교류가 활발해지는 가운데 한국 현대미술의 일본진출이 가장 눈에 띄는 현상으로 지목할 수 있을 듯하다. 양국 간의 교류란 대등한 입지에서 전개되어야 하는데 당시 한일간의 미술 교류는 한국 현대미술의 일본진출이란 일방적인 차원으로 이루어진 느낌을 주고 있다.

일본에서의 첫 전시는 1968년 일본 도쿄국립근대 미술관에서 열린 《한국현대회화전》이었다. 회화분야, 그것도 서양화 중심으로 이루어졌었다. 출품 작가는 변종하, 최영림, 김훈, 김영주, 권옥연, 이세득, 남관, 유영국, 이성자, 유강열, 정창섭, 전성우, 하종현, 박서보, 김종학, 김상유, 윤명로, 곽인식, 이우환 등이다. 물론 아카데믹한 경향이 제외된 현대미술의 주류를 이룬 추상미술 중심이었다. 일본 현대미술과 비교했을 때 당시 중심을 이루고 있었던 기하학적 추상 내지는 옵티컬 아트가 돋보인다는 평가였다. 이 전시는 약간 의례적인 측면이 없지 않으나 이어지는 1970년대의 한국미술 진출의 붐을 일으키는 교두보 역할을 했다는 데서 그 의미를 찾을 수 있을 것 같다.

1975년의 도쿄갤러리에서 열린 《한국 5인의 작가—다섯 가지의 흰색》전은 1970년대 이후로 이어지는 첫 전시라는데 관심을 불러일으켰다. 이 전시는 일본의 비평가 나카하라 유스케가 기획과 작가선정에 참여하였다. 선정된 작가는 권영우, 박서보, 이동엽, 서승원, 허황 등이다. 소규모의 기획전이긴 하나 흰색을 주조로 한 작가들로 구성되었다는 데서 주목을 끌었다. 당시 젊은 세대를 중심으로 흰색의 단색이 새로운 경향으로 떠올라있었다는 점을 파악했다는 점에서 어쩌면 이 전시가 이후 단색화의 출범을 알리는 기폭제가 되지 않았나 생각된다. 왜 흰색이냐는 물음은 일본의 현대미술과 비교해 보았을 때 대단히 상대적이었다는 점에서 답을 찾을 수 있을 것 같다. 나카하라는 흰색을 색의 차원으로 본 것이 아니라 한국 특유의 반유채(反油彩)적 정서에 기인한다고 하였다. 보편적인 관점에서 본다면 모노크롬의 범주에서 벗어나지 않으나 색채가 아니라 색채를 벗어난다는 점에서 이는 어디에도 볼 수 없는 독특한 한국의 정서에 다름없다고 한 것이다.

With the opening of Korea-Japan relations, Japanese visitors to Korea became more frequent. Art figures visited Insa-dong, where antique and modern galleries clustered around. They encountered a unique culture unlike their own. It was not just a discovery from the tourism experience but a distinctive sense of culture that was ignored in themselves for a long time. No exaggeration to say the beauty of white porcelain was taken as a shock with white clothes, Korean paper (hanji), and ceramics. The concrete background of the exhibition was the white colour, which was highly coded throughout Korean life, also appeared in contemporary Korean art. It is the most consequential factor that we have discovered in Korean art's unique nature. For example, can such an inner side be easily found by Westerners? Japan, which is in our vicinity, shares the East Asian civilisation. It was also a shock that the nearest neighbour discovered our uniqueness beyond such universality.

Following *Five Korean Artists, Five Kinds of White*, large-scale Korean exhibitions were held in various regions of Japan. Representative examples include the Korean Contemporary Art Cross-sectional held at the Tokyo Central Museum of Art in 1977 with Quac Insik, Kwon Youngwoo, KIM Kulim, KIM Gui-line, Kim Yongik, Kim Jinsuk, Kim Tschang-yeul, Park Seobo, Park Jangnyun, Suh Seungwon, Shim Moon seup, Yun Hyongkeun, Lee Kangso, Lee Dongyoub, Lee Sangnam, Lee Seungjio, Lee Ufan, Chin Ohcsun, Choi Byungso. The scale of these exhibitions was magnificent. Participating artists are as follows: KIM Kulim, KIM Gui-line, Kim Sunwhoe, Kim Tschang-yeul, Kim Taeho, Kim Hongjoo, Park Seobo, Ahn Byeongseok, Lee Dooshik, Chung Sanghwa, Tchine Yuyeung, Ha Dongchul, Lee Seungjio, Park Choong-heum, Lee Kangso, Kwak Namsin, Kwon Young woo, Kim Yongmin, Kim Jinsuk, Kim Hongseuk, Suh Seungwon, Shin Sunghy, Yun Hyongkeun, Youn Myeongro, Lee Dongyoub, Lee Bann, Lee Bongreal, Chung Changsup, Chin Ohcsun, Choi Myoungyoung, Ha Chonghyun, Kim Yongik, Kim Tschang-yeul, Park Suk-won, Park Hyunki, Shim Moonseup, Lee Kunyong, Lim Choongsup, Ji Seokcheol. In addition, major participating artists, classified as Dansaekhwa painters (monochrome paintings), presented their artworks, as well as some hyperrealistic painters who appeared in the late 1970s also participated.

3.

The 1980s shows that our art's global advancement became more pronounced. It is an impression that the era of globalisation has opened widely. The 1980s, which can be called a kind of the era of openness, always had to refine itself in a comparative measurement, different from the situation so far. Reflection and confirmation were required as much as the opening toward the outside. Fortunately, the challenge was naturally carried out through exhibitions held in Japan and Taiwan from the late 70s to the 80s. Because the Korean art world was confident in entering the international world and, at the same time, explored their identity in art.

The Korean monochrome group has been steadily forming the mainstream since the 1970s. It is regarded that Korean art has had an independent inner side as it corresponds to the so-called international trend. This tendency destroyed the mainstream and marginal relationship that ensued at that time. Until the 20th century, the international art scene had been composed of the so-called central and surrounding structures. The global movement took place as a new wave in Paris and New York, then spread around. However, the situation after the 1980s is gradually breaking away from this structure and entering an era without a centre. Not only Paris and New York, but also Berlin, London, and Tokyo have entered a period where they can be centred at the same time. From this point of view, the status of the Korean monochrome movement should be considered. They say that monochrome is minimalism and is nothing more than a subclass of minimalism. Monochrome is not an influence nor an imitation of a trend. It has its uniqueness and must be considered autonomously. I think it is the achievement of the globalisation of Korean art.

한일 관계가 열리면서 일본인들의 한국 내방이 잦아지기
시작했다. 그 가운데서 미술계 인사들이 고미술상과
현대적 성격의 화랑들이 몰려있던 인사동 일대를
답사하면서 자신들과 다른 독특한 문화가 있다는 것을
체험하게 되었다고 할까. 단순한 관광 차원이 아닌
자신들 속에선 찾을 수 없는 독특한 문화의 향기에 빠져들게
되었던 것이다. 백의(白衣)와 한지, 도자 가운데서도
백자의 아름다움은 충격으로 받아들였다고 해도 과언이
아니다. 생활 전반에 포만되어있는 흰색이 현대미술
속에서도 나타나고 있음을 발견하게 된 것이 흰색전이
열리게 된 구체적인 배경이었다고 할 수 있다. 타자에 의한
우리 미술의 독특한 내면이 발견되었다는 것에 더욱
의미가 크다고 하지 않을 수 없다. 예컨대 서구인들에 의해
이 같은 내면이 쉽게 발견될 수 있을까. 우리와는
가장 가까운 거리에 있는 일본은 극동이란 지역의 문화적
보편성을 공유하고 있는 국가이기도 하다. 그러한
보편성을 넘는 고유성에 대한 발견이 가장 가까운 이웃에
의해 이루어졌다는 것은 우리에게도 충격이 아닐 수
없었다.

《한국 5인의 작가―다섯 가지의 흰색》에 이어 대규모
한국전이 일본 여러 지역에서 열렸다. 대표적으로 1977년
도쿄 센트럴미술관에서 열린 《한국 현대미술의 단면》
(출품작가: 곽인식, 권영우, 김구림, 김기린, 김용익, 김진석,
김창열, 박서보, 박장년, 서승원, 심문섭, 윤형근, 이강소,
이동엽, 이상남, 이승조, 이우환, 진옥선, 최병소)과
1983년 도쿄도미술관, 도치기현립미술관, 국립국제미술관,
후쿠오카시 미술관, 홋카이도 도미술관 등 5개 공공
미술관에서 순회전으로 열린 《한국현대미술전―70년대
후반 하나의 양상전》이 될 것이다. 이들 전시는 한국전의
결정판이라 할 수 있는 규모의 전시였다(출품작가:
김구림, 김기린, 김선회, 김창열, 김태호, 김홍주, 박서보,
안병석, 이두식, 정상화, 진유영, 하동철, 이승조, 박충흠,
이강소, 곽남신, 권영우, 김용민, 김진석, 김홍석, 서승원,
신성희, 윤형근, 윤명로, 이동엽, 이반, 이봉열, 정창섭,
진옥선, 최명영, 하종현, 김용익, 김창열, 박석원, 박현기,
심문섭, 이건용, 임충섭, 지석철). 출품작가들의 경향을 보면
모노크롬 계통의 단색화가 주류를 이루는 가운데
70년대 후반에 등장하기 시작한 극사실적 경향, 장소성이
강한 입체물, 드로잉적인 요소가 강한 작품들로 분류된다.

3.

80년대는 우리 미술의 국제 진출이 더욱 현저해지고
있음을 보여주고 있다. 국제화의 시대가 활짝 열린
인상이다. 개방의 시대라고 부를 수 있는 80년대는 이로
인해 지금까지의 상황과는 다른 언제나 자신을 비교
차원에서 가다듬지 않으면 안 되었다. 밖으로 향한 열기만큼
내부에서의 자기성찰과 검증이 요구되었다고 할 수 있다.
70년대 후반에서 80년대로 이어지는 시점에 일본과
대만에서의 잇따른 전시를 통해 우리 미술에 대한 검증이
자연스럽게 이루어진 것은 여간 다행한 일이 아니다.
국제사회로의 진출에 자신감을 갖는 동시에 자국 미술에
대한 정체성의 탐구가 동시에 이루어졌기 때문이다.

70년대 이후 꾸준히 주류를 형성해 온 단색화는 국제적으로
일어난 이른바 중심과 주변의 관계상황을 와해시킨
기류에 상응되면서 더욱 독자한 내면을 갖출 수 있었다고
본다. 20세기에 이르기까지 국제미술의 판도는 이른바
중심과 주변의 구도로 이루어져 왔다. 파리나 뉴욕에서
일어난 새로운 기류가 주변으로 파급되면서 국제미술이
형성되는 형국이었다. 그러나 80년대 이후의 상황은
점차 이 같은 구도에서 벗어나 이른바 중심이 없는 시대로
돌입하고 있다. 파리나 뉴욕뿐 아니라 베를린, 런던,
도쿄가 동시에 중심이 될 수 있는 시대로 진입한 것이다.
이 같은 관점에서 단색화의 위상을 점검할 수 있다는
것이다. 단색화가 미니멀리즘이나 모노크롬의 아류에
지나지 않는다는 지금까지의 관점에서 벗어나 단색화는
어느 경향의 영향과 모방이 아니라 그 자체 고유한
것으로서 자립된 것으로 보지 않으면 안 된다는 것이다.
한국미술의 국제화가 도달한 성과이지 않나 생각된다.

One of the characteristics of the 80s is that there is no mainstream. Meanwhile, until the 1990s, the monochrome movement was still advancing toward Korea's representative trend. Hence, the discrete tendency for representing Korean art is frequently noted as a monochrome group. However, it cannot be denied that the wind of change was coming when we were selected for participation or exchange exhibitions in major international exhibitions in the 1990s. It is also directly related to the sudden generational shift, which should not be overlooked. It is time to witness the so-called postmodernist era forming a giant wave.

Suppose modernism, which has been mainstream till then, is fine dining. On the other hand, postmodernism can be compared with a McDonald's menu from which you can choose. Free-spirited thinking and actions outside of formality are in full swing. As it is linked to the explosive popular culture, the transfer of values across society is rapidly taking place. If we suppose that art had an elite system before, nowadays, it is changing into a multi-centred system called the democratisation of art. Choice and concentration are cultural strategies. If elite artists have been selected previously, opportunities are now spread. The rising of emerging and mid-career artists is a trend that replaces established artists.

4.

The Venice Biennale was the first step to advance Korean art to the international level in the 1990s. The site of the Venice Biennale is a structure in which each country has to build its pavilion on the park site because participating countries display their exhibition according to their installation plan. The long-cherished Korean art world idea had not yet come true until 1995. Venice is no available site anymore, so the Korean Pavilion became the last national pavilion. Before 1995, Korea had to rent Italian halls or lend exhibition venues to hold the exhibitions. Even now, a few countries still have no choice but to comply with this situation.

In 1995, the year of the inauguration of the Korean pavilion, Kwak Hoon, Kim Inkyum, Yun Hyongkeun, and Jheon Soocheon were selected to represent. In 1997, the Korean pavilion presented Kang Ikjoong, Lee Hyungwoo, and in 1999 Lee Bul and Noh Sangkyoon. We should note that the biennale organisation deviated from the existing standard in selecting only elite artists to embrace a more diverse group of artists. It is noteworthy that Jheon Soocheon received an honourable mention at the 46th International Art Exhibition of the Venice Biennale 1995 with two more consecutive special mentions to Kang Ikjoong at the 47th International Art Exhibition in 1997 and Lee Bul at the 48th Exhibition in 1999. It reflects the international interest in Korean art.

The special exhibition *The Tiger's Tail: 15 Korean Contemporary Artists for Venice 95* (Ahn Sungkeum, Cho Duckhyun, Cho Sungmook, Ha Chonghyun, Kimsooja, Kwak Duckjun, Lee Hyungwoo, Lee Jongsang, Lee Kyusun, Lim Oksang, Shim Moonseup, Youn Myeongro, Nam June Paik, Younhee CHUNG PAIK, Yun Suknam) was held at different venues in Venice. Compared to the '80s, it effectively showed a remarkable change in Korean art.

80년대가 열린 시대로 불리는 요인 가운데 먼저 꼽을 수 있는 것이 주류가 없다는 데 있다고 할 수 있다. 그러면서도 90년대 이르기까지 여전히 단색화 계통이 한국을 대표하는 경향으로 진출하는 것을 엿볼 수 있다. 아마도 그것은 우리의 정체성을 이야기할 때 빈번히 거론되는 대표적인 경향이 단색화이기 때문일 것이다. 그러나 90년대의 주요 국제전의 참여나 교류전에 선정되는 작가군의 색깔은 점차적으로 변해가고 있음을 부정할 수 없을 듯하다. 그것은 세대교체란 변화와 직결되기도 한다. 기성세대와 신진세대의 세대교체가 급속히 이루어지고 있음을 간과할 수 없을 듯하다. 이른바 포스트 모더니즘의 시대가 거대한 물결을 이루어가고 있음을 목격하는 시점이다.

지금까지 주류를 이루었던 모더니즘이 잘 차려진 밥상이라고 한다면 포스트모더니즘은 맥도날드류의 햄버거와 같은 잡식의 밥상이라고 할 수 있을 듯하다. 격식을 벗어난 자유분방한 사고와 행위가 활개를 치는 형국이다. 폭발하는 대중문화와도 연계되면서 사회 전반에 걸친 가치의 전도가 급속히 이루어져 가는 추세에 있다. 지금까지의 예술이 엘리트중심이었다면 예술의 민주화 현상으로 불리는 다중중심의 구도로 변해가는 양상이다. 선택과 집중은 일종의 문화적 전략으로서 엘리트중심의 작가선정이 이루어졌다면 이제는 기회의 확산이라고나 할까, 중견과 신진의 대두가 엘리트중심을 대신하는 기류임이 분명하다.

4.

90년대에 들어와 먼저 꼽을 수 있는 국제전의 진출은 베니스비엔날레이다. 베니스비엔날레의 구조는 참여국가가 자국관을 통해 작품전시를 하기 때문에 각국이 공원부지에 자국관을 건설하지 않으면 안되는 구조이다. 오랫동안 염원했던 한국관이 1995년에야 이룩된 것이다. 그것도 부지가 없어 한국관이 가까스로 건설된 마지막 국가관이 된 행운을 차지한 셈이다. 1995년 이전 한국의 출품은 이탈리아관이나 종합기획전이 열리는 장소를 빌리는 형국이었다. 지금도 적지 않은 국가들이 이런 구차함을 벗어나지 못하고 있는 실정이다.

국가관 건설 이후 첫해인 1995년에는 곽훈 김인겸, 윤형근, 전수천이 1997년은 강익중, 이형우, 1999년은 이불, 노상균이 각각 참여하였다. 참여작가들의 면면을 보면 지금까지의 엘리트 중심의 작가선정에서 벗어나고 있음을 엿볼 수 있다. 이들 중 전수천(1995), 강익중(1997), 이불(1999)이 3회 연속으로 특별상을 수상한 것은 특기할 사항이다. 한국미술에 대한 국제적 관심이 높았다는 것을 반영해준 것이라 하지 않을 수 없다.

베니스비엔날레가 열리는 시기에 맞추어 베니스 팔라초 벤드라민에서 열린 특별전 《호랑이의 꼬리》(안성금, 조덕현, 조성묵, 하종현, 김수자, 곽덕준, 이형우, 이종상, 이규선, 임옥상, 심문섭, 윤명로, 백남준, 정연희, 윤석남)는 제한된 비엔날레 본 전시와는 다른 한국미술의 현주소를 알리는 계기가 되었다. 80년대에 비해 변화가 현저한 한국미술을 효과적으로 보여준 것이었다.

In addition, Yook Keunbyung was invited to the ninth edition of documenta in Kassel. Sydney Biennale presented Nam June Paik, Moon Joo, Cha Ouhi in 1992. At the exhibition of Tate Liverpool Working with Nature—Traditional Thoughts in Contemporary Art from Korea (Chung Changsup, Yun Hyongkeun, Kim Tschang-yeul, Lee Ufan, Lee Kangso). Kim Bongjun and another artists such as Kim Hosuk, Kim Hongjoo, Park Buldong, Son Jangsup, Ahn Kyuchul. Yun Suknam, Yeesookyung, Lee Jonggu, Choi Min-Hwa, Choi Jinkook, Sungho Choi, Shim Hyungsoo, Bahc Yiso, Kim Jinsoo, Kim Young, Yoon Jinmee, Lee jin, Min Youngsoon, Michael Joo, Byron Kim, David Jung presented at Across the Pacific: Contemporary Korean and Korean American Art at Queens Museum in 1993. In 1995, Circulating Currents—Japanese and Korean Contemporary Art at Nagoya Museum of Art and Aichi Museum of Art in Japan ((Park Hyunki, Shim Moonseup, Cha Ouhi, Choi Insu, Choi Jae-eun, Won Gye-hwan, Kim Keunjoong, Kim Chandong, Cho Duckhyun, Yook Keunbyung, Kimsooja, Kim Tschoonsu, Yoon Hee-Chang). In 1996, The Painters of Silence (Les Peintres du Silence) presented Korean artists (Chung Changsup, Yun Hyongkeun, Kim Tschang-yeul, Suh Seok, Park Seobo, Ha Chonghyun, Lee Ufan, Lee Kangso) at Montbéliard in France. In 1997, in Secession at Vienna and Bordeaux, at the Fine Arts Museum of the city of Bordeaux, Choi Jeonghwa, Kimsooja, Koo Jeonga, Lee Bul, Choi Uk, Kim Soojin, Tae Kyungsun, Minn Sohn Joo, Kim Jinbae, Seung H-sang participated Cities on the Move. In 1998, a touring exhibition, In the Year of the Tiger: Contemporary Art from Korea, presented 15 Korean artists. (KANG Yongmeon, Kang Ikjoong, Kim Yeojin, Park Sinyoung, Bae Bien-u, Bae Joonsung, Shin Kyunghee, Ahn Sungkeum, Yoo Youngho, Yook Keunbyung, Lee Hyungwoo, Lim Youngsun, Jheon Soocheon, Cho Duckhyun, Choi Jeonghwa)

I classified other significant exhibitions by year below:

1990
- *Contemporary Korean paintings* in Poland

1991
- *Ten Contemporary Korean Women Artists* in Mexico and Washington, at the National Museum of women in the art Modern Prints from Korea in Yugoslavia

1992
- The first edition of *Korean and Chinese Artist* at the Fine Art Museum of Research Institute of Traditional Chinese Painting

1995
- *Information & Reality—Korean contemporary art*, Scotland

1999
- A touring exhibition, *Contemporary Korean Print: A Reflection of a Culture* (LE ESTAMPA COREANA CONTEMPORÁNEA: REFLEJO DE UNA CULTURA) in Spain
- *Contemporary Korean paper art*, at the Gorcum museum in Netherland
- *The Korean artists*, Düsseldorf

Furthermore, Korean artists regularly participate in international exhibitions includes the India Triennale, the Cagnes International Painting Festival, and the Bangladesh Biennale. Korean art's dynamism is at the national level indeed. Individual promotions also increase rapidly.

This enthusiastic international expansion of Korean art led to international exhibitions in Korea. The advancement to the outside world appears to embrace global art energetically. For Korea, this phenomenon can be a hope of developing into a new eye of international art, playing an ambitious role as the hub of Asia.

이외 90년대 주목되는 국제전의 참여는 1990년 독일
카셀 도큐멘타에 육근병이 초대된 것과 1990년 시드니
비엔날레(백남준, 문주, 차우희), 1992년 영국 테이트
갤러리의 기획전《자연과 함께》(정창섭, 윤형근,
김창열, 박서보, 이우환, 이강소), 1993년의 뉴욕 퀸즈
미술관의《태평양을 건너서: 오늘의 한국미술》(김봉준,
김호석, 김홍주, 박불똥, 손장섭, 안규철, 윤석남, 이수경,
이종구, 최민화, 최진국, 최성호, 심형수, 박모, 김진수,
김영, 윤진미, 이진, 민영순, 마이클 주, 바이런 김,
데이빗 정), 1995년 일본 나고야시립미술관, 아이치현립
미술관의《환류—일한현대미술전》(박현기, 심문섭,
차우희, 최인수, 최재은, 원계환, 김근중, 김찬동, 조덕현,
육근병, 김수자, 김춘수, 윤희창), 1998년 프랑스
몽벨리아르 뷔르템베르크미술관의《침묵의 화가》(정창섭,
윤형근, 김창열, 서세옥, 박서보, 하종현, 이우환, 이강소),
1997년 오스트리아 비엔나 서세션, 프랑스 보르도
현대미술관의《시티즈 온 더 무브》(최정화, 김수자, 구정아,
이불, 최욱, 김수진, 태경선, 민선주, 김진배, 승효상),
1998년《한국현대미술 독일 순회전—호랑이의 해》
(강용면, 강익중, 김여진, 박신영, 배병우, 배준성,
신경희, 안성금, 유영호, 육근병, 이형우, 임영선, 전수천,
조덕현, 최정화)등이 있고 이외 꼽을 수 있는 전시로는
1990년 폴란드의《한국현대회화의 오늘전》, 1991년
멕시코의《한국현대미술전》, 1991년 미국 워싱턴 국립
여성미술관《한국현대미술 여성 10인전》, 구 유고
류블랴나《한국현대판화전》, 1992년 중국 베이징 중국화
연구원《한중 대표작가전》, 1995년 영국 스코틀랜드
《정보와 현실》, 1999년《한국현대판화스페인 순회전》,
1999년 네덜란드 호르쿰미술관《한국현대 종이
조형전》, 1999년 독일 뒤셀도르프《뒤셀도르프 한국작가
특별전》등을 꼽을 수 있을 것 같다.

이외 정기적인 국제전의 참여는 인도트리엔날레,
《카뉴국제회화제》, 방글라데시비엔날레 등이 있다. 국가
단위 외에 개별적인 초대도 급증하고 있는 추세다.

이 같은 국제진출의 왕성한 양상은 국내에 국제전의 창설로
이어졌다. 밖으로의 진출이 해외의 미술을 적극적으로
포용하는 추이로 나타나고 있다. 이러한 현상은 국제미술의
또 하나의 중심을 꿈꾸는 것이라 하지 않을 수 없다.
아시아의 중심의 역할을 담당하려는 야심찬 의욕을 반영함이
분명하다.

Olympiad of the Art (1988)
Postwar International Art Exhibition and Changes in Art World in Korea

Yang Eunhee
Director, Space D

The Change of Art World in the 1980s

Korean art and its art world in the 1980s had significantly changed that had undergone Park Chung-hee's death who had been in a long regime under the Cold War ideology from the 1970s, struggle to establish a new government, and political turmoil preceded by May 18 Democratisation Movement. Fortunately, due to export-driven policy, Korea achieved rapid economic growth by more than a 10 percent growth rate that further continued to expand by leading conglomerates. Moreover, the aspiration of the military regime to raise the country as one of the 'Four Asian Dragons' led to considerable investment in the cultural and sports sectors. Within the said structure, the Korean art world expanded in size as many aspects, such as its markets and systems, started to diversify.

The 1980s could be defined as the period of the emergence of diverse perspectives on a fundamental topic of 'What is Art'. The most significant one is the appearance of Minjung Art under the influence of the Democratisation Movement that came to challenge the leading Abstract Art in the 70s. The appearance of Minjung Art, which pursued social criticism and engagement of reality through representational and realistic images, stirred up the art world who used to comply with anti-Communistic government-led cultural policies.

Beyond the conflicting structure of Modernism against Minjung Art, diverse ideologies and gestures in making artwork have emerged. Disappointed by Minjung Art's patriarchal views, female artists gathered to bring up a discussion on the 'Feminist art' to the male-driven art industry gravitating toward patriarchal culture. In addition, seeking changes in Korean Paintings, which have long been marginalized from the art world dominated by western paintings, had been witnessed, and small groups amongst emerging artists, in particular, have been active during this period. Toward the late 1980s, the introduction of Feminism and Postmodernism expanded the idea of artists' bodies and means of making work, e.g. gender, appropriation, and Fetishism. Artists from the new generation rejected the concept of classical art, instead explored various mediums like installation and performance and dealt with topics like gender and consumer culture that had been neglected till then.

The increase in the art population and the growth of the art world accounted for the motivation for changes. As art schools and their student bodies grew in quantity, many college graduates became prospective practicing artists and future art critics due to the establishment of art history and art aesthetics majors. Instead of depending only on selected schools, a wide range of schools started to produce talented workers in the art field in which later demanded structural changes.

As Korea's economy grew, so did the demand for art collections and art galleries consequently. Not just the gallery spaces, department stores started to run spaces to fulfill the demand for exhibitions for Korean painting, photography, ceramics, etc. Nine out of twenty-two department stores in 1985 ran the showrooms under the name of art museums. Around 60 galleries in Seoul and 120 nationwide were in business which is ten times bigger in quantity than that of the mid-1970s.[1]

However, the art market did not grow enough to hold all the emerging artists. Only a selected number of artists could make a living off of selling their works like in the past. The new generation of artists who could not find art-related jobs and the old generation with vested interest sometimes conflicted.

1. Jung Joongheon, "Art Market In Recession — Yet New Galleries Continues to Open," *Chosun Ilbo*, April 18, 1985.

세계현대미술제(1988) 전후의 외국 작가 전시와
국내 미술계의 변화

양은희
스페이스 D 디렉터

1. 정중헌, 「미술품경기 아직 불황이라는데...
새 화랑 잇따라 개업」, 『조선일보』, 1985년 4월
18일 자, 7면.

1980년대 미술계의 변화

1980년대 한국 미술과 미술계는 1970년대부터 이어진
냉전 이데올로기 하에서 장기 집권하던 박정희 대통령의
사망, 그리고 이후 새로운 정권 수립을 위한 진통,
5·18 이후 이어진 민주화 운동으로 인해 혼란스러운
정치적 환경 속에서 많은 변화를 거쳤다. 다행히도
수출주의 정책은 10% 이상의 성장률을 기록하며 경제가
크게 발전했고 대기업 주도의 성장이 지속되고 있었다.
이에 힘입어 '아시아의 용'으로 부상하려는 군사정권의
열망은 문화와 스포츠에 대한 투자 확대로 나타났으며 이런
구도 속에서 미술계도 규모가 커지고 시장과 제도 등
여러 측면에서 다변화되기 시작했다.

1980년대는 '미술이란 무엇인가'라는 근본적 화두를 두고
다양한 관점이 대두된 시기라고 볼 수 있다. 가장 큰
변화는 민주화 운동의 영향 속에서 등장한 민중미술이
1970년대를 주도하던 추상미술에 도전한 것이다.
재현적 그리고 사실적 이미지를 통해 사회 비판과 현실
참여를 지향한 미술의 등장은 그동안 반공 이념을
내세운 정부 주도의 문화 정책에 순응하던 미술계를 뒤흔든
사건이었다.

그러나 곧 '모더니즘 계열'과 민중미술의 대립 구도를
넘어 다양한 창작 이념과 태도가 나타났다. 먼저 민중미술의
남성중심적 시각에 실망한 여성 작가들이 모여 가부장
문화에 익숙한 미술계에 '여성주의 미술'이라는 화두를
던졌다. 이외에도 서양화 주도의 미술계에서 소외된
한국화(또는 동양화) 진영의 변화 모색, 젊은 예술가를
중심으로 등장한 소그룹 활동이 두드러진 시기이기도
하다. 1980년대 후반에는 페미니즘과 포스트모더니즘
이론이 도입되어 젠더, 차용, 패스티시 등 예술가
주체와 창작 방법에 관한 새로운 개념들이 확산되기
시작했다. 신세대 작가들은 고답적인 미술 개념을 거부하고
설치, 퍼포먼스 등 다양한 매체와 젠더, 소비문화 등
그동안 흔하지 않았던 주제를 탐구하곤 했다.

새로운 변화의 동력은 미술 인구 증가와 미술계의 성장에
힘입었다고 할 수 있다. 대학 정원이 늘어나고 다수의
미술 대학이 들어서자 많은 작가 지망생들이 배출되었고
미학, 미술사 관련 학과의 등장으로 잠재적 평론가층도
확대되었다. 그동안 소수의 미술 대학이 인력을 배출하던
구도에서 벗어나 다양한 학교에서 재능있는 인재들이
등장하여 구조적 변화를 요구하고 있었다.

경제 성장에 힘입어 미술품 수요가 늘어났으며 작가들의
전시 개최 열망이 커지면서 전국에 화랑이 늘기
시작했다. 일반 화랑뿐만 아니라 백화점도 전시장을 만들어
동양화, 사진, 도예 등 여러 분야의 전시수요를 충족하고
있었는데 1985년경 서울의 22개 백화점 중에서 9곳이
미술관이라는 명칭하에 전시장을 운영하고 있었다.
일반 화랑의 경우도 서울에만 60여 개의 화랑이 있었으며
전국에 1백 20여 개가 있었는데 이는 1970년 중반에
비해 10배 증가한 것이었다고 한다.[1]

그러나 미술시장이 새로 등장한 신진작가들을 모두 수용할
정도로 거래 규모가 커진 것은 아니었다. 과거처럼
창작으로만 생계를 유지한다는 것은 극소수의 작가에게
해당하는 일이었다. 그래서 미술 관련 직업의 기회를
얻지 못한 젊은 세대와 기득권을 확보한 기성세대 간의
갈등도 벌어지곤 했다.

미술 인구의 증가는 재능있는 작가 발굴을 위한 제도로
귀결되는데, 1970년대 말 등장한 동아미술제(1978
설립)와 중앙미술대전(1978 설립)은 80년대를 거치며
유력한 신인 등용문으로 성장했다. 특히 오랫동안
권위를 잃고 심사와 작가선정을 두고 논란이 많았던
국전이 1981년 폐지되자 그에 대한 대안으로
자리를 잡게 된다. 『계간미술』(1975), 『선미술』(1979)
등 소수에 그치던 미술 잡지도 『미술평단』(1986),
『가나아트』(1988) 등의 등장에 힘입어 미술평론 및
이론 분야의 인력이 활동할 수 있는 공간을 넓히기
시작한다.

The increase of infrastructure in art resulted in the open calls for talented artists. Through the 1980s, *Dong-A International Fine Art Exhibition* (est.1978) and *JoongAng Fine Arts Prize* (est.1978) grew to be the entry gate for promising emerging artists. When the National Exhibition was discontinued in 1981 after losing their authority due to a long controversy in their jury process, the two previously mentioned open calls became the alternative. Furthermore, the new launch of art magazines like *Korean Art Critics Review* (1986) and *Gana Art* (1988) in addition to previously launched ones, *Art Quarterly* (1975) and *SUN Art Quarterly* (1979), broadened the ground for workers in art criticism and theory.

Increase of International Artist Exhibitions in the 1980s and Introduction of Contemporary Art

According to statistics, international art exhibitions opened in Korea grew dramatically in numbers from 17 in the 1950s, 13 in the 1960s, 80 in the 1970s, 383 in the 1980s, and 973 in the 1990s.[2] The sudden increase in the 1980s is partially due to previously mentioned economic growth and consequent growth of the art world.

While exhibitions were mostly of well-known traditional artists like Pablo Picasso and Jean-François Millet in the 1970s, interest in art was expanded with increased art viewers and art lovers in the 1980's. This phenomenon was due to the Korean art field's tendency to respond sensitively to international art trends from the United States, France, etc. In particular, diverse international artworks were imported depending on the gallery owner's interest.

Above all, Chaebols' (the Korean conglomerates) art collections grew in quantity. Private collectors started to build art museums, going beyond merely collecting artworks, to fulfill the craving for international art. Seoul Museum (est.1981), founded by Yim Setaik, a France based artist; Walkerhill Art Museum (est.1984) located in Sheraton Walkerhill Hotel, founded by Park Gye-hee, the wife of Sunkyoung groups' (current SK group) chairman; Ho-Am Art Museum (est.1982), run by Samsung; Hoam Gallery (est.1985), located in JoongAng Ilbo Building, would be the typical example of such private art museums. Newly founded private art museums became outposts to introduce contemporary arts from foreign countries due to the conglomerates' funds and prompt decision-making.

Of course, the National Museum of Modern and Contemporary Art continued to introduce international art. In the 1980s, MMCA introduced European and American art through *German Contemporary Art* (Deoksugung, 1983), *Auguste Rodin* (Deoksugung, 1985), *Frederick R. Weisman Collection* (Gwacheon, 1986), and private art museums hosted *Nouvelles Figurations en France* (Seoul Museum, 1981), *Contemporary Art Prints London & New York* (Walkerhill Art Museum, 1984), *Exposition Des Sculptures de Bourdelle Corée* (Hoam Gallery, 1985), *Contemporary Art Prints of Eastern Europe* (Walkerhill Art Museum, 1985), *Africa: African Primitive Art in Contemporary Art* (Hoam Gallery, 1987), *Marcel Duchamp–Seoul* (Seoul Museum, 1987), *Contemporary Art from New York* (Hoam Gallery, 1988). Thus, not only master artists' works from the west like Duchamp, Rodin, and Bourdelle were shown, but diverse arts from East Europe that were difficult to encounter and relatively unknown African art were also introduced.[3]

These exhibitions did not connect Korea and the world to share trends in contemporary art extensively and proactively. Amid the tension of the Cold War and due to political ties with the US, Korean art was more sensitive toward American art like POP Art, Conceptual Art, Postmodernism, etc. Nonetheless, the Korean art world ended up just introducing already known artists. Yet the exception would be *Nouvelles Figurations en France* (Seoul Museum, 1982) which showed works by figurative painters like Balthus and R. Matta, and responded to the contemporaneity of Minjung Art. It showed that figuration and representation are not out of style but go beyond the boundaries of countries and cultures that show universally valid problems in the Art.

The introduction of contemporary artists in the 1980s did not only happen within the existing systems like artist associations, galleries, and museums but also was done by art figures who stayed abroad. Along with the said Yim Setaik, the director of the Seoul Museum, Nam June Paik, a video artist, and Hong Ga Yi, a philosopher and an art critic, should be noted. They introduced changes in the western art world, like France and the United States, and contributed to the process of globalization of contemporary Korean art.

2. Cho Eunjung, "60 years of the international art exhibition in Korea," *Art in Culture*, July, 2012., "60 years of history of domestic exhibitions of foreign art," *60 years of the international art exhibition in Korea: 1950–2011*, (Seoul: KimDaljin Art Archives & Museum, 2012), 232.

3. Please see, *60 years of the international art exhibition in Korea: 1950–2011*, (Seoul: KimDaljin Art Archives & Museum, 2012).

1980년대 해외작가 전시 증가와 동시대 미술의 소개

국내에서 열린 외국 미술 전시의 수를 집계한 한 통계 결과를 보면 1950년대 17회, 1960년대 13회, 1970년대 80회였던 것이, 1980년대 들어 383회, 1990년대는 973회로 크게 증가했다는 것을 알 수 있다.[2] 1980년대 외국 작가 전시의 증가는 위에서 언급한 경제 성장과 미술계의 팽창에 힘입었다고 할 수 있다.

1970년대 주로 국립현대미술관을 중심으로 피카소, 밀레 등 전통적인 서양의 유명작가의 전시가 기획되던 것과 달리, 1980년대는 늘어난 미술 인구와 미술애호가를 토대로 외국 미술에 대한 관심이 확산되는데 그동안 프랑스, 미국 등 해외 미술 동향에 민감하게 반응했던 국내 미술계의 특성상 자연스러운 현상이었다. 특히 전시장을 설립한 주체의 관심에 따라 다양한 외국 미술이 수입되곤 했다.

무엇보다 '재벌'/자본가의 미술품 컬렉션이 늘고 있었다. 자본가/컬렉터들은 개인 컬렉션을 넘어 미술관을 설립하여 해외 미술에 목마른 수요를 채우곤 했다. 프랑스에서 활동하던 작가 임세택이 만든 서울미술관(1981 설립), 그리고 선경(현재의 SK) 그룹 회장 부인 박계희가 쉐라톤 워커힐 호텔에 만든 워커힐미술관(1984 개관)과 삼성이 만든 호암미술관(1982 개관), 중앙일보 건물에 들어선 호암갤러리(1985 개관)는 당시 등장한 대표적인 사립 미술관이다. 새로 등장한 사립 미술관들은 대기업의 자본과 빠른 의사결정에 힘입어 외국의 현대미술을 선보이는 새로운 전초기지가 되었다.

물론 국립현대미술관 주도의 외국 미술 소개도 이어지고 있었다. 1980년대 국립현대미술관은 《독일현대미술전》(1983), 《로댕전》(1985), 《프레데릭 R. 와이즈만 컬렉션》(1986) 등 유럽과 미국의 미술을 전시했고 사립 미술관은 《프랑스 신구상회화전》(1981, 서울미술관), 《현대 판화 런던-뉴욕》전 (1984, 워커힐미술관), 《브루델 조각전》(1985, 호암갤러리), 《동구의 현대판화》(1985, 워커힐미술관), 《아프리카 미술전》(1987, 호암갤러리), 《뒤샹-서울》전(1987, 서울미술관), 《뉴욕현대미술》전 (1988, 호암갤러리) 등을 개최했다. 뒤샹, 로댕, 브루델과 같은 서구의 거장을 소개하는 전시뿐만 아니라 냉전으로 인해 접하기 어려웠던 동유럽에서부터 상대적으로 잘 알려지지 않았던 아프리카에 이르는 다양한 국제미술이 소개되고 있었다.[3]

이러한 전시들이 동시대 미술을 공유할 정도로 한국과 한국 외부 사이에 광범위하고 적극적인 접촉을 보여준 것은 아니다. 냉전 구도 속에서 한국은 미국과 정치적 동맹관계 속에서 팝아트, 개념미술, 포스트모더니즘 미술 등 미국 중심의 미술에 촉각을 세우곤 했다. 그럼에도 불구하고 대부분 이미 알려진 작가를 소개하는 경우가 많았다. 그나마 예외적인 경우는 《프랑스 신구상회화전》(1982, 서울미술관)으로 이 전시는 발튀스(Balthus, 1908-2001), 마타(R. Matta, 1911-2002) 등 프랑스 주요 구상작가를 선보이며 자연스럽게 민중미술의 동시대성을 옹호하게 된다. 구상과 재현이 지나간 유행이 아니라 국가 간, 문화 간 경계를 초월하는 보편타당한 예술의 문제라는 점을 보여준 것이다.

1980년대 동시대 해외 미술 소개는 작가협회, 화랑, 미술관 등 기존의 제도권뿐만 아니라 해외 체류 경험이 있는 인물들을 통해서도 이루어지곤 했다. 그중에서 위에서 언급한 서울미술관의 임세택뿐만 아니라 비디오 아트로 유명한 백남준, 그리고 철학자이자 미술평론가 홍가이도 빼놓을 수 없는 인물이다. 이들은 프랑스와 미국 등 서양의 변화를 소개하며 1990년대 한국 동시대 미술의 전 지구화 과정에 기여한 바 있다.

2. 조은정, 「외국미술 국내전시 60년전」, 『아트인컬처』, 2012년 7월; 김달진미술자료박물관, 『외국미술 국내전시 60년: 1950-2011』(서울: 김달진미술자료박물관, 2012), 232. 재인용. 또한 같은 책에 실린 글, 김달진, 「외국미술 국내전시 60년 소사」를 참고할 것.

3. 김달진미술자료박물관, 『외국미술 국내전시 60년: 1950-2011』 참조.

Nam June Paik introduced three satellite installation projects that connected Korea and other countries. When his first project, *Good Morning, Mr. Orwell* (1984), was presented in Korea, public interest was surging all of a sudden that led to his visit to Korea after a long leave of several decades. Later through *Bye Bye Kipling* (1986) and *Wrap around the World* (1988), he introduced the phrase, 'Electronic Space Opera' to expand the range of art to the universe and completed the legend of 'the international artist, Nam June Paik'. His satellite installation project series was the transnational media art that implanted broadcasting, satellite, and performance that came possible with the development of satellite technology in the late 1970s to connect the public residing in Seoul, New York, Paris, Tokyo, etc. His media art was a mind-blowing spectacle that was relatively unknown to the Korean art world and the viewers.

Nam June Paik's open attitude and the use of advanced technology influenced young artists in particular that his name was always mentioned from the artists' interviews like Kang Ik-Joong and Jeon Soocheon, who received attention in the 1990s. Nam June Paik, working back and forth between Seoul and New York, advised governmental institutions like MMCA and supported exhibition funding thus having a good influence on the Korean art world. Significant art events in the Korean art world in the 1990s, such as the *Whitney Biennial in Seoul* (1993), the *SeOUL of Fluxus Festival* (1993), Gwangju Biennale (founded in 1995), and the inauguration of the Korean Pavilion in Venice Biennale(1995), were realized with his persistent effort and persuasion.

Hong Ga Yi developed discourses on modern art and postmodernism in the magazine called *Space* and published *30 essays on Contemporary art: Major critique on Modernism and Late Modernism with socio-political perspective over the past 20 years* in 1987. This book introduced writings of influential critics from Arthur Danto to Rosalind Krauss when translated versions of books on art theory were scarce. He was also a playwright and staged his own play, actively working across genres. Embracing theory and creative practice, he was unprecedentedly international and manifested his cosmopolitan aspect.

Context of *Olympiad of the Art* (1988): from Internationalism to Globalism

Olympiad of the Art, which occurred as a highlight program for the 1988 Summer Olympics in Seoul, became the catalyst for opening up the Korean art world. Despite ideological conflict during the Cold War, expectations for cultural exchanges and communications beyond the ideology were higher than ever for artists who became aware of the need for a common language to communicate with the art world abroad.

This international art event connected many countries around the world which was divided into two due to the Cold War and promoted the cultural status of Korea hosting the Olympics. The amount of nine billion won, record-high amount of the time, was invested in building Olympic Park, covering 165 hectares, located in Bangi-dong, Songpa-gu, Seoul. To celebrate the establishment of the structure, the following exhibitions were opened: *International Outdoor Sculpture Exhibition* (Aug–Oct, 1988) and *International Open-Air Sculpture Symposium* (Summer 1987, Spring 1988); and *International Contemporary Painting Exhibition* (Aug–Oct 1988, MMCA), *Exhibition of Contemporary Calligraphy* (Sept–Nov 1988, Seoul Arts Center) were opened to show paintings from Korea and abroad.[4]

Despite the Olympic organizing committee's intention to make the event a cultural exchange ground, the Korean art world struggled to decide the direction of the event. As it turned to be a ground for political conflict from accumulated power struggle amongst groups, discourses on the identity of modern art were inevitable because selected artists would be granted the honor of representing Korea like Olympic athletes. Not only social status, cultural identity and background mattered, did the organizing committee consider artists' main media, alma mater, age and many other criteria for artist selection. Thus, qualifications for who represents Korean modern art created intense conflict amongst committee members.

From 1987 to 1988, criticism from excluded artists and critic groups in the selection process was raised from all groups of Minjung Art, Korean painting, figurative art, etc. Amid the criticism, problems occurred through the process of localizing imported 'Art' with modernization started to emerge. Long-existing tensions between groups with different political lines and backgrounds arose simultaneously: representation vs abstract, Korean painting vs Western painting, young vs old generation, and Minjung Art vs Modernism. As a result, *Olympiad of the Art* came to be on trial to solve structural problems that the Korean art world had.

4. Korean People's Artists Association, "Is It Really Okay?: Reality and Illusion of *Olympiad of the Art*," *Minjok Misul*, no. 4 (July 1987), 44.

백남준은 한국과 해외를 연결하는 위성중계 프로젝트 3개를 선보이며 미디어 시대를 알렸다. 그 첫 번째 작업 〈굿모닝 미스터 오웰(Good Morning, Mr. Orwell)〉(1984)이 국내에서 펼쳐지자 갑자기 그에 대한 대중적 관심이 촉발되었고 그로 인해 한국을 떠난 지 수십 년 만에 처음으로 귀국하게 된다. 이후 〈바이 바이 키플링(Bye Bye Kipling)〉(1986), 〈세계와 손잡고〉(1988)를 연속으로 선보이며 '우주 오페라'라는 신조어를 알리고 '세계적인 작가 백남준'의 신화를 형성하기 시작한다. 그의 위성중계 프로젝트 시리즈는 1970년대 후반 위성기술의 발달에 힘입어 방송, 위성, 공연을 접목하여 서울, 뉴욕, 파리, 도쿄 등 여러 도시에 거주하는 대중에 다가가려는 초국가적 미디어아트로 이 분야에 생소한 국내 미술계와 일반 관객들에게는 놀라운 스펙터클로 다가왔다.

백남준의 개방적 태도와 첨단 기술을 이용한 예술은 특히 젊은 작가들에게 큰 영향을 미쳤으며 강익중, 전수천 등 1990년대 주목받은 작가들이 인터뷰마다 백남준을 언급할 정도였다. 백남준은 서울과 뉴욕을 오가며 국립현대미술관 등 정부 관련 기관에 자문을 하거나 직접 전시 예산을 후원하며 영향력을 확대해 갔다. 1990년대 한국미술계의 주요 사건들—《1993 휘트니비엔날레 서울》(1993), 《서울 플럭서스 페스티벌》(1993), 광주비엔날레 설립(1995), 베니스비엔날레 한국관 개관(1995)—뒤에는 백남준의 노력과 설득이 있었다.

홍가이는 1980년대 『공간』지를 중심으로 현대미술과 포스트모더니즘에 대한 논의를 전개했으며 『현대미술비평 30선: 최근 20년간 모더니즘과 후기 모더니즘, 사회정치적 관점의 주요비평집』(1987)을 발간하기도 했다. 이 책은 아서 단토(Arthur Danto)부터 로잘린드 크라우스(Rosalind Krauss)에 이르는 주요 평론가의 글을 소개하며 미술이론에 대한 번역서가 거의 없던 시절 큰 반향을 불러일으켰다. 또한 직접 쓴 연극을 무대에 올리고 장르를 초월하여 이론과 창작을 아우르는 활동으로 당시로서는 파격적일 정도로 국제적이며 코스모폴리탄적인 면모를 보여준 바 있다.

4. 민족미술협의회,「정말 이래도 되는 것인가: 〈88 세계현대미술제〉의 실상과 허상」,『민족미술』 4, 1987년 7월, 44.

세계현대미술제(1988)의 맥락: 국제화에서 전 지구화로

돌이켜보면 세계현대미술제는 1988년 서울 올림픽의 부대행사로 열린 전시였으나 한국미술계의 개방화를 촉진한 계기였으며 냉전 시대의 이념 갈등에도 불구하고 예술가들이 그 이념을 넘어 문화적 교류와 소통이 가능하다는 기대를 높였으며 해외 미술계와 소통할 수 있는 공통의 언어가 필요하다는 자각을 유발한 장이었다.

이 전시는 국제 행사를 통해 냉전체제로 인해 양분된 세계 여러 국가 간의 연결망을 모색하는 한편 올림픽을 개최하는 한국의 문화적 위상을 선전하는 장이었다. 당시의 기준으로 역대 최고 예산인 90억 원이 투입되어 서울시 송파구 방이동에 50만평에 달하는 올림픽조각공원을 조성하고 이를 위해 《국제야외조각초대전》(1988년 8월 15일-10월 5일), 《국제야외조각전》(1987년 여름, 1988년 봄, 2회 개최), 그리고 국내외 회화를 소개하는 《국제현대회화전》(8월 17일-10월 5일, 국립현대미술관), 《국제현대서예전》(9월 12일-11월 12일, 예술의 전당) 등을 포함시킨 매머드급 행사였다.[4]

그러나 올림픽 조직위원회가 동서 화해와 교류의 장으로서 의도했던 것과 달리 국내미술계는 추진 방향을 두고 갈등하곤 했고 그동안 축적된 각 분파별 권력이 충돌하는 '정치적' 장이자 현대미술의 정체성에 대한 논쟁의 장을 피할 수 없었다. 한국을 대표하는 작가로서 올림픽 선수처럼 영예를 얻는 기회였기 때문이다. 작가선정을 맡은 운영위원의 사회적 위상, 문화적 정체성과 배경뿐만 아니라 작가가 다루는 매체, 출신학교, 연령 등 여러 요인도 선정과정에 작용하곤 했기에 한국 현대미술의 대표 자격을 두고 첨예한 대립의 장이 될 수밖에 없었다.

1987년부터 1988년까지 약 1년여에 걸쳐 민중미술 진영, 한국화 진영, 구상미술 진영 등 선정과정에서 소외된 작가와 평론가 그룹에서 비판이 제기되곤 했으며 그 비판 속에서 근대화 속에서 수입된 '미술'이 토착화하는 과정에서 구축된 문제들이 불거져 나왔다. 구상/추상, 동양화/서양화, 젊은 세대/기성세대, 민중미술/모더니즘 계열 등 여러 노선과 진영에 따라 축적된 문제가 동시다발적으로 나타났다. 그 결과 세계현대미술제는 한국미술계가 가진 구조적 문제의 해결 가능성을 타진하는 시험대가 되기도 했다.

5. Art Criticism Research Group, "Olympiad of the Art, what did it leave behind?", *Whitepaper of Olympiad of the Art—What's left?*, edited by The antitrust committee of artists on 88 Olympics World Contemporary Art Festival, (Seoul: Ulgul publication, 1989). 319–323.

6. Park Sehun, "Economy Agora: Surplus in Economy Opened Art Importation Era," *Chosun Ilbo*, June 19, 1988.

7. Lee Yongwoo, "Opening to Artwork, Big Changes In Prices," *Dong-a Ilbo*, January 17, 1990.

8. Jung Cheolsoo, "'Opening of Art Market' Preparation In Progress," *Kyunghyang Shinmun*, May 15, 1990.

Participating international artists and curators from other countries in *Olympiad of the Art* also came to be subjects of criticism. In the doubt of their adequate authenticity standard, the resignation of the international organizing committee consisting of Gerard Xuriguera, Thomas Messer, Nakahara Yusuke, Ante Glibota, Pierre Restany was mentioned. Art Criticism Research Group, closely related to Minjung Art, held conferences several times to criticize the event as bureaucratic and undemocratic, which continued after the event to have "an aspect of cultural panorama by Neo-Colonialism". A negative response to the influx of international art was quite intense in which dominating groups in the art world "was imposing international trends, Modernism and Postmodernism, to Korean artists in suppressing manners" through the spectacle of cultural events made by the military regime.[5]

Nevertheless, the art festival served as an impetus for MMCA's collection of artworks by international artists. For the museum that opened in 1986 yet with few international artists' works, this was the opportunity to take the advantage of, proactively. Several artists' maquettes, who participated in *International Outdoor Sculpture Exhibition* in *Olympiad of the Art*, were donated. The museum's current collection list included maquettes for Dennis Oppenheim's *Glass* (1988), Gunther Uecker's *Sword* (1988). Some participating artists also donated their works which included Jean Messagier's *Encounter of Gian Battista Tiepolo and Vincent van Gogh* (1987) and Bernard Schultze's *Ophelia* (1985).

Growth of International Artists' Exhibition and the Art Market in the 1990s

The result of the Seoul Olympics and *Olympiad of the Art* was that the import regulations on the international artists' artworks was substantially lowered. Until 1988, the importation of international artworks required recommendation letters from the Ministry of Culture and Information. Yet, the receipt of recommendation from the government required submission of complicated documents such as an art critic's recommendation letter, a certificate of origin of artwork, a certificate of authenticity, and a certificate of proof of price that only conglomerates could follow proactively. The Samsung Group, founded by Lee Byung-chul, after the establishment of Ho-Am Art Museum, started to collect artworks abroad from the 1980s that opened a number of exhibitions of Henry Moore and August Rodin and later purchased the exhibited works for their private collection. It is also known that the Sunkyoung Group, after the establishment of Walkerhill Art Museum, purchased artworks by Alexander Calder and David Smith after their exhibition for their private collection.[6]

Since the hosting of the Seoul Olympics, the government adopted the open culture policy that pushed the import liberalization policy. More items became subjects of the import liberalization policy which was applied on antiques in 1989, on sculpture in 1990, and on painting and prints in 1991.[7] Consequently, from 1991, artworks started to be legally imported and cleared customs just like any other imported goods. Around then, as an aspiration toward international art by collectors grew enormously with the collapse of the Cold War, galleries in Korea, such as Gana Art Center, Gallery Hyundai, Sun Gallery, started to focus on exhibitions of international artists. Excited by the open Korean art market, Choi Woncheol, a Korean art collector and gallerist from Spain, opened the Union de Arte Seoul branch, which marked the milestone for the establishment of a branch gallery in Korea by prominent galleries overseas.[8]

세계현대미술제에 참여한 외국 작가와 외국인 전시기획자들도 비판을 피할 수 없었다. 객관성을 담보할 수 없다는 이유로 국제운영위원—제라르 슈리게라(Gerard Xuriguera), 토마스 메서(Thomas Messer), 나카하라 유스케(Nakahara Yusuke), 안테 글리보타(Ante Glibota), 피에르 레스타니(Pierre Restany)—의 사퇴가 거론되기도 했다. 민중미술 진영과 가까운 미술비평연구회는 여러 차례 좌담회를 열어 "관료적이고 비민주적인 성격"의 행사라고 비판했으며 미술제가 끝난 후에도 "신식민주의가 펼치는 문화적 파노라마의 양태"를 보이는 행사이자 군사정권이 만든 스펙터클한 문화행사를 통해 미술계 지배집단이 "모더니즘과 포스트모더니즘의 대세를 국제적으로 압도시키는 방식으로 국내 미술인에게 강요"하고 있다고 진단할 정도로 해외 미술의 도입에 부정적인 태도도 상당했다.[5]

그럼에도 불구하고 이 미술제는 국내에 들어온 해외작가의 작품이 국립현대미술관에 소장되는 직접적인 계기가 되었다. 1986년 문을 열었으나 해외작가 작품이 많지 않았던 국립현대미술관으로서는 적극적으로 이 기회를 활용할 수밖에 없었던 것이다. 정확하게 어떤 과정을 거쳤는지 알 수 없으나 세계현대미술제의 《국제야외조각 초대전》에 참여한 일부 작가들의 마케트(maquette)가 다수 국립현대미술관에 기증되었다. 현재 이 미술관 소장품 목록에는 데니스 오펜하임(Dennis Oppenheim, 1938-2011)의 〈유리잔〉(1988), 귄터 위커(Günther Uecker, 1930-)의 〈칼〉(1988) 등의 마케트 작업이 보인다. 또한 《국제현대회화전》에 포함되었던 작가들 일부도 작품을 기증했는데 장 메사지에(Jean Messagier, 1920-1999)의 〈쟝 바티스타 티에폴로와 빈센트 반 고흐의 만남〉(1987), 베르나르트 슐체(Bernard Schultze, 1915-2005)의 〈오필리아〉(1985) 등이 국립현대미술관의 소장품 목록에 들어가 있다.

5. 미술비평연구회, 「서울올림픽미술제, 무엇을 남겼나」, 『서울올림픽미술제 백서— 무엇을 남겼나?』, 88올림픽세계현대미술제 변칙운영저지를 위한 범미술인 대책위원회 편집 (서울: 도서출판 얼굴, 1989), 319-323.

6. 박세훈, 「경제広場(광장) 黑字(흑자)경제 미술품도 輸入(수입) 개방시대」, 『조선일보』, 1988년 6월 19일 자, 7면.

7. 이용우, 「美術品(미술품)개방...값 대변화 예고」, 『동아일보』, 1990년 12월 17일 자, 17면.

8. 정철수, 「"美術(미술)시장개방" 대비 한창」, 『경향신문』, 1990년 5월 15일 자, 8면.

1990년대 해외작가 전시 증가와 미술시장

서울 올림픽과 세계현대미술제가 남긴 첫 번째 성과는 해외작가의 작품을 국내에 들여오는 법적 문턱을 낮추었다는 점이다. 1988년까지 외국의 미술작품은 문화공보부의 추천을 받아야 하는 수입 추천제를 통해야 했다. 그러나 정부의 추천을 받기까지 미술평론가의 추천서, 작품의 원산지증명, 진위증명, 가격증명 등 까다로운 서류를 제출해야 했고 대기업 정도나 적극적으로 이 제도를 활용할 뿐이었다. 이병철 회장의 삼성그룹은 호암미술관을 설립한 후 1980년대 초반부터 해외에서 미술품을 구입하곤 했으며 헨리 무어(Henry Moore, 1898-1986), 오귀스트 로댕(August Rodin, 1840-1917) 등의 작업을 전시한 후 다수 소장품으로 구입한 바 있다. 선경그룹 역시 워커힐미술관을 설립한 후 알렉산더 칼더(Alexander Calder, 1898-1976), 데이비드 스미스(David Smith, 1906-1965) 등의 작품을 전시한 후 소장했다고 알려져 있다.[6]

그러나 올림픽을 계기로 정부는 문화개방정책을 취하며 미술품 수입자유화가 추진된다. 1989년 골동품 수입자유화, 1990년 조각, 1991년 회화와 판화 등 모든 장르로 수입 대상이 확대되기 시작했다.[7] 따라서 1991년부터 적어도 법적으로 미술작품도 다른 일반 물품처럼 통관시킬 수 있게 된 것이다. 바로 이즈음 냉전 구도가 붕괴되고 자본가의 해외 미술에 대한 갈망이 늘어나며 가나화랑, 현대화랑, 선화랑 등 국내 갤러리들이 해외작가 전시에 공을 들이기 시작한 것도 바로 이 시기이다. 갑자기 개방된 시장에 고무되어 스페인 거주 한인 컬렉터이자 화상인 최원철이 1990년 서울에 유니언 데 아르테(Union de Arte) 갤러리 분점을 여는데 해외 화랑의 국내 진출이라는 이정표를 세우기도 했다.[8]

9. Yi Jooheon, "Art Market Awaits New Order: Overseas Artwork In Black Markets," *Hankyoreh*, September 2, 1990.

10. Ulirich Beck, "The Cosmopolitan Society and its Enemies," *Theory, Culture & Society* 19 (April 2002), 17.

However, imported artworks were sold at a higher price than their local price. Sometimes, art sales were made expediently to avoid the radar of governmental monitors. Some artworks that were on view in exhibitions in Korea were sold locally, and instead, the forged ones were returned which were caught later; fabrication of sales documents in the form of donations also happened in order to protect collectors' identity and pursue tax evasion.[9]

As international artists' exhibitions increased, more art-related personalities abroad visited Korea which led to diverse ways to own international artworks. The artworks from *Seoul International Art Festival* in 1990 were collected in museums in Korea; some curators abroad sold artworks to the museums before they returned home. When archives on museums' collection lists become available for viewing, we would figure out how the museums acquired international artworks in their collection.

Growth of International Art Exhibition in the 1990s and Problems of Globalism

The Seoul Olympics and *Olympiad of the Art* triggered the public interest in international arts. The opening of art markets by the government created the foundation for connection between the Korean and international art world and the networking expansion. With the changes in the Korean art scene were introduced more international artists. The artworks by Kathe Kollwitz at Walkerhill Art Museum, Jasper Johns, and Jim Dine were on view in 1991; and in 1992, artworks by Christo and Jenny Holzer were introduced. Artworks by Robert Rauschenberg, César Baldaccini, and Niki de Saint Phalle were on view in the Daejeon Expo (1993); and commercial galleries held shows by Andy Warhol, Tom Wesselmann, and Dan Flavin in 1994. As promising international artists' exhibitions increased, international art sales in the Korean art market grew while that of Korean artists diminished.

The significant phenomenon was that more art critics and curators' visited Korea after 1988. Pierre Restany, a member of the organizing committee for *Olympiad of the Art*, was an invited juror for *Seoul International Print Biennale* (1990), and René Block was invited as a curator to *the SeOUL of Fluxus Festival* (1993) to connect the Korean art world and contemporary global art world consequently.

Nam June Paik played a key role in inviting international art critics to Korea. For international symposiums in his retrospectives, which opened in MMCA in 1992, he invited Pierre Restany, Irving Sandler, Achille Bonito Oliva, John G. Hanhardt, and many important figures. Moreover, he also set the ground for discussion on important topics in modern art, such as postmodernism and feminism in Korean art world.

Nam June Paik also worked hard to realize Whitney Biennial in Seoul in 1993. He voluntarily worked as a cultural diplomat and met the mayor of Venice to establish the Korean Pavilion in Venice Biennale in 1995. Through the Korean Pavilion, Korean artists, Jeon Soocheon and Kang Ik-Joong, won the Special Award to change the course of the Korean Modern Art to global Modern Art and encouraged cosmopolitanization or "internationalization from within".[10] His sincere effort for the Korean art world put behind long-debated issues on imitating art from other countries, modernity, and the very Korean art and instead focused on naturalizing western art in Korea voluntarily by Korean artists that later shared the 'Art' in global levels with global communities of 'Artists'. In this context, globalism and cosmopolitanization of Korean art accelerated from 1988 to 1995.

In the 1990s, international artists' exhibitions were ubiquitous in art museums and galleries; with large scale art events, such as Whitney Biennial in Seoul, Daejeon Expo, and later Gwangju Biennale, international arts arrived in Korea almost simultaneously. Also, more artists were selected to represent Korea in the international art biennales, from São Paulo Art Biennial to Venice Biennale, which further triggered exchanges in contemporary art. At the same time, in addition to artists, curators and art critics expanded their awareness to the global ground and responded flexibly to the changes of international art. In the process of so-called globalization of the art world or the entry to the Global art world, various values and discourses like cultural pluralism and postcolonial attitude emerged to demand strong awareness from the Korean art field.

9. 이주헌, 「미술시장 새질서 기다린다: 해외 미술품 암거래 불법 판쳐」, 『한겨레』, 1990년 9월 2일 자, 9면.

10. Ulirich Beck, "The Cosmopolitan Society and its Enemies," *Theory, Culture & Society* 19 (April 2002), 17.

그러나 수입된 작품들은 해외 현지의 가격보다 비싸게 거래되었고 그나마 거래된 경우라도 정부의 감시망을 피하기 위한 편법을 사용하곤 했다고 한다. 전시를 위해 수입했던 미술품을 국내에 판매하고 위작을 만들어 돌려보내다가 적발된 사건이 있었는가 하면, 세금 추적을 피하고 컬렉터의 신분을 보호하기 위해 표면적으로는 기증의 형식을 취하는 등 법적 제도를 우회하려는 시도는 계속 이어졌다.[9]

해외작가 전시가 늘어나자 해외 미술인들의 내한이 빈번해지며 해외 작품 소장 기회도 다변화된다. 1990년 열린 《서울국제미술제》에 전시된 작품이 국내 미술관에 소장되기도 했고 해외에서 온 기획자가 작품을 전시한 후 돌아가기 전에 미술관에 판매하는 경우도 있었다. 향후 국내 미술관의 소장품 이력에 관련된 정보가 개방되면 구체적으로 누가 어떤 경로로 해외작가 작품을 미술관에 판매했는지 파악될 것이다.

1990년대 해외 미술 전시 증가와 전 지구화의 문제

서울 올림픽과 세계현대미술제가 해외 미술에 대한 관심을 촉진시키고 미술품 시장을 개방하며 외국 미술계와의 접촉과 네트워크를 확장하는 계기가 된 것도 사실이다. 이런 환경의 변화에 힘입어 1990년대 많은 해외 작가들이 국내에 소개되었다. 1991년 케테 콜비츠 (Kathe Kollwitz, 1867-1945) 전(워커힐미술관), 재스퍼 존스(Jasper Johns, 1930-), 짐 다인(Jim Dine, 1935-), 1992년에는 크리스토(Christo, 1935-2020), 제니 홀저(Jenny Holzer, 1950-) 등이 전시되었다. 대전 엑스포(1993)의 미술전람회에 라우센버그 (R. Rauschenberg, 1925-2008), 세자르(César Baldaccini, 1921-1998), 니키 드 생팔(Niki de Saint-Phalle, 1930-2002) 등이 전시되었으며 1994년에는 앤디 워홀(Andy Warhol, 1928-1987), 탐 웨슬만(Tom Wesselmann, 1931-2004), 댄 플래빈(Dan Flavin, 1933-1996) 등이 화랑을 통해 전시된다. 해외 유망 작가들의 전시가 늘어나자 자연스럽게 국내 미술시장에서 외국 작가 작품 판매가 늘었으며 상대적으로 국내작가 판매가 위축되기도 했다.

주목할 만한 현상은 1988년 이후 해외 미술평론가/ 전시기획자의 한국 방문이 늘기 시작한 것이다. 세계현대미술제 국제운영위원을 지낸 피에르 레스타니가 서울국제판화비엔날레(1990)에 심사위원으로 초대되었으며 《서울 플럭서스 페스티벌》(1993)에 르네 블록(René Block) 이 기획자로 참여하며 동시대 미술의 교감을 나눌 기회가 늘기 시작했다.

백남준은 해외 평론가들의 한국 방문의 촉매제 역할을 하기도 했다. 자신의 회고전(국립현대미술관, 1992)을 계기로 연 국제심포지엄에는 피에르 레스타니, 어빙 샌들러(Irving Sandler), 아킬레 보니토 올리바 (Achille Bonito Oliva), 존 핸하르트(John G. Hanhardt) 등 국제미술계의 저명인사들을 초대하여 백남준의 네트워크를 보여주는 한편 포스트모더니즘, 페미니즘을 비롯한 현대미술의 주요 의제를 심화할 수 있는 자리를 만든 바 있다.

백남준은 이외에도 1993년 휘트니비엔날레 서울전에 많은 공을 들였고 1995년 베니스비엔날레 한국관 개관을 성사시키기 위해 베니스 시장을 만나는 등 스스로 '문화 대사'의 역할을 자청하기도 했다. 이 한국관을 통해 전수천, 강익중 등 한국의 현대미술작가들이 특별상을 수상하며 한국 현대미술의 방향을 글로벌 현대미술로 돌리며 코스모폴리탄화(cosmopolitanization) 또는 "내부로부터의 세계화"를 강화했다고 할 수 있다.[10] 그동안 모방, 현대성, 한국적 미술을 두고 오랫동안 이어진 논란을 뒤로 하고 서구의 미술이 한국 작가의 자발적 노력에 의해 토착화되고 다시 '미술'이라는 세계적 장과 '예술가'라는 세계적 공동체를 공유하게 된 것이다. 그래서 1988년부터 1995년 사이는 한국 미술의 전 지구화와 코스모폴리탄화가 빠르게 전개된 시기라고 할 수 있다.

따라서 1990년대는 미술관과 화랑에 해외작가 전시가 빈번해졌으며, 휘트니비엔날레 서울전, 대전 엑스포, 그리고 이후 광주비엔날레 등 대형 전시를 통해 해외의 미술이 거의 실시간으로 국내에 도착한 시대라고 할 수 있다. 또한 상파울루비엔날레부터 베니스비엔날레까지 해외 비엔날레 참여 기회의 확대로 인해 동시대 미술의 가치 교류가 더욱 촉진되곤 했다. 동시에 작가를 비롯해 새로이 등장한 전시기획자와 평론가들의 인식이 국제적 지평으로 확장되었고 해외 미술의 변화에 관대하게 반응하게 된다. 미술계의 전 지구화 또는 글로벌 미술계로의 진입이라고 할 수 있는 이 과정에서 문화다원주의, 탈식민주의적 태도 등 여러 가치와 담론이 대두되어 국내 미술인들의 성찰을 더욱 강하게 요구한 것도 사실이다.

1969년 국립현대미술관은 대한민국미술전람회의 전시공간으로서 전문 학예인력은 물론
소장품 또한 전무한 상태로 경복궁 내 옛 조선총독부 건물에 개관하였다.
그리고 1971년에 이르러서야 소장품 수집이 시작되었다.
전문 문화예술기관으로서의 요건에는 못 미쳤지만, 국립미술관을 열망하는 미술계 안과 밖의
관심은 상당했다.
개관 이후 끊임없이 소장품 부족과 상설전시 운영의 어려움이 제기되었으며,
1973년 덕수궁으로 이전한 뒤에도 마찬가지였다. 특히 과천관 신축 계획 발표 전후로는
소장품 부실과 운영 문제가 더욱 구체적으로 제기되었다.

In 1969, MMCA was established as an exhibition space for National Art Exhibition of
The Republic of Korea.
It was opened in the former the Japanese Government General of Korea
building in Gyeongbokgung Palace with no professional curators and no collections.
And it wasn't until 1971 that the collection began.
Although it did not meet the requirements as a specialized cultural and artistic institution,
it was Interest in and outside the art world was considerable. Since its opening, the
National Museum of Modern and Contemporary Art has been constantly experiencing
difficulties in operating permanent exhibitions and lack of collections even if it was
moved to Deoksugung in 1973. Operational issues for collection-insufficieny were raised
more specifically as the Gwacheongwan construction plan was announced.

1969. 8. 27.

경향신문
이뤄진 20년 숙원(宿願) 국립현대미술관 발족

과거 20년 동안 전체 미술계의 최대의 숙원이었고
국가적으로도 하나의 문화적 허부(虛部)가 되어오던
현대미술관이 빈약한 출발이긴 해도 마침내
실현된다는 문공부의 움직임. 한국근대미술사에 획기적인
한 이정표로 기록될 현대미술관 발족은 그러나 너무
사전의 연구, 검토가 결여된 강행이라 관계 사회에선
일단 쌍수 환영을 보내면서도 장차의 그 실체와
운영에 비상한 관심을 모으고 있다.

그 난제를 놓고, 경복궁 뒤뜰의 국립미술관(사실은
전시관에 불과하지만)에 국전 추천작가급의 작품들을
한동안 계속 진열시키는 등의 과도기적인 노력도
보였었다.

Kyunghyang Shinmun
**Launch of the National Museum of Modern
and Contemporary Art—A long-cherished
desire realized.**

The Ministry of Culture and Education moves to
open the Museum of Modern Art. Though it might
be a poor start, it is the realization of what had
been the art world's greatest desire for 20 years,
as well as the appeasing of cultural weakness.
However, the Museum's launch — which history
will remember as a milestone in the history of
Korean modern art — lacks prior research and
proper review. Therefore, though interested
parties wholeheartedly rejoice, their interests are
focused on its future substance and operation.

1979. 3. 28.

경향신문
볼 작품 없는 국립현대미술관

우리 미술관의 기증작품 현황은 외국미술관과 비교할 때
창피할 만큼 적다. 1947년에 개관된 파리국립
근대미술관은 60년부터 65년까지 5년 사이에 모두
1천 84점의 작품을 모았지만, 이중 작가 자신이나
유족들에게서 기증받은 작품이 전체의 85%에 이르며
구입은 불과 16%에 지나지 않는다.

국립현대미술관이 책정하고 있는 작품구입비를 보면
더욱 아연해질 수밖에 없다. 올해 예산은 4천 7백 50만원.

Kyunghyang Shinmun
Nothing to See at MMCA.

Compared with foreign art galleries, the status of
donated works in Korea's Museum is embarrassing.
For example, the National Museum of Modern
and Contemporary Art in Paris, which opened in
1947, collected 1,884 pieces between 1960 to
1965 — of which 85% were donated by artists or
their families, with only 16% being purchased
by the Museum.

A look at the purchasing budget for MMCA only
makes for a more woeful picture. This year's budget
is 47.5 million won.

작고한 동양화가 朴崍賢화백의 작품 「영광」(1967년作·134cm×168cm)。이 작품은 朴씨의 부군인 雲甫 金基昶화백이 지난해 기증했다.

볼 作品없는 국립現代美術館

체계별로 整理안되고 짜임새도 없어
기증에 크게 인색…올들어 全無상태

현대 美術館 所藏品

구분	구 입	기 증	관리전환	계
동양화 각예	34	17	8	59
동서양화 각예	60	77	9	146
조소	18	31	3	52
서예	4	5	19	28
공예축	2	2		5
			11	11
계	118 (40%)	132 (45%)	41 (15%)	291 (100%)

1983. 4. 16.

동아일보
현대미술관 어떤 작품으로 채우나

최근 국립현대미술관 건립에 대한 세부 계획의 발표는
미술인들이나 문화종사자들은 물론 일반 국민들에게도
큰 자부심과 긍지를 불어넣어 주고 있다.

그러나 미술 관계자들은 "실제의 문제는 이제부터"라고
은근히 걱정하고 있다. 1만여 평이 넘는 각종 전시 공간을
과연 어떤 작품으로 채울 것이며 미술관 운영의 핵심인
전문 연구원이나 큐레이터를 어떻게 확보하느냐가
미술관 운영의 제1 관건이기 때문. (...) 외국 작품도 꼭
갖춰야

새로 지어지는 현대미술관에 과연 어떤 작품들이
전시되느냐 하는 것이 무엇보다 제일 중요하다.

Dong-A Ilbo
How to fill the Museum of Modern Art?

The recent announcement of a detailed plan for
constructing MMCA has instilled incredible
pride in artists, cultural workers, and the general
public.

However, art officials are worried that "the real
problem is from now." The key to operating a
museum is deciding which works will fill the more
than 330㎡ of exhibition space and how to
procure professional researchers or curators.

1984. 11. 15.

조선일보
과천 현대미술관 예산 부족 '작품 없는 전시실' 우려

과천에 신축 중인 국립현대미술관이 완공 후 공간을
채울 작품이 부족, 대책 마련에 부심 중이다. 미술관 측은
향후 4년간 작품구입비 20억 원과 외국 작품구매비
8억 원을 책정하고 이를 85년 정부예산에 반영해줄 것을
요청했다. 그러나 정부에서 책정한 내년도(1985)
작품구입비는 1억 2천만 원에 그쳐 준공을 3년 앞두고
작품구입에 큰 차질을 빚게 되었다.

외국 작가들의 작품을 전시할 특별전시실은 현재로선
텅 비어 있는 상태다. (...) 한나라의 국립미술관에
외국 작품이 한 점도 없다는 것은 국가적인 수치라는 게
미술인들의 이구동성이다. 그러나 외국의 유명작가
작품은 엄청나게 호가, 미술관 1년 작품 구입비로는
한점도 넘나 보기 힘든 형편이다.

"예산만 뒷받침되면 외국의 유능한 작가를 초치,
워크숍 등을 통해 제작된 작품을 남길 수 있는 방안도
강구 중"이라고 밝혔다.

Chosun Ilbo
**Lack of budget at the Gwacheon Museum
of Modern and Contemporary Art —
Concern regarding 'empty exhibition rooms'.**

MMCA under construction in Gwacheon is struggling to develop measures regarding a lack
of art to fill the space after completion. The government's purchase fee for next year (1985) is
set at 120 million won — a significant setback just
three years before construction is complete.

The special exhibition room, which will display
the work of foreign artists, is currently empty.
Artists agree that it is a national embarrassment
for there to be no foreign pieces in a country's
National Museum of Art. However, famous foreign
artists' works are particularly expensive, with
it being difficult to consider buying even a single
piece of art with the entire one-year budget
of a museum.

◇지난 3월 착공, 경기도 과천 서울대공원내에 건설증인 현대미술관
전경. 건물은 번듯하나 채울 작품은 막연하다.

조선일보 西紀 1984年 11月 15日 木曜日

果川 현대미술관 예산부족
"作品없는 展示室" 우려

購入費 8억 요청, 정부선 냉담
기증에 기대… 外國작품은 더 對策 없어

單行本 출판협의회 19일 출범
이미 160여개社서 加入 신청

1986. 11. 28.

조선일보
현대미술관 '예상 밖 인기'

규모가 커진 현대미술관은 이에 걸맞는 작품수집을
못 하고 있다. 특히 외국 작가 작품은 전무한 실정이어서
체면이 말이 아니다. 이(李) 관장은 "금년에는 국내의
30-50대 작가 작품 55점과 아시아 작가 작품 20여 점을
구입했다"며 "내년에는 외국 작품 구입에 주력하기 위해
예산을 신청해 놓고 있다."고 밝혔다.

Chosun Ilbo
MMCA 'Unexpectedly popular'.

MMCA has yet to collect works suitable for its
more extensive scale. In particular, it is disgraceful
that there are no pieces by foreign artists.
According to Director Lee, "This year, we purchased
55 works by Korean artists in their 30s to 50s, and
20 works by Asian artists." adding, "We are currently
applying for a budget to be able to focus on
purchasing foreign works next year."

현대미술관 예상밖 "人氣"

개관 3개월…… 관람객 21만명 돌파

◇아시아 현대미술전을 감상하는 관람객들. 果川 현대
미술관은 외진 지리적 여건에도 불구, 관람객들의 발길
이 잦다.

音樂会 등 다양한 프로그램 곁들여
市民들 「週末 휴식공간」으로 愛用

국립현대미술관 과천 개관 직후 관람객 모습 1986. 8. 26.
MMCA, Gwacheon crowded with visitors at the time of its openiing August 26, 1986

1978. 6. 9.

조선일보
유업소(劉業昭) 화백 전시품 1점 기증

조선일보사 주최로 1일부터 7일까지 서울 신문회관에서
특별전시회를 가졌던 자유중국의 유업소(劉業昭) 화백이
전시작품 중 1점을 8일 국립현대미술관에 기증했다.
기증작품은 유화백의 특징이 담긴 발묵산수(潑墨山水)
중 공산불견인(空山不見人).^{88쪽} 이를 유화백의 사위인
손계서(孫契瑞)씨(국립대만대인(臺灣大人) 교수)가
윤치오 관장에게 전달했는데, 윤관장은 "중국의 현역
화가로서는 첫 기증작품"이라며 "이를 계기로 양국의
문화교류가 보다 활발해지길 바란다"고 말했다.

Chosun Ilbo
Exhibition piece donated by artist LIU Ye Zhao.

Taiwanese artist LIU Ye Zhao donated *Vacant Mountain*, ^{p. 88} one of his exhibition works to MMCA on
January 8, after holding a special exhibit hosted
by Chosun Ilbo from the 1st to the 7th at the Seoul
Newspaper Center. Yoon Chi-oh, director of the
National Museum of Modern and Contemporary
Art, said, "It is the first piece donated by a currently
active Taiwanese painter." adding, "I hope this will
lead to more active cultural exchanges between
the two countries."

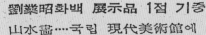

劉業昭화백 展示品 1점 기증
山水畵……국립 現代美術館에

◇孫啓瑞교수가 劉業昭화백의 작품 「空山
不見人」을 尹致五관장에게 전달하고 있다.

1981. 4. 16.

동아일보
서울서 전시회 흑인 화가 '호워드'씨 93쪽

한국 풍물 소재로 다섯 번째 개인전

그의 그림은 추상 쪽이지만 이번 전시회엔 한국을
소재로 한 한국의 인상들을 강렬하면서도 촉촉이 젖어
나는 유동감으로 표현하고 있다.

Dong-A Ilbo
Black artist 'Hoard' p.93 **holds an exhibition in Seoul.**

The 5th solo exhibition is based on Korean
traditional music.

Though her paintings are abstract, this exhibition
presents impressions of Korea with a robust yet moist
flow that expresses fluidity.

1981. 8. 3.

동아일보
한국미술 국제화 바람

한국미술의 국제화 시대는 멀기만 한 것일까. 아닌 것
같다. 아직은 성급한 판단이 될지 모르지만 그러나 서서히
우리 미술이 해외에 대량으로 소개되고 국제적으로
평가를 받는 작업이 진행되고 있는 것으로 보아 우리
미술의 국제화 시대도 머지않아 열릴 전망이다.

요즘 들어 해외에 나가 있는 우리 미술인들이 서로 모여
스스로 단체를 만들고 우리 작품들을 현지에 소개하고
교류전을 갖자는 작업이 일어나고 있는가 하면
저명미술관이나 화랑들이 한국현대작가들의 작품전시를
요구해오고 있어 그 전망은 더욱 밝다.

Dong-A Ilbo
The Globalization of Korean art.

Is the era of the internationalization of Korean art
far off? Probably not. It may be too early to call,
but as Korean art is gradually being introduced in
large quantities and evaluated internationally,
it can be predicted that an era of globalization for
Korean art is not far off.

1981. 7. 25.

조선일보
미국서 선보이는 한국현대미술

70년대 이후 한국현대미술은 일본과 유럽 쪽에 주로
진출했을 뿐, 현대미술의 중심지인 뉴욕에는 거의
진출할 기회를 갖지 못했다는 것이다. 또 이번 전시는
한국미술의 국제교류의 길을 넓히고, 적극적인
방향모색의 한 계기가 될 것으로 내다보는 견해도 있다.

《한국현대드로잉》전 개막식에는 브루클린 박물관
측에서 보트 윙크 관장, 전문위원 진 바로씨 등 간부
50여명과 한국 측에서 주유엔대사, 문화원장, 재미화가
60여명 등이 참가했다. 미술기자-평론가 400여명의
초청 관람객들은 전시장을 둘러보고, "참신한
전람회"라는 반응을 보였다고 현지를 다녀온 평론가
오광수 씨는 말했다.

이번 전시는 브루클린 미술관의 전문위원 진 바로씨가
지난 4월 내한, 현대미술관에서 열렸던 《드로잉 81》전을
관람하고 초대작가를 직접 선정하여 이루어졌다.

이번 전시회 기획에 적극 참여했던 재미화가 황규백씨는
"앞으로는 영향력 있는 미국의 미술전문가들을 자주
한국에 초청, 미술 현실을 인식시키는 것이 한국미술의
미국진출 발판을 굳히는 방안"이라며 "이를 위한 정책적
뒷받침이 필요할 때"라는 의견을 전해왔다.

Chosun Ilbo
Korean contemporary art in the U.S.

Since the 1970s, Korean contemporary art had
only expanded towards Japan and Europe and
never into the cultural center of modern art —
New York. Some predict that this exhibition will open
the way for international exchanges of Korean
art, and serve as the catalyst for many
opportunities.

The opening ceremony of the *Korea Modern
Drawing* exhibition saw the attendance of about
50 executives, including Director and expert
committee member Gene Baro, as well as about 60
U.N. ambassadors, important cultural figures, and
Korean painters who live in the U.S.

The exhibition was held by Baro, an expert
committee member of the Brooklyn Museum of Art,
who personally invited artists after attending
Korean Drawing 81 exhibition held at the Museum
of Modern and Contemporary Art in Korea in April.

"In the future, inviting influential American art
experts to Korea to recognize the reality of our art
is a means to solidify the expansion of Korean
art into the United States."
A Korean painter Hwang Gyu Baek, living in the
U.S., actively participated in the planning of the
exhibition said.

1979. 7. 24.

경향신문
"누구나 관심 갖고 참여를…"
애호가 찾는 '현대미술관회'

구미 각국 멤버십 제도를 도입
작년(1978년) 8월 발족

국립현대미술관의 운영을 도우며 문화·예술적 삶을 즐기려는 시민과 미술관과의 밀착을 도모한다는 두 가지 목적을 띤 이 회는 순수미술애호가들의 자발적인 모임.

현대미술관회가 비록 외국의 멤버십 제도를 모방했다고 하더라도 우리의 풍토로서는 그 어느 나라보다 더욱 필요한 존재 가치를 지닌다.

그 까닭은 국립현대미술관이 체제나 기구, 예산에 있어 너무도 전근대적인 초기 단계를 못 벗어나고 있기 때문이다. 국립현대미술관이 개관된 지 어언 10년.

그럼에도 미술관으로서의 각종 기능은 물론 가장 중요한 작품 구입과 보관, 전시조차도 잘 안 되고 있는 실정이다.

Kyunghyang Shinmun
"Anyone can be interested and participate …"
'Membership Society for MMCA' seeks enthusiasts.

Introduced membership systems in several countries
Launched in August of the Previous Year (1978)

The voluntary meeting of pure art lovers has two objectives — assisting the operation of MMCA, and in so doing, enjoying culture and art.

Though these Membership Society imitate foreign membership systems, they are necessary, considering Korea's traditional climate.

The reason is that MMCA failed to escape pre-modern restrictions in terms of system, organization, and budget. It has been ten years since MMCA opened.

And yet the reality is that it still fails to properly perform the various functions of an art museum, including key aspects such as the purchase, storage, and exhibition of works.

(제3종우편물인가) 1979년7월24일(화요일)

"누구나 關心갖고 參與를…"

「愛好家찾는 現代美術館會」

歐美각국 멤버십制度를 도입

작년 8월發足…會員에 無料출입등 特典

지난5월30일 건축가 尹一根교수(成大)가「韓國 現代美術史(건축)」를 강의하고있다.

現代美術館會(회장 閔丙燾)가 미술애호가들을 찾고있다. 국립현대미술관의 운영을 도우며 文化·藝術的 삶을 즐기려는 시민과 미술관과의 밀착을 도모한다는 두가지 목적을띤 이회는 순수미술애호가들의 자발적인 모임. 지난해 8월 발족되어 이제 겨우걸음마를 시작한 단계지만 이회의 회원이 누릴수있는 갖가지 특전은 미술을 아끼거나 알고자하는 사람들에게 더없이 좋은기회를 제공한다는 점에서 미술계의 주목을 끌고있다.

歐美각국의 미술관 멤버십제도를 살펴보면「現代美術館會」의 참뜻을 쉽게 이해할수있다. 우리것이 외국미술관의 멤버십제도를 도입했기 때문이다.

「미국의루브르」라고불리는 뉴욕의 메트로폴리탄 미술관의 멤버십은 1년회비 15달러의 학생회원 35달러의 일반회원, 50달러의 참여회원, 1백달러의 협조회원, 그리고 후원회원으로서의 일시불 2백50달러의 현금회원, 5백달러의 증여회원, 1천달러의 스폰서회원, 2천5백달러의 패트런 회원등으로 구분이된다.

이 구분에 따른특전도 서로 달라 학생회원은 미술관 자유출입, 미술관 뉴스·잡지·캘린더를보내주고 미술관연주회와 강좌참가의 우선권, 미술관의 사진·슬라이드 사용료 할인의혜택이 주어진다. 일반회원은 앞의 모든특전외에 1년에2회 특별전 사전관람과 봄·가을의 회원강좌초대, 미술관출판의 서적·판화·복제품의 할인이 더해진다.

그러나 참여회원이 되면 패스가 2개가 주어지며 협조회원에게는 미술관 간행서적중 2권을 무료로 주기도 한다.

이같은 멤버십제도는 외국의 유수한 미술관이라면 어디든지 있다. 英國의 테이트 갤러리, 캐나다 터론토의 로열 온타리오미술관의 멤버십은 세계적으로 명성을 날린다.

멤버십을 통해 들어온 돈으로 각미술관들은 작품을 구입하거나 교육및 보급을위한 사업을 전개하며 국가예산은 유지비나 인건비로 쓸뿐이다.

現代美術館會가 비록 외국의 멤버십제도를 모방했다하더라도 우리의 풍토로서는 그 어느나라보다 더욱 필요한 존재가치를 지닌다.

그까닭은 국립현대미술관이 체제나 기구, 예산에 있어 너무도 전근대적인초기단계를 못벗어나고 있기 때문이다. 국립현대미술관이 개관된지 어언 10년.

그럼에도 미술관으로서의 각종 기능은 물론 가장 중요한 작품구입과 보관, 전시조차도 잘안되고 있는 실정이다. 이는 그동안 미술관이 관(官)주도로 운영되어왔고 국가예산에만 의존했기 때문. 그러다보니 아이디어를 짜낼수도 없고 혹 있다해도 예산의 뒷받침이 없어 死藏되곤했다.

이뿐아니라 국가나 국민이 과거의 유산보존에는 큰관심을 기울이면서도 현재의 문화재산의 보존·계승에는 별관심을 쏟지 않는 풍조가 팽배돼있다는 점이다. 오늘의 문화가 단절될때 미래는 기약될수없다.

거기다 최근 일기 시작한 미술품의 방향이 잘못가고있다는 점에도 미술에 관심있는 사람들의 적극적인 노력이 뒤따라야할 필연성을 갖는다.

이런점으로 볼때 現代美術館會가 짊어진 책임은 더욱 무거워진다.

현재 現代美術館會의 회원은 일반·가족·영구회원등 3종류. 일반회원과 가족회원은 각각 매년 5천원과 1만원의 회비를내는 사람이며 영구회원은 한번에 10만원이상을낸 사람. 그러나 회원의 구별없이 주어지는 특전은 똑같다.

국립현대미술관의 무료출입, 미술강좌 무료청강, 미술관간행물의 할인제공, 현대미술관의 각종행사초청등이 특전의 내용이다.

그러나 現代美術館會는 규모에서부터 취약점을 면할수없는 실정. 현재 연구회원 72명, 가족회원 29명, 일반회원 2백86명으로 회원은 모두 3백87명. 모금된 회비도 겨우 7백만~8백만원에 불과하다.

『최소한 3천만원이상은 적립되어야 그이자로 운영이 원만히 된다』는 현대미술관회 사무국장 李鳳順씨는 『그럼에도 올해 들어 2월부터 6월까지 월2회씩의 미술강좌를 열어 왔다』며 기초는 다져 놓은 셈이라고 밝힌다.

李국장의 자신있는 설명에도 불구하고 실제미술관회를 들여다보면 앞으로해결해야할 문제가 산적돼있음을 곧발견하게 된다.

겨우 국립현대미술관 3층에 방1간을빌어 사용할뿐인 現代美術館會는 회원확충과 함께 슬라이드, 필름, 미술서적등 자료실의 설치와 외부에서찾아와 이를 활용할수있는 도서실개관등은 하루빨리 해결되어야할 문제다. 크게볼때 현대미술관회의 발전은 곧현대미술의 발전을 의미하기 때문이다. 【崔金錫기자】

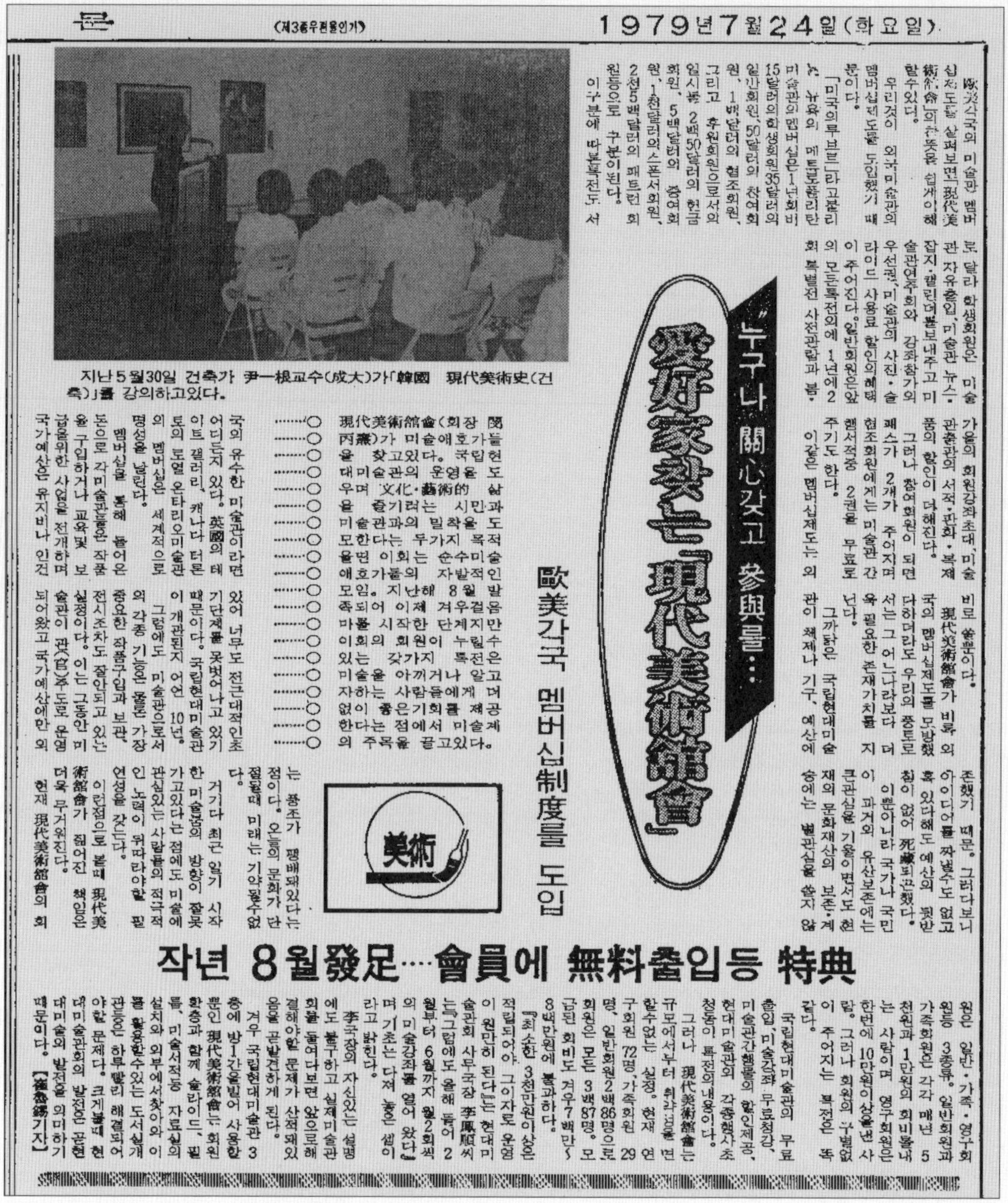

1978년 현대미술관회는 미술애호가들의 자발적 모임이자 미술관을 돕기 위한 민간후원단체로 시작되었다.
1981년 사단법인으로 발족 후 작성한 정관에 따르면 "국립현대미술관의 국가적, 사회적 기능 및 발전을 돕고 현대미술에
대한 일반인의 인식과 이해를 증진하는 것을 목적으로 한다"고 명시되어 있다.

In 1978, Membership Society for MMCA was started as a privately sponsored organization to support
the museum. In 1981 the articles of Membership Society stated "The Purpose of Membership Society
for MMCA is to improve museum's national role and to increase the public's awareness and understanding
of the art."

1978년 `현대미술관회' 창립 총회
당시 회장은 민병도 前한국은행 총재, 부회장은 건축가 김수근이었다.
단상에 올라가 있는 사람이 당시 윤치오 국립현대미술관장이다.

Inaugural Meeting, 1978
Min Byungdo, the Chairman and former president of Bank of Korea.
Kim Swoogeun, Vice-chairman and Archtect.
Yoon Chio, former Director of MMCA.

(사)현대미술관회에서는 국내외 경제, 문화계의 네트워크를 동원하여 국립현대미술관을 보좌하기 위한 국제교류의
지평을 넓히고자 했다. 다수의 해외 미술계 인사와 20명 이상의 국립현대미술관 국제미술 주요 소장작가를 직접 초청해
강좌를 열었다. 또한 해외미술품으로는 데이비드 호크니의 포토콜라주 작업 〈레일이 있는 그랜드캐년 남쪽 끝〉,
로스 블렉크너 〈노란심장〉 등 6점을 국립현대미술관에 기증했다.

Membership Society for MMCA tried to broaden range of international exchange for MMCA networking of
global economic and culture. More than 20 artists in the MMCA global art collection and leading personages
in global art were invited by the association. Each of them gave a lecture to public in Korea. In addition,
it donated 6 pieces of international artwork to MMCA including David Hockney's photomontage *The Grand
Canyon South Rim with Rail, Oct 1982*, Ross Beckner, *Yellow Heart*.

'85 피에르 레스타니 초청 강좌 〈프랑스 현대미술 10년의 동향〉
Pierre Restany at MMCA for a lecture *10 Years of French Contemporary Art* in 1985

'88 데니스 오펜하임 강좌
Lecture by Dennis Oppenheim, 1988

'90 클로드 비알라 강좌
Lecture by Claude Viallat, 1990

'91 도널드 저드 강좌
Lecture by Donald Judd, 1991

'92 크리스토, 잔 클로드 강좌
Christo and Jeanne-Claude at MMCA for a lecture, 1992

'93 프랭크 스텔라 강좌
Frank Stella at MMCA for a lecture, 1993

'94 앤서니 카로 강좌
Anthony Caro at MMCA for a lecture in 1994

'95 조나단 보로프스키 강좌
Lecture by Jonathan BOROFSKY, 1995

53

1987. 12. 17.

경향신문
국립현대미술관 외국작품 컬렉션 한창

국립현대미술관(관장 이경성)이 서울 올림픽을 앞두고 외국작품 확충작업에 열을 올리고 있다.

지난 8월 미국의 대표적인 작가 故 앤디 워홀의 〈자화상〉을 사들인 국립현대미술관은 내년을 국제적인 미술관으로서의 면모를 일신시킬 내실화의 해로 정하고 본격적인 확충작업에 들어간다.

특히 가장 큰 취약점으로 나타났던 외국작품 소장 품목을 대폭 늘린다는 방침아래 《프랑스현대미술전》 등 외국미술 국내전 유치에 주력할 계획이다.

현재 국립현대미술관의 외국작품 소장품 내용은 동양화 4점, 서양화 31점, 판화 123점, 조각 11점, 공예 5점. 6만 달러를 들여 사들인 故 앤디 워홀의 〈자화상〉106~107쪽 한 쌍을 비롯, 라우센버그의 프린트 작품 1점,109쪽 크리스토의 〈대지(大地)예술을 위한 에스키스〉 작품,108쪽 비알라의 페인팅 대작 2점,208~209쪽 故 요셉 보이스의 작품 6점이 대표적인 소장품으로 올라있다.

미술평론가 유준상씨(국립현대미술관 전문위원실장)는 미술관으로서 성과를 높이는 길은 시설도 중요하지만, 외국의 저명 작가 작품을 확보하고 이것을 국내미술 발전에 수용시키는 길임을 전제, 외국작품 구입에 정부 차원의 지원이 절실하다고 지적하고 있다.

한편 미술계에서도 국제화 시대에 부응할 수 있도록 최소한 1천여 점의 외국작품 수장이 필요하다며 보다 적극적인 대책이 아쉽다고 말하고 있다.

Kyunghyang Shinmun
Increased collection of foreign works at MMCA.

The National Museum of Modern and Contemporary Art (Director Lee Kyung-sung) is eagerly working on expanding foreign works ahead of the Seoul Olympics. The Museum, which bought the late Andy Warhol's *Self-Portrait* in August, has begun a full-scale expansion in preparation for making next year one that will affirm its reputation as an international art museum.

Particular focus was put into opening foreign exhibitions, such as *the French Rye University Art Exhibition*, following the policy of making up for the Museum's greatest vulnerability — a significant lack of foreign works.

Currently, the collection of foreign works at the National Museum of Modern and Contemporary Art consists of 4 Eastern paintings, 31 Western paintings, 123 prints, 11 sculptures, and five crafts.

These include a pair of self-portraits pp. 106–107 by the late Andy Warhol, A print by Robert Rauschenberg, p. 109 Christo *A Valley Curtain*, p. 108 two great paintings by Claude Viallat, pp. 208–209 and six works by the late Joseph Beuys.

Art critic Yoo Joon-sang (Chief Curator of the National Museum of Modern and Contemporary Art) points out that though the venue is an important means to improve an art museum's performance, it only goes so far as the capacity to attain works by famed foreign artists and utilize them for the development of domestic art culture. Thus an urgent need for government-level support in procuring foreign works. Meanwhile, the art community agrees that more active measures are necessary, saying that at least 1,000 pieces of foreign art are needed to meet the era of globalization.

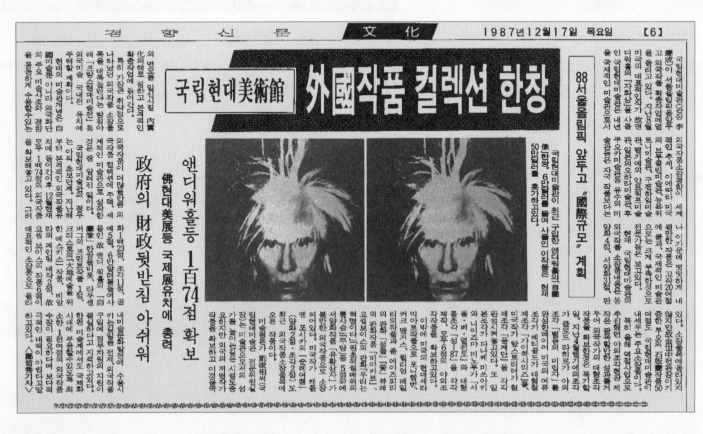

54

동아일보
현대미술관 미술품 5년간 50억 원어치 구입

국립현대미술관은 88년부터 92년까지 5개년 계획으로
매년 10억 원씩 50억 원 상당의 미술품을 영구
소장작품으로 구입할 계획이다. 국립현대미술관은
근대미술 도입기인 1910년대의 작품에서부터
최근의 것에 이르기까지 단계적으로 매입한다.

한편 현대미술관은 지난 한 해 동안 2억 80여만 원을
들여 34점의 외국작품을 구입한 것으로 밝혀졌다.
특히 이 가운데는 1점당 2천 5백만 원짜리 앤디 워홀
(미국)의 자화상 2점과 1천7백여만 원짜리의
로버트 라우센버그(미국) 크리스토(불가리아) 등 5명의
작품 5점도 포함되어 있다. 구입방법은 화랑을 통해
구입한 것이 19점, 작가에게 직접 구입한 것이 15점이다.
또 작가의 국적별로는 일본이 19점으로 가장 많다.

이렇게 5개년 계획에 의한 작품구입이 끝나도 선진
외국의 대형미술관 수준에는 못 미치지만, 그런대로
국립미술관으로서의 면모는 갖추게 된다.

Dong-A Ilbo
**MMCA to Purchase 5 billion won worth of art
in 5 years.**

MMCA plans to spend one billion won a year from
1988 to 1992 in buying artwork for their permanent
collection for a grand total of five billion won.
The Museum has planned a step by step purchasing plan starting with pieces from the introduction
of modern art in the 1910s to more recent works.

Recently, it was revealed that the Museum
had spent 2.8 million won over the past year to
purchase 34 pieces of foreign art.

국립현대미술관이 지난해 구입한 「앤디 워홀」
(미국)作 「자화상」.

1984. 1. 15.

조선일보
「굿모닝 오웰」 우주예술제 세 주역 서울서 공연 — 판화전

정초 인공위성으로 중계된 우주예술제 「굿모닝미스터
오웰」의 세 주역, 즉 비디오아트의 백남준, 현대음악의
존 케이지, 현대무용의 머스 커닝햄의 이색 판화작품들이
서울에 왔다. 원(圓)화랑 대표 정기용씨가 백남준씨와
직접 교섭하여 보내진 이 판화들은 28일 우리나라에 오는
존 케이지와 머스 커닝햄의 한국공연과 때를 맞춰
2월1일부터 10일까지 원화랑에서 일반에서 선보인다.

Chosun Ilbo
Good Morning Orwell Space Arts Festival Leads
Perform in Seoul — Print Exhibition.

The three leading artists of *Good Morning Orwell*
Space Arts Festival broadcast by satellite early in
January — video art's Paik Namjune, contemporary
music's John Cage, and contemporary dance's
Merce Cunningham, came to Seoul's Print Exhibi-
tion. The prints, sent by representative of Gallery
Won Jung Ki-Yong in direct negotiation with Paik
Namjune, will be presented at Gallery Won from
February 1 to 10 in conjunction with the arrival of
John Cage and Merce Cunningham's
exhibitions in Korea.

「굿모닝 오웰」宇宙예술제 세主役
서울서 公演-版画展

2월1~10일

정초 인공위성으로 중계된
우주예술제 「굿모닝 미스터 오
웰」의 세主役, 즉 비디오아트
의 白南準, 현대음악의 존 케이
지, 현대무용의 머스 커닝햄의
이색 판화작품들이 서울에 왔
다. 圓화랑대표 鄭基容씨가 白
南準씨와 직접 교섭하여 보내
진 이 판화들은 28일 우리나라
에 오는 존 케이지와 머스 커
닝햄의 한국공연과 때를 맞춰
2월1일부터 10일까지 원화랑에
서 일반에게 선보인다.

이들 3인은 각기 개성이 다
른 종합예술가로서, 수차례의공
동작업을 통해 화제를 모았지
만, 판화만을 함께 발표하기는
흔치않은 경우에 속한다.

비디오예술의 창시자로 유명
한 한국인 白씨는 케이지와 커
닝햄을 각각 모델로 삼아 실크

스크린技法으로 제작한 트럼프
카드 2組를 비롯, 손의 영상을
추상적으로 배열한 「無題」세트
(9장), 마샬 맥루한의 영상속에
TV안테나를 대비시킨 실크스
크린판화등을 출품했다. 白씨
는 또 TV수상기를 주제로 구
성한 드로잉 3점도 보내왔다.

현대음악의 巨匠으로 꼽히는
존 케이지는 자신의 樂譜를 입
체적으로 구성한 판화 「존타나
믹스」 3점을, 현대음악의 혁명
가로 불리는 머스 커닝햄은 기
린, 말등의 동물들을 사실적으
로 형상화한 실크스크린 판화
1점을 각각 선보인다.

이색적인 판화로는 우주예술
제 「굿모닝…」을 위해 白南準
과 앨런 긴즈버그가 공동제작
한 판화인데, 앞면엔 白씨가, 뒷
면엔 긴즈버그의 작품이 실려
있다.

원화랑은 전시기간중 白南準

과 존 케이지의 예술행위를 담
은 비디오 필름도 상영할 계획
이다. 「굿모닝 미스터 오웰」로
세계적 관심을 모은 예술가 3

인의 판화와 비디오예술, 그리
고 특별공연을 감상할수 있는
보처럼의 기회에 애호가들이 거
는 기대가 클것으로 보인다.

◇白南準씨의 트럼프 판화. 존 케이지등 예술가들을 모델로하여
각종 영상을 표현했다.

매일경제
유토피아 실현 예술만이 가능

펠트 모자와 청바지, 공군 조끼 차림의 가난한 외모와
기상천외한 작품으로 독일미술에서 가장 혁신적인
예술가이자 영향력 있는 작가로 평가되고 있는 보이스는
작년 1월 23일 심장마비로 64세의 생을 마감했는데
원(圓)화랑은 14일부터 28일까지 보이스의 《1주기》
전을 개최한다. "84년 말 비디오 아티스트인
백남준씨와 함께 보이스의 작업실을 방문, 87년에
보이스가 우리나라에 오기로 약속을 받아 백(白)씨와
함께 퍼포먼스를 계획했었는데 보이스의 죽음으로
실연은 못 하고 유작으로 대신하게 됐다."고 정기용
원화랑 사장은 4년 전부터 추진해온 이 작품전의 과정을
설명한다.

Maeil Business Newspaper
Only Utopian art is possible.

Beuys — considered the most innovative and
influential artist in Germany for his unique works
and modest attire of felt hats, jeans, and air
force vests — died of a heart attack on January 23
last year. Gallery Won will host Joseph Beuys's
1-year memorial exhibition from the 14th to
the 28th. "At the end of 1984, I visited Beuys's studio
with video artist Paik Namjune, and in 1987,
Beuys was scheduled to come to Korea and open
an exhibit with Paik. However, Beuys's passing
prevented this, so there will be a posthumous exhibit instead," said Jung Ki-Yong, representative of
Gallery Won.

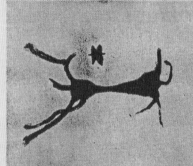

독 현대미술가 J・보이스 1周展

"유토피아 實現 藝術만이 가능"

◇ J・보이스

기상천외 작품 人間主義 표방
오브제・판화 등 21점 선보여
遺作品 국제미술시장서 最高가격 호가

◇올해 한국이 낳은 세계적인 비디오 아티스트 白南準과 함께 서울서 퍼포먼스를 벌일 예정이었던 J・보이스의 작품 「무당」.

〈丁英秀기자〉

1963. 9. 15.

조선일보
생활의 미술 판화

작품의 크기가 크지 않고, 따라서 운반이 편리하며
몇 점을 찍어 보내어도 원판이 있기 때문에 별로 아쉽지
않다는 점에서 요즈음 판화의 국제적 교류가 잦다.
또한 판화는 미술가뿐만이 아니라 누구든지 제작할 수
있다는데서 판화의 일반화가 세계적으로 '붐'을
이루다시피 하고 있다.

Chosun Ilbo
Art prints of everyday life.

International print trade has recently become
frequent due to their manageable size allowing for
convenient transportation and because molds
allow for repeated printing. In addition, the fact that
anyone — not just artists — can make a print
has contributed to the medium's worldwide 'boom'
and popularization.

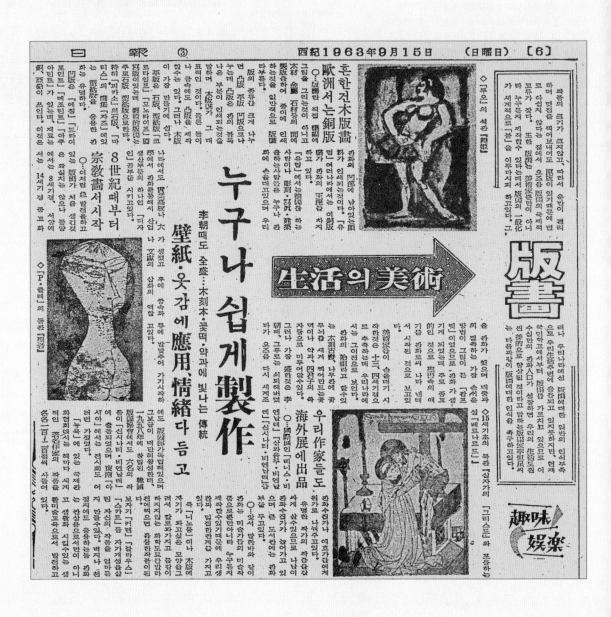

1972. 6. 8.

동아일보
동아 국제 판화 비엔날레 단체관람 등 연일 큰 성황

Dong-A Ilbo
Dong-A International Print Biennale a Success.

1970년 동아일보사가 창설하고 국립현대미술관에서 진행된 동아 국제판화비엔날레는
'판화'를 매개로 국제교류를 확장하고자한 국내 미술계의 시도를 보여준다.
국립현대미술관과 공동개최했던 제4회 서울국제판화비엔날레에서 미술관은 수상작을 포함한
10점의 작품을 소장품으로 구입했다.

The Dong-A International Print Biennale was founded in 1970 by *Dong-A Ilbo* and
held at MMCA. It shows the attempts of the domestic art world to expand
international exchange through 'print work'. At the 4th International Print Biennale,
co-hosted with MMCA, 10 works were purchased as a collection.

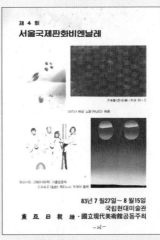

제4회 서울국제판화비엔날레 리플릿, 1983
Leaflet of the 4th Seoul International Print Biennale, 1983

제3회 동아국제판화비엔날레 리플릿, 1981
Leaflet of the 3rd Dong-A International Print Biennale, 1981

1983. 7. 20.

동아일보
제4회 서울국제판화비엔날레 수상작 발표

동아일보와 국립현대미술관이 공동 주최한
제4회 서울국제판화비엔날레의 심사 결과가 밝혀졌다.
최고상인 대상 수상작에는 윤미란(한국)의
〈정(靜)｜화음(和音) 83｜5〉와 모토나가 사다마사
(일본), 〈두개의 부유물〉, 레오나드 그레이(미국),
〈겨울관광객〉, 루나 버넬 노블(캐나다)의 〈무제〉 등
4편이 뽑혔다.

또 우수상에는 한국의 이강소, 곽덕준씨를 비롯
요코 야마모토(일본), 키무라코스케(일본), 알렉산드라
해서카(캐나다),[129쪽] 폴 야누스 입센과 벤트 칼 야콥슨
(덴마크)의 합작[128쪽] 등 6점이 결정됐다.

Dong-A Ilbo
Winners Announced for the 4th International Print Biennale.

The results of the 4th International Print Biennale
co-hosted by *Dong-A Ilbo* and MMCA have
been announced. Four pieces were selected for the
Grand Prize — including Yoon Mi-ran's *Stillness,
Chord*, Motonaga Sadamasa (Japan), *Two Floating
Objects*.

In addition, six runner-ups were awarded,
including a collaboration between Alexandra
Haeseker (Canada),[p.129] Paul Janus Ipsen, and
Bent Karl Jacopson (Denmark).[p.128]

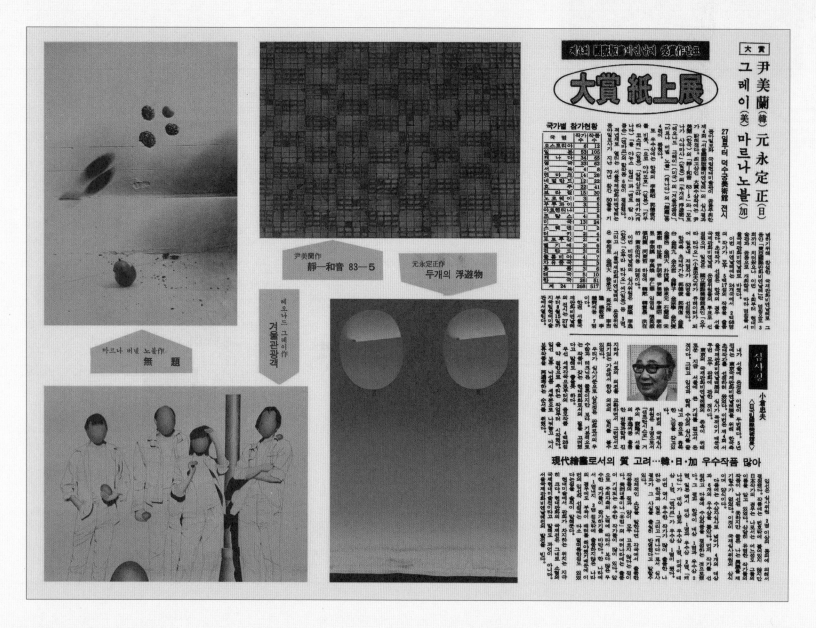

동아일보
'해외판화 국내전' 관심 집중

최근 들어 '프랑스'와 미국을 중심으로 한 해외판화의
국내전이 크게 늘어나면서 해외판화작품의 국내유통이
일반화되어가고 있다.

금년만해도 《아르비방파리》서울전을 비롯,
서울미술관의 《유럽》판화전, 《장포트리에》판화전,
《앙드레브라질리에》판화전, 일본작가 7인 판화전,
《폴 아이즈피리》판화전, 국제판화비엔날레,
현대판화가협회 주최의 《서울국제판화교류전》 등 (...)
10여 개의 수준급 판화전이 열렸다.

Dong-A Ilbo
*'Domestic Exhibition of Foreign Prints' Garnering
Attention.*

Recent increases in the domestic exhibitions of
overseas prints (centered around France and the
United States) normalize the distribution of
overseas prints in Korea.

This year alone, more than ten engraving exhibi-
tions were held, including *the Art Vivant Paris
Seoul Exhibition,* the *Jean Fautrier Exhibition,* the
Andre Brasilier Exhibition, seven exhibits by
Japanese artists, *the Paul Aizpiri Exhibition,* the
International Print Biennale, and *the Seoul
International Print Exchange Exhibition* hosted by
the Modern Engraving Association.

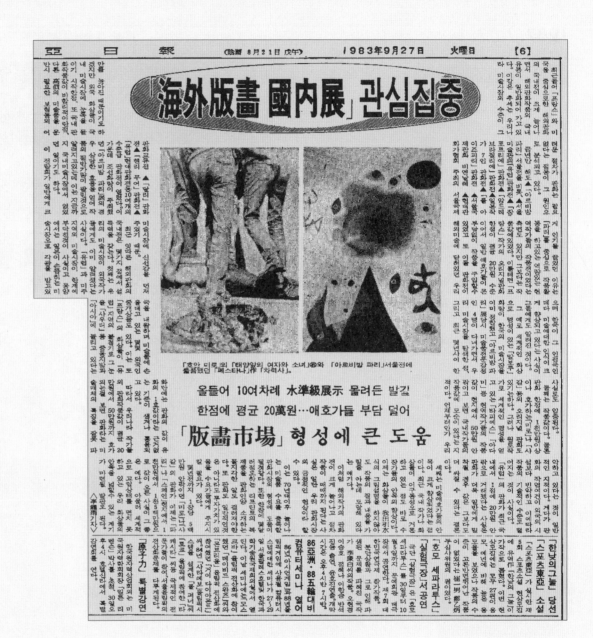

1987. 7. 17.

조선일보
세계현대미술제 논란 가열

작가들 의견 도외시... 대안을—미술계
몽촌토성 훼손... 장소 옮겨야—학계

서울 올림픽 세계현대미술제를 둘러싸고 미술계 일각에서
반대서명운동을 펴는가 하면 학계 쪽에서도 국가 사적
훼손이라고 주장하는 등 논란이 가열되고 있다.

Chosun Ilbo
**Controversy over *The Olympiad of the Art*
Intensifies.**

Ignoring artists' input... The Art world demands
alternatives.
Damage to Mongchontoseong... Academia is
demanding location change.

Controversy over *Olympiad of the Art* at the Seoul
Olympics is intensifying, with some in the art
community campaigning against it, and academia
claiming damage to national history.

『서울올림픽미술제 백서: 무엇을 남겼나』,
88올림픽세계현대미술제 변칙운영저지를 위한
범미술인대책위원회 편집.

Whitepaper of Olympiad of the Art—What's left?, edited by
The antitrust committee of artists on 88 Olympics
World Contemporary Art Festival, (Seoul: Ulgul publication,
1989).

西紀 1987年 7月 17日 金曜日

「세계현대미술제」논란 加熱

작가들 의견 도외시...대안을 美術界
夢村土城 훼손...장소 옮겨야 學界
허가범위서 시공...대화할 터 組織委

1987. 12. 21.

매일경제
'87 문화계 미술 민주화 '훈풍' … 사건 속출

88미술제 '비민주적 운영' 말썽
평단 '이념분쟁' 양분… 국제화랑 가압류 소동도
외국 작품 전시 활발 국제화 향한 도약 고무

Maeil Business Newspaper
The winds of change in '87 signal the democratization of art and culture … related incidents emerge.

Vigorous exhibition of foreign art, encouraging internationalization.

民主化「薰風」…사건 속출

'87 文化界 美術

88미술제 "非民主 운영" 말썽

◇지난 7, 8월 16개국 17명의 작가가 참여한 가운데 올림픽공원에서 국제야외조각전이 열렸다.<사진은 쿠바의 카르테나스作「가족」>

評壇「이념분쟁」양분…국제화랑 가압류 소동도

외국작품 전시활발 국제화향한 도약고무

조선일보
올림픽 미술 행사 주체성 시비

원로 등 '한국화 소외' 반발
화단 일부에서는 자성론(自省論) 대두

《국제현대회화전》 한국화와 서양화가 3대 18이라는
비율과 한국현대미술전 작가 161명 중 한국화는
14명이라는 10%에도 미치지 못하는 비율은 한국 화단에
대한 근본적인 도외시라며 선정기준의 편협성을
들고나왔다.

서명인들은 국립현대미술관 학예관 중에 한국화 부문의
전문인이 없는 점, 국제전 작가선정에서 한국화
도외시 현상, 동-서양화의 전공별 모집, 서구적 시각에
입각한 평론 등의 부당성도 꼽았다.

Chosun Ilbo
Disputes over the identity of Olympic art events.

Senior members and others oppose the 'Alienation
of Korean art'
Some in the art world claim the necessity of
introspection.

Some call into question the fairness of the selective
process claiming that the ratio of Korean and
Western paintings being 3:18, and only 14 of the
161 artists in *International Contemporary Painting
Exhibition* being Korean traditional art artists (less
than 10%) signifies a fundamental exclusion of
Korean paintings.

올림픽美術行事주체성是非

元老등 "韓國畵소외" 반발
画壇 일부선 自省論 대두

◇「한국현대미술전」 초대작가로 선정된 申山沐씨의 한국화 「풍경」. 작가선정을 둘러싸고 한국화쪽이 부담성을 주장하고 있다.

1988. 8. 2.

조선일보
서울이여 세계여 인류의 숨결이여

세계 80여 개국 3천여 명의 예술인들이 서울에 모여
펼칠 사상 최대규모의 지구촌 축제―88올림픽
문화축전(Seoul Olympic Arts Festival 88)이 8월 16일
화려한 막을 올려 장장 50일간 신명 나는 인류의 한마당
잔치를 벌인다.

이중 세계현대미술제 등 전시행사가 24건, 음악-연극-
무용축제 등 공연행사가 11건, 거리축제, 한강 축제 등
경축 행사가 6건이다.

Chosun Ilbo
Seoul, the world, the breath of humankind.

The '88 Seoul Olympic Arts Festival — the largest-
ever global festival to be held in Seoul by
more than 3,000 artists from 80 countries around
the world — will begin in spectacular fashion
on August 16 and have an exciting 50-day
banquet for humanity.

◇오페라 「투란도트」에서 열연하는 투란도트공주역의 소프라노 게나 디미트로바, 4백여명이 출연하는 라 스칼라오페라단의 한국공연은 쉽게 접하기 어려운 세계최고의 화려한 무대로, 스칼라극장의 품격과 규모를 고스란히 서울에서 펼치는 올림픽문화축전의 최대 이벤트다.

첫 公演 라 스칼라 오페라

세계현대미술제
— 1, 2차 국제야외조각전
— 국제야외조각초대전

《제1회 국제야외조각 심포지엄》에는 동구권을 포함한 16개국 17명의 작가가 참여하여 '돌'과
'콘크리트'를 재료로 한 조각 17점을, 《제2회 국제야외조각전》에 17개국 19명의 작가들이
철, 브론즈, 합성수지, 목재를 재료로 한 작품 19점을 현장 제작, 설치했다.
뒤이은 《국제야외조각초대전》에서는 64개국 158명의 작가들이 자국에서 제작한
야외 조각을 국내로 이송하여 올림픽공원에 기증, 영구 설치하였다.

Olympiad of the Art
— *1st, 2nd International Open-Air Sculpture Symposium*
— *International Outdoor Sculpture Exhibition*

17 artists from 16 countries, including Eastern Europe, participated in *the 1st International Open-Air Sculpture Symposium* made 17 pieces of sculpture of 'concrete' and 'stone'. And 19 artists from 17 countries participated in *the 2nd International Open-Air Sculpture Symposium* made 19 pieces of works of iron, bronze, synthetic resin, and wood. Those sculptures were produced and installed on site.
In the subsequent *International Outdoor Sculpture Exhibition*, 158 artists from 64 countries presented their own outdoor sculptures. It was transported to Korea, donated to Olympic Park and permanently installed.

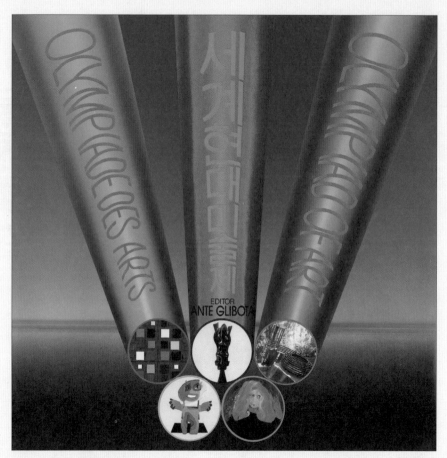

세계현대미술제 도록
Catalog of *Olympiad of Art*

세계현대미술제 올림픽 문화예술축전 행사
Culture and Art Festival Dinner, *Olympiad of the Art*, 1988

세계현대미술제 전시
Exhibition of *Olympiad of Art*, 1988

세계현대미술제 운영회의
Operation Meeting of *Olympiad of Art*, 1988

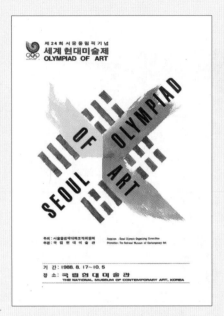

《한국현대미술전》홍보물 표지, 세계현대미술제, 1988
Korean Contemporary Art Exhibition Promotional material, 1988

국립현대미술관은 64개국의 해외작가 158명의 158점이 전시되었던 《국제현대회화전》(1988. 8. 17–10. 5.)의
운영과 진행을 맡았고, 전시에 참여했던 42개국(공산권 8개국 포함)의 작가로부터 회화 62점을 기증받았다.
이 기증작들은 1988년 연말까지 《국제현대회화전 기증작품 특별전》을 통해 관람객에게 공개되었고, 1990년까지 부산,
대구, 대전, 전주에서 네 차례의 순회전을 진행했다.

MMCA exhibits 158 works by 158 foreign artists from 64 countries in *International Contemporary Painting
Exhibition* (1988. 8. 17–10. 5.). 62 paintings were donated by artists from 42 countries (including 8 communist
countries) who participated in the exhibition. These paintings were displayed until the end of 1988.
The special exhibition of donations from International Contemporary Painting of Exhibition went around in
Busan, Daegu, Daejeon, and Jeonju as provincial tour.

《국제현대회화특별전》 도록
Catalog of *the Special Exhibitions of International Contemporary Painting*

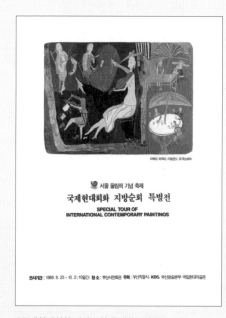

《국제현대회화 지방순회 특별전》 리플릿
Leaflet of *Special Tour International Contemporay Paintings*

《국제현대회화전》 개막식
Opening Ceremony of *International Contemporary Painting Exhibition*

《국제현대회화전》 전시 장면, 1988
Exhibition scene of *International Contemporary Painting of Exhibition*, 1988

경향신문
《국제현대회화전》 64국서 걸작 속속 반입

이태리 작품 〈신부〉 보험료 48만불
종묘제례 햇불 켜고 야간연주 이채
〈투란〉 무대 세트 한국 기증
알파벳순으로 진열

세계현대미술제 행사의 하나인 《국제현대회화전》에
참가할 64개국 작가의 작품 160점 중 12일
현재 145점이 국립현대미술관에 반입을 완료.

국내 작가 27명은 모두 작품을 냈는데 미술품 작가
15명은 스페인의 타피에스 등 교섭이 늦어진 사람들로
늦어도 15일 안으로는 도착할 것이라고 미술관 측은
전망.

미술관 측은 작품이 도착하는 대로 세관원의 입회하에
일일이 포장을 풀어 통관 절차를 밟은 뒤 예정된 장소에
옮겨 놓고 디스플레이의 효과를 점검.

작품은 나라별 알파벳 순으로 배열, 최종 확정을 거쳐
벽면에 걸게 되는데 전시회의 국제운영위원 중 한 사람인
파리아트센터 대표인 길보타(유고)씨는 일주일째
작품배열과 전시를 자문하는 등 열성적으로 일해 눈길.

Kyunghyang Shinmun
International Contemporary Painting Exhibition
importing masterpieces from 64 countries.

As of the 12th, 145 out of 160 works by artists
from 64 countries who will participate in
International Contemporary Painting Exhibition —
one of *Olympiad of the Art* events — have
been brought into MMCA.

All 27 Korean artists have submitted their works.
The Museum predicts that works by the 15 artists
with which communications were delayed,
such as Spain's Tapis, will arrive within 15 days at
the latest.

As soon as the pieces arrive, the Museum
unpacks them and moves them through customs
clearance procedures before having them
transferred to their designated location and
evaluating the effectiveness of the display.

After final confirmation, the works will be arranged
alphabetically by country and hung on the
wall. A member of the international management
committee, representative of the Pairs Art Center
Gilbota (Yugo), has been noticed passionately
consulting the arrangement and exhibition of the
pieces.

1988. 8. 16.

경향신문
"캔버스 올림픽"… 인류의 이상 화폭 마다

참여작가는 프랑스의 레스티니, 뉴욕 구겐하임 미술관장
메서를 비롯한 5명의 외국 미술평론가들이 세계를
다섯 구역으로 나누어 선정했다. 때문에 이들 작가는
국제적인 동일 양식보다는 이질적인 지역 양식을 대표해
다양한 작품세계를 펼친다.

작가들은 특히 서울에서의 초청에 응하면서 사상
최대·최고의 이 인류제전을 통해 평화와 화합·전진을
기원, 자신들의 작품을 기꺼이 국립현대미술관에
기증할 예정.

Kyunghyang Shinmun
"Canvas Olympics"… Canvases as humanitarian
ideals.

Participating artists, who include France's Restini
and the Director Thomas Maria Messer of
New York's Guggenheim Museum, were selected
by five foreign art critics based on a division of
the world into five sections. Therefore, these artists
represent various works on behalf of heteroge-
neous local styles rather than an identical international style.

The artists accepted their invitations to Seoul in
hopes of promoting peace, harmony, and
progress — and are planning on donating their
works to MMCA.

1988. 8. 12.

동아일보
현대회화의 흐름 한눈에

세계 속 한국미술 위상 확인
서구 모방에서 벗어날 계기
(윤명로, 서울대 미대 교수)

Dong-A Ilbo
The flow of modern painting at a glance.

Affirming the prestige of Korean art in the world.
A stimulant to escape imitating the West
(Yun Mteong-Ro, Professor emeritus of the College
of Fine Arts, Seoul National University)

A R 펭크, 〈서독〉作 출력이란 무엇인가...

현대繪畵의 흐름 한눈에

尹明老
〈서울大 美大교수〉

世界속 한국美術 位相확인
西歐모방에서 벗어날 계기

1988. 8. 18.

경향신문
인터뷰 88현대미술제 포스터 디자인한 스위스 화가
피터 크나프씨 "태극기 팔괘서 힌트 얻었죠."

Kyunghyang Shinmun
Interview of the poster-designer for the *the
Olympiad of the Art,* Swiss painter Peter Knauf
"I got a hint from the Palgwa of the Taegeukgi."

세계현대미술제의 포스터 디자인 도안
Poster Design of Olympiad of Art

1988. 7. 7.

동아일보
외국 작가 전시회 러시

《세자르》전 신사실주의 20여 점 선보여
뉴욕현대미술 미국현대미술 흐름 한눈에
개방영향... 88아트판화 《아르망》전은 내달 열려

이달 1일부터 해외미술품의 수입이 허용된 것을 계기로
외국 작가의 개인전이나 그룹전이 잇따라 기획되고 있다.
해외 작가전을 기획하고 있는 화랑 중에는 해외미술품
수입을 허용한다는 정부의 발표가 있기 전부터 올림픽을
앞두고 미술품의 수입 개방 조치가 이루어질 것이라는
예측에 따라 미리 준비해온 화랑도 있고 정부 조치 발표
후 서둘러 준비하는 곳도 있다.

Dong-A Ilbo
Rush for Foreign Artist Exhibits.

In *Cesar's solo Exhibition*, about 20 Neo-Realism
works are presented.
Shows New York Contemporary Art and American
Contemporary Art at a glance
Impact on openness ... *Arman solo Exhibition* to be
held next month.

With the legalization of the importation of foreign
art on the 1st of this month, individual and
group exhibitions of foreign artists have been
planned one after another.

外國작가 전시회 러시

이달 1일부터 해외미술품의 수입이 허용된 것을 계기로 외국작가의 개인전이나 그룹전이 잇따라 기획되고 있어 해외작가전을 기획하고 있는 화랑중에는 해외미술품수입을 허용한다는 점

부의 발표가 있기전부터 올림픽을 앞두고 미술품의 수입개방조치가 이루어 질것이라는 예측에 따라 미리 준비해온 화랑도 있고 정부조치 발표후 서둘러 준비하는 곳도 있다.

「세자르」의 조각 「새가 된 인간」

「세자르」展 新사실주의 20여點 선보여
뉴욕현대미술 美國 현대미술흐름 한눈에

개방영향…88아트판화·「아르망」展은 내달열려

1990. 11. 21.

동아일보
한지에 펼친 세계 화가들의 꿈

한국의 전통 한지를 주요 소재로 한 제1회 서울국제
미술제의 개막식이 20일 오후 5시 국립현대미술관에서
열렸다. 이날 개막식에는 이어령 문화부 장관과
이민섭 국회문공위원장 김성진 서울국제미술제이사장 등
국내관계인사와 이번 미술제의 대상 수상자인 미국의
브라이언 헌트,[173쪽] 특별 초청작가인 조지 시걸(미국),
다니엘 뷔렌(프랑스) 등 모두 200여 명이 참석, 성황을
이루었다.

이날 개막식에서 심사위원을 맡았던 프랑스의 미술평론가
피에르 레스타니는 "한지라는 독특한 소재를 통해
동서양이 함께 만났고 한지는 이제 더 이상 한국이라는
지역적 소재가 아닌 세계적 미술 매체가 되었다."고 강조.

Dong-A Ilbo
International dreams are unfolding on Korean paper.

The opening ceremony of the first *Seoul International-
al Art Festival* — the primary subject matter of
which was traditional Korean paper — was held at
5 p.m. on the 20th at MMCA. More than 200 people
attended the opening ceremony, including
Minister of Culture Lee Eoryeong, National Assembly
Chairman Lee Min-Seop, Seoul International Art
Festival Chairman Kim Sung-jin, the grand prize
winner of the art festival, the U.S.'s Bryan Hunt,[p.173]
as well as special guests artists George Segal and
Daniel Buren (France).

Pierre Restany, a French art critic who served as
a judge at the opening ceremony, emphasized that
"The East and West met through the unique
subject of Hanji, which is no longer a regional
subject of Korea, but a global art medium."

韓紙에 펼친 세계화가들의 꿈

서울국제미술제 개막

한국의 전통한지를 주요소
재로한 제1회 서울국제미술
제의 개막식이 20일 오후5
시 국립현대미술관에서 열렸
다. 이날 개막식에는 李御寧
문화부장관과 李敏燮국회문
공위원장 金聖鎭서울국제미
술제이사장 등 국내관계인사
와 이번 미술제의 대상수상
자인 미국의 브라이언 헌트,

특별초청작가인 조지 시걸
(미국) 다니엘 뷔렌(프랑스)
등 모두 2백여명이 참석, 성
황을 이루었다.

특히 이날 개막식에서는
우리의 전통한지를 제작하는
기법을 시연하여 국내관계자
는 물론 외국작가및 외교사
절들로부터 큰 관심을 불러
일으켰다.

이날 개막식에서 심사위원
을 맡았던 프랑스의 미술

평론가 피에르 레스타니는
"한지라는 독특한 소재를 통
해 동서양이 함께 만났고 한
지는 이제 더이상 한국이라
는 지역적 소재가 아닌 세계
적 미술매체가 되었다"고 강
조. 전시는 91년 2월 20일까지.

75

동아일보
서울국제미술제 외국인 심사위원 좌담 한국현대미술
모방 탈피 자기 세계 찾았다

서울국제미술제를 위해 내한했던 심사위원 커미셔너 등 국제적 명성을 얻고 있는 미술평론가들은 한국현대미술의 현주소를 놓고 자생력을 가진 독특한 형식미를 창조하고 있다고 평했다. 특히 이들은 한국미술이 전통에 대한 자의식이 강한 반면 모방도 많다고 말하고 젊은 작가들의 왕성한 작업 의식이 태평양 문화권의 주역이 될 것이라고 내다봤다. 80년대 현대미술의 대표적 경향 중 하나였던 트랜스아방가르드를 창시한 이탈리아의 아킬레 보나토 올리바, 누보레알리즘을 주창한 프랑스의 피에르 레스타니, 미국 팝아트의 이론적 근거를 마련한 데이비드 버튼, 미국 조각계의 거장 조지 시걸 등 네 사람이 한국미술에 관한 인상기를 좌담으로 엮어봤다.

Dong-A Ilbo
Foreign judges for *Seoul International Art Festival* declare Korean contemporary art has found a vision apart from imitation.

Art critics gaining international fame — including the judge commissioner who visited Korea for *Seoul International Art Festival* — have commented that Korean contemporary art has manifested a self-sustainable, unique, formal beauty. In particular, they said that Korean art has a strong sense of self-consciousness regarding tradition, though with a tendency towards imitation. Furthermore, they predicted that the vigorous work ethic of young artists would be the dominant force in shaping Pacific culture. Four people shared their impressions on Korean arts: Achille Bonito Oliva of Italy (who created one of the contemporary art trends that represent the 1980s, Transavantgarde), Pierre Rastany of France (who advocated Nouveau réalisme), David Burdeny (who laid the theoretical foundations for American pop art) and George Segal (a master of American sculpting).

모방탈피 자기세계 찾았다

韓國현대미술

「서울국제미술제」外國人심사위원 좌담

강한 전통의식 절제美 돋보여
독특한 形式에 자생력도 가져
작품質못따르는 초라한 전시장에 놀라

아킬레 올리바

데이비드 버튼

피에르 레스타니

조지 시걸

1990. 12. 19.

동아일보
서양화가들 한지에 흠뻑 매료

헤럴드 트리뷴 12월 8일 자에 「서구 작가들 동양재료에 매료」란 제목으로 소개된 이 기사는 한지의 질감 및 보존성 등 우수성에 관한 내용과 최근 한국미술계의 활발한 움직임 등을 소개하고 있다. 또 짧은 준비기간에도 불구, 국제적 작가들이 대거 참가하여 서울국제미술제의 격을 높였으며 낯선 한지라는 소재가 서구 작가들에게 새로운 가능성으로 등장했다고 소개했다.

특히 이 기사는 한지라는 매우 개성적인 재료를 작가들에게 나누어 주어 한국을 체험시켰으며 60명의 참가작가 중 카렐 아펠, 아르망, 대니얼 뷔렌, 존 챔벌레인, 샘 프란시스, 브라이언 헌트(대상수상자),^{173쪽} 일랴 카바코프,^{176-177쪽} 대니 카라반, 로버트 라우센버그, 조지 시걸 등이 매우 우수한 작품을 제작했다고 평했다.

Dong-A Ilbo
Western artists fascinated by Korean Paper (Hanji).

A December 8 article by the *Herald Tribune* entitled "Western Artists Fascinated by Eastern Materials" introduces the excellence of Hanji's texture and longevity and the recent proactivity of the Korean art world.

In particular, the article distributed a very unique material called Hanji to writers to allow them to experience Korea. Of the 60 participating artists, positively reviewed works include Karel Appel, Arman, Daniel Buren, John Chamberlain, Sam Francis, Bryan Hunt,^{p. 173} Ilya Kabanov,^{pp. 176-177} Danni Karavan, Robert Rauschenberg, and George Segal.

"서양화가들 韓紙에 흠뻑 매료"

─ 헤럴드 트리뷰紙 서울국제미술祭 크게 소개

"質感 뛰어나고 독특한 맛" 격찬

새로운 미술소재 가능성 열어

"서울 새화랑 한달에 몇개씩 생긴다"

국립현대미술관에서 진행된 1990년 《서울국제미술제》는 '한지'를 소재로 한 서구권 작가들의 열띤 작업과 경쟁의 장으로 국내외의 주목을 받았다. 프랑스의 피에르 레스타니, 미국의 데이비드 버든(David Burden)과 이탈리아의 보니토 올리바(Bonito Oliva)가 국외 심사위원, 국내 심사위원은 이경성(국립현대미술관장)과 이일(미술평론가)이 맡았다. 다니엘 뷔렝, 조지 시걸 등 200여명의 참여작가들이 우리 고유의 재료 '한지(닥종이)'를 이용한 독특한 작업을 선보였다.

1990 *Seoul International Art Festival* attracted domestic and international attention as a venue for passionate works and competition of artists from the West working on Hanji. Pierre Restany (France), David Burden (USA) and Bonito Oliva (Italy) were the international judges, while the domestic judges were Lee Kyungsung (Director of MMCA) and Lee Il (Art critic). About 200 participating artists, such as Daniel Buren and George Segal presented their unique works using 'Korean paper (Hanji)', drawing attention both at home and abroad.

대상 수상작인 미국 작가 브라이언 헌트의 〈가을폭포 I〉를 감상 중인 이어령 문화부 장관
Lee Oyoung, the former minister of Culture and Information was viewing Grand Prize Painting, *Autumn Falls I* by Brian Hunt

1990 서울국제현대미술제 포스터
Poster of *Seoul International Art Festival*, 1990

대상 수상자인 미국 작가 브라이언 헌트와 심사위원 피에르 레스타니
Brian Hunt, Grand Prize Winner and Pierre Restany, International Panel of Judge

1992. 9. 6.

조선일보
국립현대미술관 "무상기증 안 받겠다"

소장품 수준 향상 위해
"수상작 등 심의 후 구입료 지불"

국립현대미술관의 미술품 수장-보존 업무가 크게 변한다. 임영방 현대미술관장은 5일 "앞으로 국립현대미술관은 국내외의 어떤 작가로부터도 무상으로 작품을 기증받는 일이 없을 것"이라고 밝혀 이 미술관이 보다 주체적인 입장에서 작품 수집에 나설 것임을 분명히 했다.

작가들의 작품 기증은 초기 국립현대미술관의 빈약한 작품 구입료를 보완하는 방편의 하나로 시작됐으나 후에 빈도가 늘어가면서 미술관 소장작품들의 질적 저하 요인으로 작용했다는 게 임 관장의 생각이다.
이와 아울러 임관장은 "구입할 때도 청탁이나 정실에 의한 구입은 일체 배격할 것"이라고 말했다.

현대미술관은 또 외국 작가들 작품의 경우, 앞으로는 판화보다는 양이 적더라도 유화 수입에 주력할 계획이다.

Chosun Ilbo
MMCA "Free donations not accepted."

To improve the prestige of the collection,
"Payment for works (award-winning etc.) to be given after deliberation."

The art collection-preservation work of MMCA faces a significant change. Lim Young-bang, head of MMCA, said on the 5th, "In the future, MMCA will not receive free donations from any artist at home or abroad." making it clear that the Museum will take a more proactive stance in collecting art.

In the future, MMCA also plans to focus on collecting oil paintings, even if the amount is less than prints.

便物(가)級認可) 조 선 일 보 西紀 1992年 9月 6日 日曜日

국립현대미술관 '무상기증 안받겠다.

수장품 수준향상 위해

"수상작등 심의후 구입료 지불"

국립 현대미술관의 미술품 수장·보존 업무가 크게 변한다. 林英芳현대미술관장은 5일 『앞으로 국립 현대미술관은 국내외의 어떤 작가로부터도 무상으로 작품을 기증받는 일이 없을 것』이라고 밝혀 이 미술관이 보다 주체적인 입장에서 작품 수집에 나설 것임을 분명히 했다.

아울러 林관장은 『국립현대미술관의 수장품들은 심의 기구의 엄정한 심의 절차를 거쳐 선정될 것』이라며 『선정된 작품에 대해서는 반드시 소정의 구입료를 지불하게 될 것』이라고 말했다.

林관장은 또 『우수 작품의 컬렉션은 국립 미술관의 가장 중요한 기능이란 점에서 현재 3천4백여점의 전 소장품들에 대한 면밀한 재조사가 진행되고 있다』고 밝히고 『지금까지의 조사 결과, 70세 이상의 원로 작가 작품과 각종 공모전에서의 수상작품이 현저하게 부족해 당분간 이들 작품을 수집하는 데 최대한 예산을 투입할 계획』이라고 말했다.

이같은 林관장의 발언은 국립 현대미술관이 그동안 미술계 일각으로부터 『주먹구구식』이라고 비난을 받아온 미술품 컬렉션 업무를 정비 강화하겠다는 의지의 표현으로 보여 비상한 관심을 끈다. 그동안 현대미술관의 소장품 컬렉션에 대해서는 엄정한 심사와 장기적인 계획이 결여된 게 아니냐는 의문이 있었으며, 이에따라 국내 유일의 국립 미술관인 현대미술관의 수장품 부실화에 대한 우려가 꾸준히 제기돼 왔다. 현대미술관의 컬렉션 업무 혁신 중에서 우선 두드러진 것은 작가들의 무상 기증을 일체 받지않기로 했다는 것. 특히 林관장은 지난 5월 취임이후 10여건에 달하는 작가들의 작품 기증의사를 모두 사절, 이 문제에 대한 강한 의지를 보이고 있다. 작가들의 작품 기증은 초기 국립현대미술관의 빈약한 작품 구입료를 보완하는 방편의 하나로 시작됐으나 후에 빈도가 늘어나면서 미술관 소장 작품들의 질적 저하 요인으로 작용했다는 게 林관장의 생각이다. 이와 아울러 林관장은 『구입할때도 청탁이나 정실에 의한 구입은 일체 배격할 것』이라고 말했다.

현대미술관은 또 원로작가와 역대 공모전 수상자들의 작품 수집에도 적극적이다. 미술관의 한 관계자는 『70세 이상 된 원로 작가들은 한국 현대미술 발전의 초석을 마련한 분들이지만 조사 결과, 미술관에 소장된 이들의 작품은 태반이 50-60년대 것이며, 심지어는 작품이 한점도 없는 분들이 여럿 있는 것으로 확인됐다』고 수집에 나서게 된 동기를 말했다. 이에따라 최근 林관장이 직접 金基昶 柳景埰 金興洙 李惟台 張利錫화백등 원로를 만나 작품을 구입하기로 합의했다.

문제는 이들 원로들 작품의 미술시장 가격에 비해 현대미술관의 구입가격(1점당 2천만원)이 현저하게 낮다는 것. 때문에 미술관 측은 흔쾌히 작품을 내놓는 작가들에게는 「기증」과는 별개의 차원에서 세제 혜택을 주도록 하는 방안을 국세청 등 관계기관과 적극 검토할 계획이다.

현대미술관은 또 외국 작가들 작품의 경우, 앞으로는 판화보다는 양이 적더라도 유화 수집에 주력할 계획이다.

〈金泰翼기자〉

◇果川에 있는 국립 현대미술관 전경。 현대미술관이 작가들의 작품 기증을 사절하는 등 수장·보관 업무에 새로운 혁신을 꾀하고 있다。

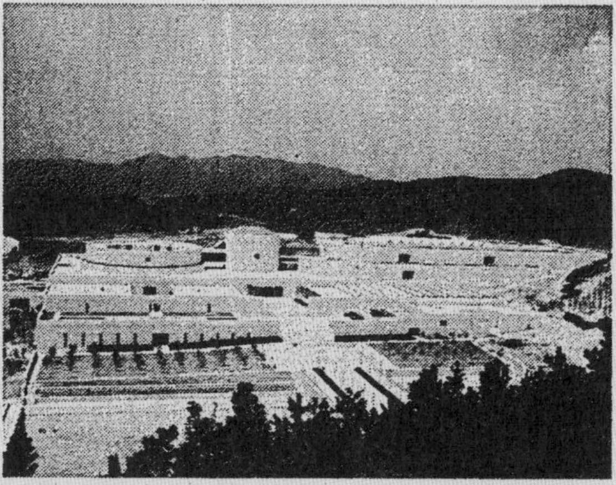

동아일보
국립현대미술관 4억짜리 조각 구입

어려운 재정 속 세계적 대가 프랑스 작가 상팔작품 매입
작년 영국서 급매물 나온 것 반값에 잡아
연 구입예산 6억원…올해 독일 키퍼 등 걸작품 사냥 나서

프랑스 출신의 세계적 여류조각가 니키드 상 팔(64)의
대형작품이 국내에 첫선을 보였다. 국립현대미술관(관장
임영방)이 지난해 11월 영국 런던에서 매입한 상팔의
작품은 지난 64년 제작된 〈검은 나나〉183쪽로 최근 미술관
현관에 놓여져 일반에 공개되고 있다.

국립현대미술관 측은 이 작품과 함께 역시 프랑스 출신의
세계적인 조각가 장 뒤뷔페(1901-1985)의 조각도
매입해 최근 전시장에 설치했다.

이밖에 지난 연말 미술관 측이 구입해 일반공개에 들어간
해외미술품 중에는 회화 분야에 조나단 브로후스키
(미국),219쪽 엔조 쿠키(이탈리아),218쪽
샘 프란시스(미국) 등의 작품이 있으며 조각으로는
짐 다인(미국)182쪽의 작품이 포함되어 있다.

Dong-A Ilbo
MMCA buys a four-million-dollar sculpture.

Despite financial difficulties, a piece by world-class
French master Niki de Saint Phalle is purchased.
Bought at half-price from a sudden sale last year in
the U.K.
Annual purchase budget of 600 million won …
This year will vie for masterpieces by those such as
German Anselm Kiefer.

A large-scale work by world-renowned female
French sculptor Niki de Saint Phalle, 64, debuted in
Korea. Saint Phalle's creation in 1964's "Black Nana"
p.183 was purchased in London in November
last year by MMCA (Director Lim Young-bang).
It was recently placed at the museum entrance
and is open to the public.

Along with this piece, MMCA also purchased
a sculpture of the world-renowned French sculptor,
Jean Dubuffet (1901-1985) and recently installed
it in the exhibition hall.

In addition, among the overseas art purchased
by the Museum at the end of last year and opened
to the public, are the work of Jonathan Borofsky
(USA),p.219 Enzo Cucchi (Italy)p.218 and Sam
Francis (USA), and the sculptures of Jim Dine
(USA). p.182

국립현대미술관

4億짜리 조각구입

어려운 財政 속 세계적 대가 佛상팔작품 매입

국립현대미술관이 국내 처음 매입한 니키드 상 팔의
「검은 나나」.

장 뒤뷔페의 「집지키는 개」.

작년 英國서 급매물 나온것 반값에 잡아

年구입예산 6억원…올해 獨키퍼등 걸작품 사냥나서

미국작가 짐 다인의 「색채의 전율」.

1999. 9. 29.

매일경제
현대미술관 구입작품 중 〈검은 나나〉가 최고가

국립현대미술관이 그동안 구입한 미술작품 중 최고가는 니키드 상팔의 조각작품 〈검은 나나〉[183쪽]인 것으로 나타났다.

문화관광부가 국회에 제출한 올해 국정감사 자료에 따르면 국립현대미술관은 94년 상팔의 조각작품을 2억 310만원에 구입해 최고 구입가를 기록했다.

구입가 2위는 같은 해 구입한 조지 시걸의 조각 〈침대 위의 소녀Ⅲ〉[187쪽]로 2억 102만 5000원, 3위는 안중식의 한국화 〈산수〉(98년 구입)로 1억 8000만원이다.

최고가 작품 10선은 조각작품이 단연 많다. 세자르의 〈승리의 여신상〉(97년)은 1억 7147만 9000원으로 4위, 장 피에르레이노의 〈붉은 화분〉(96년)[185쪽]은 1억 3020만 8000원으로 6위를 기록했다.

Maeil Business Newspaper
Black Nana is the most expensive piece purchased by MMCA.

It was found that the most expensive among the pieces purchased by MMCA was Niki de Saint Phalle's sculpture *Black Nana*. [p.183]

According to this year's parliamentary audit data submitted by the Ministry of Culture and Tourism to the National Assembly, the Museum purchased Saint Phalle sculptures for 23.1 million won in 1994, the highest purchase price to date.

Second place is George Segal's sculpture *Girl on Bed III* [p.187], which was purchased in the same year and cost KRW 28 million. The third is Ahn Joong-sink's Korean painting *Sansu*, purchased in 1998.

Predictably, there are many sculptures among the ten most expensive works. For example, Cesar's "The Statue of Victory" (97) ranked fourth with 171.479 million won, while Jean Pierre Raynaud's *Red Pot* (96) [p.185] ranked sixth with 130.208 million won.

현대미술관 구입작품 중 '검은 나나'가 최고가

황국성 기자

국립현대미술관이 그 동안 구입한 미술작품 중 최고가는 니키드 상팔의 조각작품 '검은 나나'인 것으로 나타났다.

문화관광부가 국회에 제출한 올해 국정감사 자료에 따르면 국립현대미술관은 94년 상팔의 조각작품을 2억310만원에 구입해 최고 구입가를 기록했다.

구입가 2위는 같은해 구입한 조지 시걸의 조각 '침대 위의 소녀Ⅲ'로 2억102만5000원, 3위는 안중식의 한국화 '산수'(98년 구입)로 1억8000만원이다.

최고가 작품 10선은 조각작품이 단연 많다. 세자르의 '승리의 여신상'(97년)은 1억7147만9000원으로 4위, 장 피에르 레이노의 '붉은 화분'(96년)은 1억3020만8000원으로 6위를 기록했다.

브로프스키의 '노래하는 사람'(96년)과 변관식의 한국화 '춘경산수'(98년)가 각각 1억 3000만원으로 공동 7위였다.

동아일보
국립현대미술관 해외유명작가 조각품 공개

국립현대미술관이 새로 구입한 해외 저명작가의
미술이 최근 관람객들에게 공개되고 있다. 해마다
3억 원 안팎의 예산으로 외국 저명작가의 미술품을
사들여 온 미술관은 미국의 조지 시걸(71)이
제작한 〈침대 위의 소녀 III〉187쪽와 영국작가인 앤터니
카로(71)의 철 조각 〈레몬 시퐁〉186쪽을 지난해
해외에서 구입해 들여왔다.

미국 팝아트 창시자 가운데 한사람인 조지 시걸의 작품은
석고로 되어 있으며 옷을 완전히 벗은 소녀의 모습을
실물 크기로 묘사, 고혹적인 자태를 자아낸다.

이 작품은 원래 몬테 카를로의 야외조각전에 출품된 것을
임영방 국립현대미술관장이 미국 뉴욕에 있는 작가의
집을 직접 방문해 구입했으며 한국으로 작품이 운송되기
전 작가 자신이 다시 수정작업을 했다.

시걸은 일상적이고 평범한 현대인의 모습을 담담하게
나타내온 조각가로 유명하며 그의 작품 구입은 국내에서
이번이 처음이다.

Dong-A Ilbo
MMCA unveils sculptures by famous foreign artists.

Artwork by renowned foreign artists at MMCA
recently purchased have recently been revealed to
visitors. Last year, the Museum — which buys
artworks from famous foreign artists with a budget
of around 300 million won every year — purchased
Girl on Bed III p. 187, produced by George Segal of
the United States, and *Lemon, Chiffon* p. 186, an iron
sculpture by British artist Anthony Caro.

The work by George Segal — one of the founders of
American POP Art — is made of plaster and depicts
the alluring figure of a life-sized girl who is entirely
undressed.

The work was initially exhibited in Monte Carlo's
outdoor sculpture exhibition when Lim Young-bang,
head of MMCA, visited the artist's house in
New York and purchased his art. With the artist
himself revising it before. The artwork was
shipped to Korea.

Segal is famous as a sculptor who calmly expresses
the everyday lives of ordinary modern people,
with this being the first time that Korea has purchased his work.

조지 시걸의 「침대위의 소녀」

앤터니 카로의 「레몬 시퐁」

尹錫南씨의 「어머니 2」

국립현대미술관 **海外유명작가 조각품 공개**

시걸·카로작품 사들여 첫전시

조드·불탄스키 것도 매입추진

동아일보
독일미술 봄 화단 잠 깨웠다

독일의 고속전철 ICE와 함께 상륙한 독일의 문화군단이
새봄 미술계에 신선한 충격을 주고 있다.

《테크놀로지의 예술적 전환》전시회는 산업사회에서
탄생한 다양한 기술을 어떻게 예술과 접목하며 어떻게
예술로 해석될 수 있는지에 대한 방법론을 보여주는
전시회이다. 특히 전시회는 지난해 시드니비엔날레의
디렉터로 명성을 날렸으며 〈레디메이드 부메랑〉이란
주제를 살려 찬사를 받은 독일의 미술 행정가 르네 블록이
구성했다.

참가작가는 제조업의 대량생산을 판화작업과 연결 지어
'대량생산 = 복제미술'의 등식을 보여준 지그마 폴케,
게르하르트 리히터, 브레머 등 [188-190쪽] 국내에도 널리
알려진 저명작가와 산업생산품을 작업에 직접 도입한
메첼, 사진작가 메티히, 지베르딩, 클라인 등이다.

Dong-A Ilbo
The new wave of German art awakens Korean Art world.

The impact of German culture, which landed with the country's high-speed ICE train, is sending shockwaves throughout the New Spring art world.

UMWANDLUNGEN: The Artistic Conversion of Technology shows how various industrial technologies society can be combined with and interpreted as art. The exhibition was organized by René Block, a German art administrator who made a reputation as a curator of last year's Sydney Biennale, and was praised for taking advantage of the theme *Readymade Boomerang*.

Participating artists include well-known artists such as Sigmar Polke, Gerhard Richter and K. P. Brehmer [pp. 188-190] who showed the equation of 'mass production = reproduction art' by linking mass production in the manufacturing industry with printmaking; Metzel, who introduced industrial products directly into their work; Photographers Metich, Sieverding, Klein, etc.

르네 블록은 1991년, 독일 현대미술 전시인 《테크놀로지의 예술적 전환》을
국립현대미술관과 공동기획했다. 이 전시에 출품했던 K. P. 브레머,
게르하르트 리히터와 지그마르 폴케의 합작품 2점을 미술관에 기증했다.

In 1991, René Block co-planned the German contemporary art
exhibition *UMWANDLUNGEN: The Artistic Conversion of Technology*
with MMCA. Two works by K. P. Brehmer, Gerhard Richter, and
Sigmar polke which were exhibited in the exhibition, were donated
to the museum.

《테크놀로지의 예술적 전환》 도록, 1991
Exhibition Catalog of *UMWANDLUNGEN: The Artistic Conversion of Technology*, 1991

이경성 전(前) 관장과 르네 블록
Lee Kyungsung (former director of MMCA) and René Block

The main characteristic of the early international art collections of MMCA (National Museum of Modern and Contemporary Art, Korea) is that they all have "Korean things" as their subject matter. Of the only 8 works collected until 1981, 4 are works by overseas artists of American nationality, and the remaining 4 are all works with the theme of 'Korean impressions', which is unique. Among them, Richard Franklin worked as an exchange professor at Seoul National University for three years, choosing 'hanji (Korean paper)' and 'bamboo' as traditional Korean materials. In 1979, held a solo exhibition at MMCA located in Deoksugung then. Adrian Walk Howard also toured Korea in 1981 and held a solo exhibition at the Cultural Exchange Center of the US Embassy in Korea under the title of *USA-Korean Impression*, featuring Korean landscapes such as Gyeongju tombs, Shilla earthenware, and Jeju scenery. The title of the solo exhibition of Filipino artist Manuel Valdemor, held at the Philippine Embassy in Korea and at the Green Hills Art Center in Manila in the same year, is also the title of Korean Impressions. The work that Manuel Valdemor donated to the museum after his solo exhibition is *Saemaul Undong (The New Village Movement)*, a work that emotionally depicts a day in a bustling rural area during *Saemaul Undong* in the 1970s. Although foreigners' visits to Korea increased and overseas exchanges began to expand around the 1988 Seoul Olympics, it seems to them that Korea remained in the realm of curiosity as a country in Northeast Asia with exotic customs and culture rather than a global partner.

OVERSEAS ARTISTS VISITING KOREA

한국 방문 해외 미술 1

국립현대미술관 초기 국제미술 소장품의 주된 특징은
"한국적인 것"을 소재로 하고 있다는 점이다. 1981년까지 수집된
8점의 작품 가운데, 4점은 미국 국적의 재외작가의 작품이고,
나머지 4점이 모두 '한국의 인상'을 주제로 삼은 작품이라는 점이
독특하다. 그 중에서 리처드 프랭크린(Richard Franklin)은
서울대 미대 교환교수로 지내는 3년 동안 '한지'와 '대나무' 등
한국의 전통적인 소재로 선택해 작업을 했으며, 1979년
덕수궁 국립현대미술관에서 개인전을 열었다. 에이드리언 워커
호워드(Adrienne Walker Hoard) 역시 1981년 한국의
곳곳을 다니며 경주 고분, 신라 토기, 제주 풍경 등 한국적인 풍경을
담아, 주한 미국대사관 문화교류처에서 개인전 《미국-
한국의 인상》을 개최하였다. 같은 해 주한 필리핀 대사관과 마닐라
그린힐즈 아트센터에서 열었던 마누엘 발데모어(Manuel
Baldemor)의 개인전 제목도 《한국의 인상》이었다. 발데모어는
개인전에 출품했던 작품 〈새마을 운동〉을 미술관에 기증하였다.
이 작품은 1970년대 새마을 운동이 널리 퍼진 분주한 농촌의
하루를 '비단에 채색'이라는 한국화 기법으로 밀도 있고 정감가게
표현하였다. 1988년 서울 올림픽을 전후로 외국인들의 한국
방문이 늘어나고 해외교류가 확장되기 시작했지만 외국작가에게
한국은 여전히 이국적인 풍물과 문화를 지닌 동북아시아의
한 국가로서 호기심의 영역에 머물렀던 것으로 보인다.

류예자오(중국, 1910-2003)
공산불견인(空山不見人)
1978, 종이에 수묵담채, 68×130cm
1978년 작가 기증

LIU Ye Zhao (China, 1910-2003)
Vacant Mountain
1978, Ink and color on paper, 68×130 cm
Donated by the artist in 1978

리처드 프랭크린(미국, 1939-)
경쾌한 항해 #2
1979, 한지에 대나무, 실 콜라주, 23×27 cm
1979년 작가 기증

Richard FRANKLIN (USA, 1939-)
Light Sail #2
1979, Bamboo and thread collage on paper, 23×27 cm
Donated by the artist in 1979

마누엘 발데모어(필리핀, 1947-)
새마을 운동
1981, 비단에 수채, 126×88cm
1981년 작가 기증

Manuel BALDEMOR (Philippines, 1947-)
Saemaul Undong (The New Village Movement)
1981, Watercolor on silk, 126×88 cm
Donated by the artist in 1981

헤디 터키(튀니지, 1922-2019)
한국에 대한 추억
1980, 나무판에 유채, 60.5×81 cm
1981년 작가 기증

Hedi TURKI (Tunisia, 1922-2019)
Souvenir of Korea (Souveir de Corée)
1980, Oil on panel, 60.5×81 cm
Donated by the artist in 1981

애이드리언 워커 호워드 (미국, 1946-)
제주의 정원
1981, 캔버스에 유채, 76×122cm
1981년 작가 기증

Adrienne Walker HOARD (USA, 1947-)
Garden of Jeju
1981, Oil on canvas, 76×122 cm
Donated by the artist in 1981

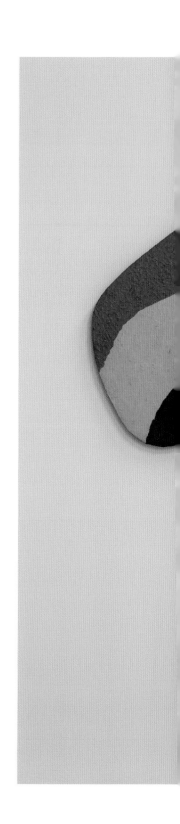

에이드리언 워커 호워드(미국, 1946-)
구름의 전당
1981, 캔버스에 유채, 48×118 cm, 37×111 cm, 66×119 cm
1981년 작가 기증

Adrienne Walker HOARD (USA, 1946-)
Temple of Clouds
1981, Oil on canvas, 48×118 cm, 37×111 cm, 66×119 cm
Donated by the artist in 1981

최르지 요바노비치(헝가리, 1939-)
경주로 가자
1987, 시멘트, 석고, 96×60×17.5cm
1988년 서울올림픽 조직위원회 기증

Gyorgy JOVANOVICS (Hungary, 1939-)
Let's go to Gyeongju
1987, Cement, plaster, 96×60×17.5 cm
Donated by Seoul Olympic Organizing Committee in 1988

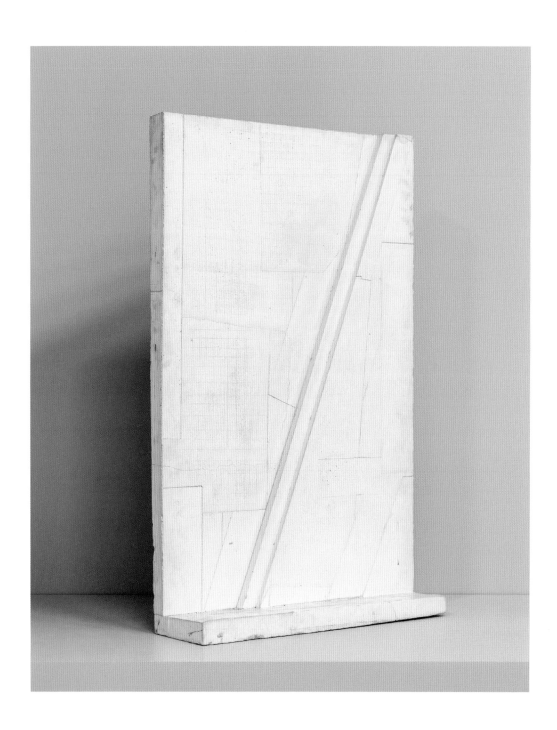

나이젤 홀(영국, 1943-)
한강
1988, 철, 47.9×68.5×36.5cm
1988년 서울올림픽 조직위원회 기증

Nigel HALL (United Kingdom, 1943-)
Han River
1988, Steel, 47.9×68.5×36.5 cm
Donated by Seoul Olympic Organizing Committee in 1988

The internationalization of Korean art can be considered from two aspects: 'Korean art's overseas expansion' and 'international inflow of foreign art'. While the overseas expansion of Korean art since the 1960s was a common goal to escape the "frog in the well," the inflow of overseas art into Korea until the early 1980s was more of an individual movement centered on public affairs offices or Korean artists abroad. Before the founding of the Gwangju Biennale, in Korea, where there were no specialized institutions for international art exchange, networks and friendships gathered and formed through knowledge and it became the starting point of international exchange. Among them, Nam June Paik is the one who gave birth to large and small issues and links in the process of globalization of Korean art in the 1980s and 1990s. MMCA (National Museum of Modern and Contemporary Art, Korea) was able to collect major works containing the autobiographical story of Nam June Paik and Joseph Beuys' relationship as artistic comrades through the 1st anniversary exhibition of Joseph Beuys, *Beuys Vox* (Won Gallery, 1987).

Meanwhile, before the construction of MMCA Gwacheon in 1986, MMCA was mainly functioning as an administrative institution that carried out exhibitions. In those days Membership Society for MMCA, a private sponsor of the museum, took on a role of supplementing the insufficient role of the museum, from donating works, to academies, lectures, and international art exchanges. More than 20 foreign artists including Donald Judd, Christo Javacheff, and Jonathan Borofsky were invited to lectures, and six international art collections, including David Hockney, were donated to the museum.

ART COMMUNICATION AND EXCHANGE AT THE GLOBAL LEVEL

미술교유交遊, 미술교류交流

한국미술의 국제화는 '한국미술의 해외진출'과 '해외미술의 국내 유입'이라는 두 가지 측면에서 생각해 볼 수 있다. 1960년대 이후 한국미술의 해외진출이 "우물 안 개구리"를 벗어나기 위한 공통의 목표였다면, 1980년대 초까지 해외미술의 국내 유입은 해외공보관이나 재외작가 중심으로 이루어지는 개별적인 움직임에 가까웠다. 광주비엔날레 창립 이전까지 국제미술교류 전문기관이 전무했던 우리나라에서는 알음알음으로 모이고 맺어진 네트워크나 교유(交遊)가 국제교류의 시발점이 되기도 했다. 그 중 백남준은 1980-90년대 한국미술의 세계화 과정에서 크고 작은 이슈와 연결고리를 낳은 장본인이다. 국립현대미술관은 요제프 보이스 (Joseph Beuys) 1주기 추모전 《보이스 복스》(원화랑, 1987)을 통해 백남준과 요제프 보이스의 예술적 동지로서의 관계와 자전적인 이야기를 담은 주요 작품을 수집할 수 있었다.

한편 1986년 과천관 신축 전까지 국립현대미술관은 전시를 실행하는 행정기관으로서의 기능이 중심이 되었다. 이 시기에 미술관의 민간후원단체인 (사)현대미술관회는 작품 기증부터 아카데미와 강좌, 국제 미술교류 등 미비했던 미술관의 역할을 보완하는 역할을 맡았다. 도널드 저드(Donald Judd), 크리스토(Christo Javacheff), 조나단 보로프스키(Jonathan Borofsky) 등 20명 이상의 해외작가 초청강좌를 마련하고, 데이비드 호크니(David Hockney) 등 6점의 국제미술 소장품을 미술관에 기증했다.

데이비드 호크니(영국, 1937-)
레일이 있는 그랜드 캐년 남쪽 끝, 1982년 10월
1982, 사진 콜라주, 95×334cm
1991년 (사)현대미술관회 기증

David HOCKNEY (United Kingdom, 1937-)
The Grand Canyon South Rim with Rail, Oct. 1982
1982, Photographic collage, 95×334 cm
Donated by Membership Society for MMCA in 1991

앤디 골즈워시(영국, 1956-)
무제(백)
1989, 종이에 크레용, 오일스틱, 엠보싱, 170×148cm
1992년 (사)현대미술관회 기증

Andy GOLDSWORTHY (United Kingdom, 1956-)
Untitled (White)
1989, Crayon, oilstick on paper, 170×148 cm
Donated by Membership Society for MMCA in 1992

앤디 골즈워시(영국, 1956-)
무제(흑)
1989, 종이에 흑연, 크레용, 오일스틱, 엠보싱, 158×146cm
1992년 (사)현대미술관회 기증

Andy GOLDSWORTHY (United Kingdom, 1956-)
Untitled (Black)
1989, Crayon, oilstick on paper, 158×146 cm
Donated by Membership Society for MMCA in 1992

앤디 골즈워시(영국, 1956-)
잎 조각
1988, 나뭇잎, 21×14.5×9cm
1992년 (사)현대미술관회 기증

Andy GOLDSWORTHY (United Kingdom, 1956-)
Leaves
1988, Leaves, 21×14.5×9 cm
Donated by Membership Society for MMCA in in 1992

로스 블렉크너(미국, 1949-)
노란심장들
1994, 캔버스에 유채, 244×320cm
1996년 (사)현대미술관회 기증
Courtesy of the Artist and Petzel Gallery, New York

Ross BLECKNER (USA, 1949-)
Yellow Hearts
1994, Oil on canvas, 244×320 cm
Donated by Membership Society for MMCA in 1996
Courtesy of the Artist and Petzel Gallery, New York

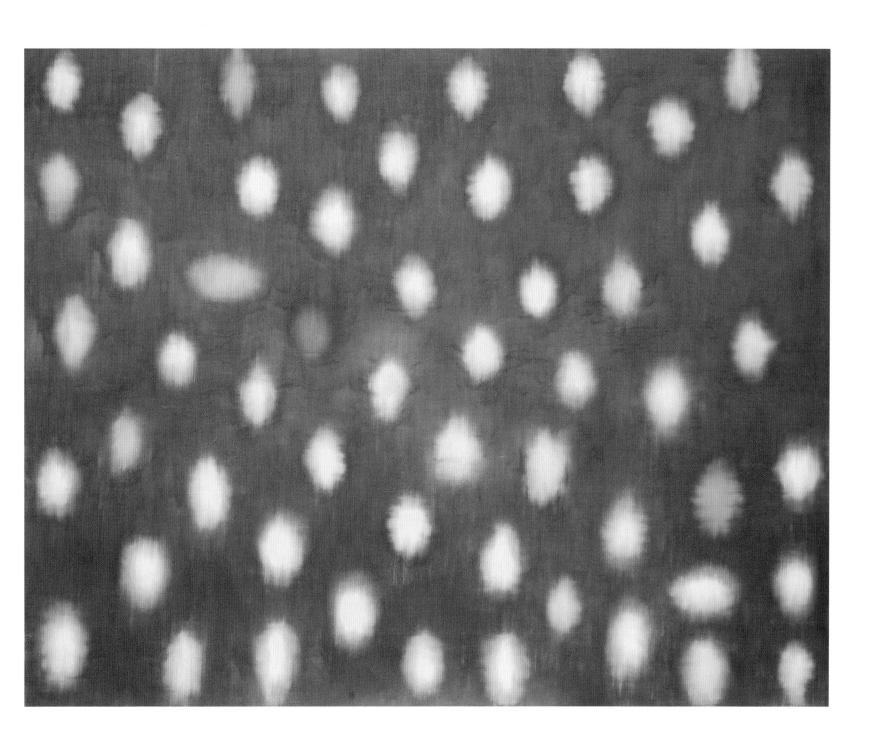

앤디 워홀(미국, 1928-1987)
자화상
1985, 캔버스에 포토 실크스크린, 100×100cm
1987년 구입

Andy WARHOL (USA, 1928-1987)
Self-Portrait
1985, Screen print on canvas, 100×100 cm
Purchased in 1987

앤디 워홀(미국, 1928-1987)
자화상
1985, 캔버스에 포토 실크스크린, 100×100cm
1987년 구입

Andy WARHOL (USA, 1928-1987)
Self-Portrait
1985, Screen print on canvas, 100×100 cm
Purchased in 1987

크리스토 야바체프(미국, 1935-2020)
계곡장막
1972, 종이에 흑연, 천, 색연필, 아크릴릭, 지도 인쇄물, 71×56cm
1987년 구입

Christo JAVACHEFF (USA, 1935-2020)
A Valley Curtain
1972, Mixed media, 71×56 cm
Purchased in 1987

로버트 라우센버그(미국, 1925-2008)
팀
1978, 종이에 직물 콜라주, 사진전사, 77.5×59cm
1987년 구입

Robert RAUSCHENBERG (USA, 1925-2008)
Teem
1978, Mixed media, 77.5×59 cm
Purchased in 1987

요제프 보이스(독일, 1921-1986)
보이스,백 카드
연도미상, 사진인쇄물, 트럼프카드, 콜라주, 49×38cm, 67.5×52cm, 38×28×(2)cm
1989년 원화랑 기증

Joseph BEUYS (Germany, 1921-1986)
Cards of Beuys and Paik
Undated, Collage, printed photograph, playing card, 49×38 cm, 67.5×52 cm, 38×28×(2) cm
Donated by Gallery Won in 1989

요제프 보이스(독일, 1921–1986)
작품 II
1983, 종이에 석판, 24×16×(2) cm
1989년 원화랑 기증

Joseph BEUYS (Germany, 1921–1986)
Work II
1983, Lithograph on paper, 24×16×(2) cm
Donated by Gallery Won in 1989

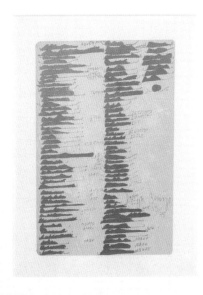
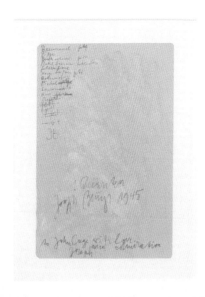

요제프 보이스(독일, 1921–1986)
보이스 작품
1966, 인화지에 흑백 인쇄, 20×29 cm
1989년 원화랑 기증

Joseph BEUYS (Germany, 1921–1986)
Work of BEUYS
1966, Print on photo paper, 20×29 cm
Donated by Gallery Won in 1989

백남준(미국, 1932-2006)
고지대 I
1988, 컬러 인쇄물 위에 연필, 50×59cm
1989년 원화랑 기증

Nam June PAIK (USA, 1932-2006)
Highland I
1988, Pencil on color print, 50×59 cm
Donated by Gallery Won in 1989

113

Nearly half of the international exhibitions held in Korea until the 1980s were print exhibitions. It was also a time when various media and experimental printmaking, which deviated from classical printmaking techniques such as engraving and woodblock prints, were recognized as a 'modern attempt' among artists. Also, as a reproduction of Western masterpieces, printmaking became an opportunity for art lovers to be aware of Western art. Because logistics and transportation between countries were not smooth, printmaking was an easier to bring into Korea compared to sculpture and painting. On July 1, 1988, the measures to open the importation of foreign art were announced, and in the early days, frequency of sales increased centered on small print works. In particular, prints reminiscent of Western paintings with an exotic atmosphere and prints by famous artists such as Picasso and Dali were popular. In the case of Paul Aïzpiri, the number of domestic exhibitions in the 1980s reached 10, including three solo exhibitions. Dong-A International Print Biennale, held at MMCA (National Museum of Modern and Contemporary Art, Korea) in 1970 proves interest in printmaking, which has been on the rise since the mid-1960s.

In the second exhibition in 1972, 446 works by 199 artists from 31 countries were submitted, and at a time when international art events were very rare, about 200 people took part in the opening ceremony. After being suspended for 9 years, the 3rd exhibition was resumed in 1981.

All of them were held at MMCA until the 4th exhibition in 1983, and at the 4th International Print Biennale, 10 works including award-winning works were purchased as collections.

THE WORLD GAZING THROUGH ART

그림으로 보는 세계

3

1980년대까지 국내에서 개최한 국제전시 가운데 절반 가까이가
판화 전시였다. 동판화, 목판화 등 고전적인 판화기법에서
벗어난 다양한 매체와 실험적인 방식의 판화가 예술가들 사이에서
'현대적인 시도'로 인식되던 때이기도 했다. 또한 서양 명화의
복제품으로서 판화는 미술애호가를 비롯한 일반인들이 서양의
미술을 접할 수 있는 계기가 되었다. 국가간 물류와 운송이 원활하지
않았던 시기에 판화는 조각과 회화에 비해 국내에 반입하기
용이한 매체였다. 1988년 7월 1일 해외미술품 수입 개방조치가
공표되고, 초창기에는 값비싼 대작보다는 소규모 판화작품을
중심으로 관심과 매매 빈도가 높아졌다. 특히 이국적인 분위기의
서양 그림을 연상시키는 판화와 피카소(Pablo Picasso),
달리(Salvador Dali) 등 유명작가의 판화가 인기를 끌었다.
폴 아이즈피리(Paul Aïzpiri)의 경우, 80년대에 국내 전시
횟수가 개인전 3회를 포함하여 10회에 다다를 정도였다. 1970년
동아일보사가 창설하고 국립현대미술관에서 개최했던 국제
판화비엔날레는 1960년대 중반부터 대두되었던 판화에 대한
관심을 반증한다. 1972년 제2회 전시에는 31개국의 작가
199명의 446점이 출품되었으며, 국제미술행사가 매우 드물었던
당시에 개막식 행사에만 200여 명이 참여하는 등 큰 주목을
받았다. 이후 9년간 중단되었다가 1981년 제3회 전시가
재개되었다. 1983년 제4회 전시까지 모두 국립현대미술관에서
개최하였으며, 제4회 국제판화비엔날레에서는 수상작을
포함한 10점의 작품을 소장품으로 구입했다.

폴 아이즈피리(프랑스, 1919-2016)
정물
1955, 캔버스에 유채, 100×80cm
1986년 기요시 다메나가 기증

Paul AIZPIRI (France, 1919-2016)
Still Life
1955, Oil on canvas, 100×80 cm
Donated by Kiyoshi Damenaga in 1986

폴 아이즈피리(프랑스, 1919-2016)
꽃
연도미상, 종이에 석판, 57×46.5cm
1986년 피에르 위까르 기증

Paul AIZPIRI (France, 1919-2016)
Flowers
Undated, Lithograph on paper, 57×46.5 cm
Donated by Pierre Wicart in 1986

이브 브라이에(프랑스, 1907-1990)
루르마랭
연도미상, 종이에 석판, 48×62cm
1986년 피에르 위까르 기증

Yves BRAYER (France, 1907-1990)
LOURMARIN
Undated, Lithograph on paper, 48×62 cm
Donated by Pierre Wicart in 1986

모리스 기리옹 그린(프랑스, 1913-1989)
야외음악당
연도미상, 종이에 석판, 45×54.5cm
1986년 피에르 위까르 기증

Maurice GHIGLION-GREEN (France, 1913-1989)
Outdoor Music Hall
Undated, Lithograph on paper, 45×54.5 cm
Donated by Pierre Wicart in 1986

기 바르돈(프랑스, 1927-2015)
아일랜드의 빛
연도미상, 종이에 석판, 67×49.5cm
1986년 피에르 위까르 기증

Guy BARDONE (France, 1927-2015)
Radiance of Ireland
Undated, Lithograph on paper, 67×49.5 cm
Donated by Pierre Wicart in 1986

폴 기라망(프랑스, 1926-2007)
로랭에게 드리다
연도미상, 종이에 석판, 64.5×47cm
1986년 피에르 위까르 기증

Paul GUIRAMAND (France, 1926-2007)
Dedicated to Lorrain
Undated, Lithograph on paper, 64.5×47 cm
Donated by Pierre Wicart in 1986

질 고리티(프랑스, 1939-)
큰 야자수나무
연도미상, 종이에 석판, 63×46cm
1986년 피에르 위까르 기증

Gilles GORRITI (France, 1939-)
Big Coconut Palm
Undated, Lithograph on paper, 63×46 cm
Donated by Pierre Wicart in 1986

장-클로드 퀼리시(프랑스, 1941-)
미꼬노의 꽃 있는 골목길
연도미상, 종이에 석판, 60.5×50.5cm
1986년 피에르 위까르 기증

Jean-Claude QUILICI (France, 1941-)
MYKONOS
Undated, Lithograph on paper, 60.5×50.5 cm
Donated by Pierre Wicart in 1986

마르셀 크라모아장(프랑스, 1915–2007)
브르타뉴의 항구
연도미상, 종이에 석판, 42.5×59.5cm
1986년 피에르 위까르 기증

Marcel CRAMOYSAN (France, 1915–2007)
Port of Brittany
Undated, Lithograph on paper, 42.5×59.5 cm
Donated by Pierre Wicart in 1986

마르셀 케르벨라(프랑스, 1930–)
베니스의 궁전
연도미상, 종이에 석판, 44.5×64.5cm
1986년 피에르 위까르 기증

Marcel KERVELLA (France, 1930–)
Palace of Venice
Undated, Lithograph on paper, 44.5×64.5 cm
Donated by Pierre Wicart in 1986

조르주 라포르트(프랑스, 1926-2000)
팽폴의 배
연도미상, 종이에 석판, 45.5×67cm
1986년 피에르 위까르 기증

Georges LAPORTE (France, 1926-2000)
Ship of Paimpol
Undated, Lithograph on paper, 45.5×67cm
Donated by Pierre Wicart in 1986

마디 드 라 지로디에르(프랑스, 1922-2018)
혁명기념일의 행진
연도미상, 종이에 석판, 64.5×42cm
1986년 피에르 위까르 기증

Mady de La Giraudière (France, 1922-2018)
French Revolution Anniversary's Parade (Le défilé du 14 juillet)
Undated, Lithograph on paper, 64.5×42 cm
Donated by Pierre Wicart in 1986

베르나르 뷔페(프랑스, 1928-1999)
패커드
연도미상, 종이에 석판, 49.5×65cm
1986년 피에르 위까르 기증

Bernard BUFFET (France, 1928-1999)
Packard
Undated, Lithograph on paper, 49.5×65 cm
Donated by Pierre Wicart in 1986

폴 야누스 입센(덴마크, 1936-)
벤트 칼 야콥슨(덴마크, 1934-2004)
센트럴 파크
1976, 종이에 실크스크린, 50.5×50.5cm
1983년 구입(제4회 서울국제판화비엔날레 우수상 수상)

Poul Janus IPSEN (Denmark, 1936-)
Bent Karl Jacobsen (Denmark, 1934-2004)
Central Park, New York
1976, Screen print on paper, 50.5×50.5 cm
Purchased in 1983 (Superior Class Prize, The 4th Seoul International Print Biennale)

알렉산드라 해세커(캐나다, 1945-)
지난 여름
1983, 종이에 석판, 56×71 cm
1983년 구입

Alexandra HAESEKER (Canada, 1945-)
Last Summer
1983, Lithograph on paper, 56×71 cm
Purchased in 1983

모토나가 사다마사(일본, 1922-2011)
떠 있는 두개의 물체
1981, 종이에 실크스크린, 55×45cm
1983년 구입(제4회 서울국제판화비엔날레 대상 수상)

MOTONAGA Sadamasa (Japan, 1922-2011)
Two Floating Objects
1981, Screen print on paper, 55×45 cm
Purchased in 1983 (Grand Prize, The 4th Seoul International Print Biennale)

A.P.   S. motonaga

"Seoul to the world, the world to Seoul" is a slogan uttered at the opening ceremony of the 1988 Seoul Olympics by IOC (International Olympic Organizing Committee) Chairman Juan Antonio Samaranch. The 1988 Seoul Olympics drew the attention of people from all over the world as they broke down the wall of the Cold War witnessed in the previous Olympics in Moscow and Los Angeles and created harmony between East and West. During the Olympics, a variety of international art events such as art, music, and performances were held as well as sports events, just like the world's festival. Among them, *Olympiad of Art* hosted by the Seoul Olympic Organizing Commitee drew attention with a budget of 9 million dollars, an international scale, and a short implementation schedule. However, it caused a massive backlash from the Korean art world against the rush management and partiality. It was at the center of constant controversy and interest in the coordination process. Meanwhile, in the promotional material for the event at the time, there is a clause that encourages participating artists to exhibit one piece and donate one piece, which stands out. *Olympiad of Art* served as a groundbreaking opportunity for the collection of the international art collections of the National Museum of Modern and Contemporary Art, Korea, as 39 small-scale sculptures by artists participating in the outdoor sculpture symposium and 62 paintings by participating artists in *International Contemporary Painting Exhibition*, were donated. It is true that it was remembered as an event with many problems due to the heated controversy and opposition of the art world, and it was difficult to properly evaluate it as an international art event. However, the meaning can be found in that it opened a prelude to the full-scale globalization and diversification of Korean contemporary art by providing a place where domestic and foreign contemporary art could be compared side by side based on the Olympic spirit of being a place of human harmony.

SEOUL TO THE WORLD, THE WORLD TO SEOUL

서울은 세계로, 세계는 서울로

"서울은 세계로, 세계는 서울로"는 1988년 서울 올림픽 개막식에서 IOC(국제올림픽조직위원회) 사마란치(Juan Antonio Samaranch) 위원장이 개회선언으로 외쳤던 구호이다. 88서울 올림픽은 이전의 모스크바와 LA 올림픽에서 목격했던 냉전의 벽을 허물고 동서간의 화합을 일궈낸 것으로 전 세계인들의 이목을 집중시켰다. 올림픽 기간에는 세계인의 축제답게 스포츠 행사뿐만 아니라 미술, 음악, 공연 등 다채로운 국제 예술행사가 펼쳐졌다. 그 가운데서도 서울올림픽 조직위원회에서 주최했던 세계현대미술제는 90억 원의 예산과 국제적인 규모, 단기간의 추진 일정으로 주목을 받았다. 그러나 졸속운영과 편파성에 대한 국내 미술계의 대대적인 반발을 초래했고, 조율 과정에서도 끊임없는 논란과 관심의 중심에 있었다. 한편 당시 행사 홍보물에는 전시 참여 작가들에게 1점은 전시하고 1점은 기증하는 것을 독려하는 조항이 있어 눈에 띈다. 세계현대미술제는 야외조각 심포지엄 참여 작가들의 소규모 조각 39점, 《국제현대회화전》에 참여 작가의 회화 62점이 기증되는 등 국립현대미술관 국제미술 소장품 수집에도 획기적인 계기가 되었다. 지금껏 미술계의 뜨거운 논란과 반발로 문제점이 많았던 행사로 기억되고 국제미술행사로서의 정당한 평가가 어려웠던 것은 사실이다. 그러나 인류화합의 장이라는 올림픽 정신을 바탕으로 국내외 현대미술을 나란히 견주어 볼 수 있었던 자리를 마련하고, 한국현대미술의 본격적인 세계화와 다원화의 서막을 열었다는 점에서 의미를 찾을 수 있다.

디오한디(그리스, 1945-)
무제
1987, 현무암, 화강석, 채색된 나무, 35×58×52 cm
1988년 서울올림픽 조직위원회 기증

DIOHANDI (Greece, 1945-)
Untitled
1987, Wood and granite, volcanic rock, 35×58×52 cm
Donated by Seoul Olympic Organizing Committee in 1988

다니 카라반(이스라엘, 1930-2021)
예루살렘
1987, 청동, 33×33×5cm
1988년 서울올림픽 조직위원회 기증

Dani KARAVAN (Israel, 1930-2021)
Jerusalem
1987, Bronze, 33×33×5 cm
Donated by Seoul Olympic Organizing Committee in 1988

히울라 코시세(아르헨티나, 1924-2016)
얽힘
1988, 플랙시글라스, 74.5×41×29cm
1988년 서울올림픽 조직위원회 기증

Gyula KOSICE (Argentina, 1924-2016)
Symbiosis
1988, Plexiglass, 74.5×41×29 cm
Donated by Seoul Olympic Organizing Committee in 1988

에드가르 네그레트(콜롬비아, 1920-2012)
무제
1988, 알루미늄, 볼트, 너트, 38.5×81.5×39cm
1988년 서울올림픽 조직위원회 기증

Edgar NEGRET (Columbia, 1920-2012)
Untitled
1988, Aluminum, bolt, nut, 38.5×81.5×39 cm
Donated by Seoul Olympic Organizing Committee in 1988

에리크 디에트만(스웨덴, 1937-2002)
무제
1987, 청동, 철, 11×66×10cm
1998년 서울 올림픽 조직위원회 기증

Erik DIETMAN (Sweden, 1937-2002)
Untitled
1987, Bronze and steel, 11×66×10 cm
Donated by Seoul Olympic Organizing Committee in 1988

모한드 아마라(알제리, 1952-)
무제
1987, 청동, 16×34×13cm
1988년 서울올림픽 조직위원회 기증

Mohand AMARA (Algeria, 1952-)
Untitled
1987, Bronze, 16×34×13 cm
Donated by Seoul Olympic Organizing Committee in 1988

권터 위커(독일, 1930-)
칼
1988, 나무에 채색, 못, 148×48×46cm
1988년 서울올림픽 조직위원회 기증

Günther UECKER (Germany, 1930-)
Sword
1988, Wood and nail, 148×48×46 cm
Donated by Seoul Olympic Organizing Committee in 1988

권터 위커, 〈칼 조각〉, 1988, 나무, 돌, 철, 로프, 320×320×400cm, 올림픽 조각공원
Gunther UECKER, *Knife Sculpture*, 1988, Wood, stone, steel, rope, 320×320×400 cm, Olympic Park

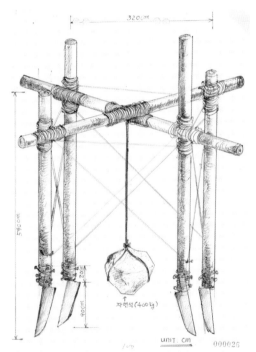

소마미술관 소장 자료
SOMA (Seoul Olympic Museum of Art) Archive

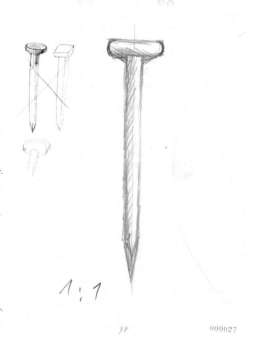

권터 위커, 《세계현대미술제》, 〈제2차 야외조각 심포지엄〉에서 현장제작한 작품의 드로잉과 자필 설명서. 권터 위커는 올림픽 조각공원에 설치한 조각의 축소모형(마케트) 대신에 그의 대표작인 못 조각(nail sculpture)을 국립현대미술관에 기증함.

Günther Uecker, Drawings and handwritten instructions of the work to be produced on site at *The 2nd International Open-Air Sculpture Symposium, Olympiad of Art*. He donated his representative *Nail Sculpture* to MMCA instead of the miniature model (Maquette) for installed in Olympic Park.

프란스 크라이츠베르그(브라질, 1921–2017)
파괴
1988, 나무, 258×109×97 cm
1998년 서울 올림픽 조직위원회 기증

Frans KRAJCBERG (Brazil, 1921–2017)
Destruction
1988, Wood, 258×109×97 cm
Donated by Seoul Olympic Organizing Committee in 1988

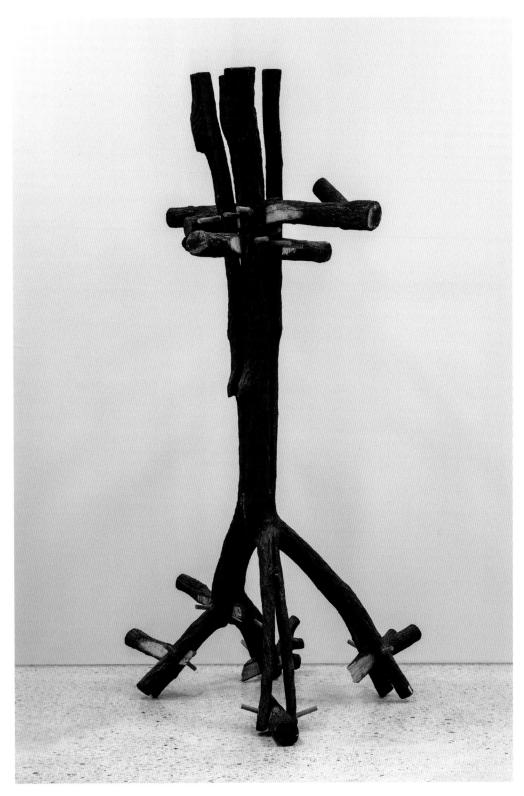

(전경)

(굵기)　(길이)

작업현장 이동 (참나무 41주)

~ 2 ~　000045

프란스 크라이츠베르그가 제작했던 올림픽 조각공원 내 〈저항의 시각〉 작품 제작 현장. 작가의 요청한 조건에 맞는 소나무를 찾아 벌목하고, 두 차례의 태우기를 거쳐 완성했다.

The production site of *Vision of Revolt* work in Olympic Park, which was produced by Frans Krajberg. A pine tree that meets the conditions requested by the artist was found and felled, and it was completed after two rounds of burning.

8. 태우기 (2차)

8-1

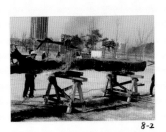

8-2

~ 10 ~　000053

2 - 3

2 - 4

~ 18 ~　000062

프란츠 크라이츠베르그, 〈저항의 시각〉, 1988, 나무, 1000×1000×600cm, 올림픽 조각공원
Frans KRAJCBERG, *Vision of Revolt*, 1988, Wood, 1000×1000×600 cm, Olympic Park

데니스 오펜하임(미국, 1938-2011)
유리잔
1988, 헝겊, 볼트, 너트, 100.5×45×41×(2)cm
1988년 서울올림픽 조직위원회 기증

Dennis OPPENHEIM (USA, 1938-2011)
Glass
1988, Fiber, 100.5×45×41×(2) cm
Donated by Seoul Olympic Organizing Committee in 1988

마그달레나 아바카노비치(폴란드, 1930-2017)
안드로진과 바퀴
1988, 나무, 합성수지에 채색, 173×104×90cm
1988년 서울올림픽 조직위원회 기증

Magdalena ABAKANOWICZ (Poland, 1930-2017)
Androgyn and the Wheel
1988, Wood and synthetic plastics, 173×104×90 cm
Donated by Seoul Olympic Organizing Committee in 1988

피터 크나프(스위스, 1931-)
동풍 IVA + 동풍 IVB
1987, 플렉시글라스, 115×180×(2)cm
1988년 서울올림픽 조직위원회 기증

Peter KNAPP (Swiss, 1931-)
Wind from East IVA + Wind from East IVB
1987, Plexiglass, 115×180×(2) cm
Donated by Seoul Olympic Organizing Committee in 1988

피터 클라센(독일, 1935-)
회색 탱크차 / 방수포
1984, 캔버스에 아크릴릭, 162×130cm
1988년 서울올림픽 조직위원회 기증

Peter KLASEN (Germany, 1935-)
Gray tank truck/Tarpauling (Wagon Citerne Gris/Bache)
1984, Acrylic on canvas, 162×130 cm
Donated by Seoul Olympic Organizing Committee in 1988

올리비에 모세(스위스, 1944-)
대한항공기
1986, 캔버스에 아크릴릭, 203×213cm
1988년 서울올림픽 조직위원회 기증

Olivier MOSSET (Swiss, 1944-)
KAL
1986, Acrylic on canvas, 203×213 cm
Donated by Seoul Olympic Organizing Committee in 1988

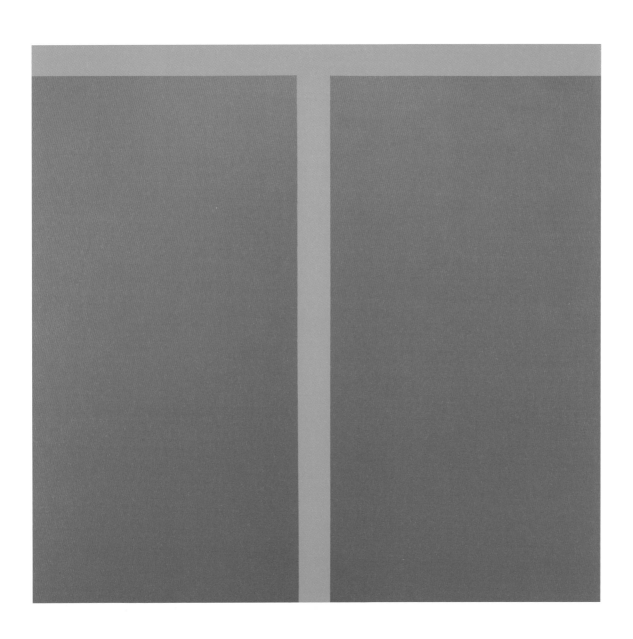

얀 방리에(벨기에, 1948-)
복수
1988, 캔버스에 유채, 크레용, 199.5×299cm
1988년 서울올림픽 조직위원회 기증

Jan VANRIET (Belgium, 1948-)
Revenge
1988, Oil and crayon on canvas, 199.5×299 cm
Donated by Seoul Olympic Organizing Committee in 1988

151

오페 르루쉬(이스라엘, 1947-)
야자수가 있는 자화상
1987, 캔버스에 유채, 197×138.2cm
1988년 서울올림픽 조직위원회 기증

Ofer LELLOUCHE (Israel, 1947–)
Self-Portrait with Coconut Palm
1987, Oil on canvas, 197×138.2 cm
Donated by Seoul Olympic Organizing Committee in 1988

일리아 하이니히(독일, 1950-)
청소년
1985, 캔버스에 유채, 250×300cm
1988년 서울올림픽 조직위원회 기증

Ilja HEINIG (Germany, 1950-)
Youth
1985, Oil on canvas, 250×300 cm
Donated by Seoul Olympic Organizing Committee in 1988

카를-헤닝 페데르센(덴마크, 1913-2007)
미로의 축제
1987, 캔버스에 유채, 206×290cm
1988년 서울올림픽 조직위원회 기증

Carl-Henning PEDERSEN (Denmark, 1913-2007)
Feast of Labyrinth
1987, Oil on canvas, 206×290 cm
Donated by Seoul Olympic Organizing Committee in 1988

아킬레 페릴리(이탈리아, 1927-2021)
영혼의 무게
1986, 캔버스에 아크릴릭, 150×150cm
1988년 서울올림픽 조직위원회 기증

Achille PERILLI (Italy, 1927-2021)
The Weight of the Soul (Il Peso dell'anima)
1986, Acrylic on canvas, 150×150 cm
Donated by Seoul Olympic Organizing Committee in 1988

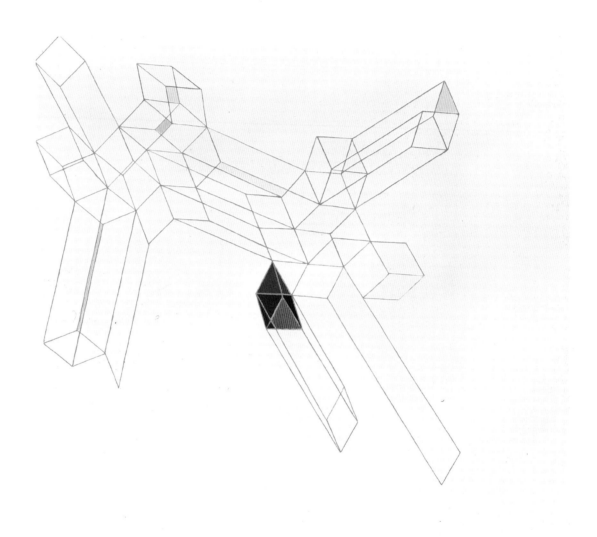

아우구스토 바로스(포르투갈, 1929-1998)
연을 가진 남자
1987, 캔버스에 템페라, 과슈, 126.2×88cm
1988년 서울올림픽 조직위원회 기증

Augusto BARROS (Portugal, 1929-1998)
The Man with the Kite (L'Homme au Cerf-Volant)
1987, Tempera and gouache on canvas, 126.2×88 cm
Donated by Seoul Olympic Organizing Committee in 1988

마리안네 헤스케(노르웨이, 1946-)
햄세달로부터
1988, 캔버스에 실크스크린, 169×219cm
1988년 서울올림픽 조직위원회 기증

Marianne HESKE (Norway, 1946-)
From Hemsedal
1988, Screen print on canvas, 169×219 cm
Donated by Seoul Olympic Organizing Committee in 1988

콘스탄틴 제나키스(프랑스, 1931–2020)
위생시설 법규에 관한 변주곡
1978, 캔버스에 아크릴릭, 200×65cm
1988년 서울올림픽 조직위원회 기증

Constantin XENAKIS (France, 1931–2020)
Variations on Sanitary Regulations
1978, Acrylic on canvas, 200×65 cm
Donated by Seoul Olympic Organizing Committee in 1988

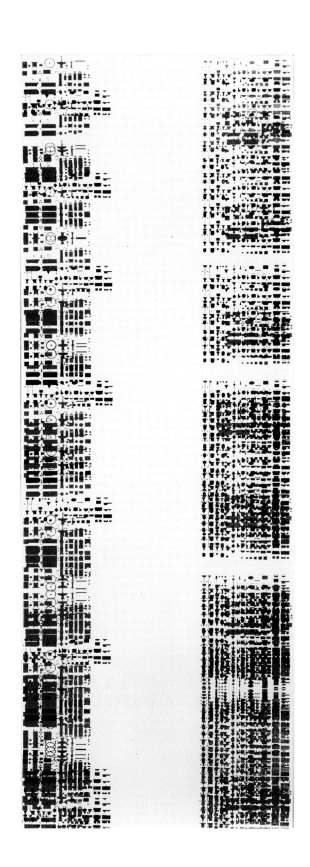

벵트 린드스트렘(스웨덴, 1925-2008)
공적
1987, 캔버스에 유채, 198×199cm
1988년 서울올림픽 조직위원회 기증

Bengt LINDSTROM (Sweden, 1925-2008)
The Feat (L'Exploit)
1987, Oil on canvas, 198×199 cm
Donated by Seoul Olympic Organizing Committee in 1988

제니 왓슨(오스트레일리아, 1951-)
미술관을 위한 작품
1987, 면천에 유채, 아크릴릭, 172.7×200.6cm
1988년 서울올림픽 조직위원회 기증

Jenny WATSON (Australia, 1951-)
Work for Museum
1987, Oil and acrylic on raw canvas, 172.7×200.6 cm
Donated by Seoul Olympic Organizing Committee in 1988

발도메로 페스타나(스페인, 1918-2015)
이면화
1988, 종이에 연필, 유채, 149×99×(2) cm
1988년 서울올림픽 조직위원회 기증

Baldomero PESTANA (Spain, 1918-2015)
Diptyque
1988, Pencil and oil on paper, 149×99×(2) cm
Donated by Seoul Olympic Organizing Committee in 1988

장 메사지에(프랑스, 1920-1999)
쟝 바티스타 티에폴로와 빈센트 반 고흐의 만남
1987, 캔버스에 유채, 205.3×217 cm
1988년 서울올림픽 조직위원회 기증

Jean MESSAGIER (France, 1920-1999)
Encounter of Gian Battista Tiepolo and Vincent van Gogh
1987, Oil on canvas, 205.3×217 cm
Donated by Seoul Olympic Organizing Committee in 1988

올리비에 드브레(프랑스, 1920-1999)
장미빛과 오렌지빛 선
1983, 캔버스에 유채, 150×150cm
1988년 서울올림픽 조직위원회 기증

Olivier DEBRE (France, 1920-1999)
Pink and Orange Lingnes (Les Lingnes Roses et Oranges)
1983, Oil on canvas, 150×150 cm
Donated by Seoul Olympic Organizing Committee in 1988

베르나르트 슐체(독일, 1915-2005)
오필리아
1985, 캔버스에 유채, 천, 200×140cm
1988년 서울올림픽 조직위원회 기증

Bernard SCHULTZE (Germany, 1915-2005)
Ophelia
1985, Oil and cloth on canvas, 200×140 cm
Donated by Seoul Olympic Organizing Committee in 1988

It is relatively recent that a pluralistic perspective, which excludes the artist's nationality, ethnicity, and cultural characteristics, and evaluates them based on their work, has been introduced in contemporary art around the world. Since mid-1980s, attempts to break away from the view of Western-centrism on International Exhibition had emerged, but they were also led by Western artists and planners with cultural bias. However, since 1988 when Seoul Olympics and *Olympiad of Art* were held, the aspect of Korea's international art exchange has changed in progressive way. The atmosphere of globalization, such as measures to open the importation of foreign art and the declaration of globalization in 1994 has been heightening. International art events, large and small, have emerged in the art world, and the number of overseas exhibitions flowing into Korea has increased. In 1990, the Seoul International Art Festival with the theme of 'Korean paper' drew attention both at home and abroad as a venue for fierce work and competition by Western artists. The establishment of Gwangju Biennale in 1995 and Korean Pavilion at Venice Biennale showed the achievements of international art exchanges that have continued to expand since Seoul Olympics in 1988. Although the number of donations in global art collection of MMCA (National Museum of Modern and Contemporary Art, Korea) has decreased compared to before, various works that fill the history of contemporary art have been collected through ambitious collection activities. MMCA global art in the 1990s is significant in that it opened a door to the world beyond the fence and beyond the window through art.

ART, A WINDOW ON THE WORLD

미술, 세계를 보는 창   5

전 세계의 동시대미술에서 작가의 국적이나 민족, 문화적 특성을
배제하고 작업만을 기준으로 평가하는 다원주의적 관점이
도입된 것은 비교적 최근의 일이다. 1980년대 중반부터 유럽과
미국 등 서구 중심 미술사관에서 벗어나고자 하는 시도가
대두되었으나 그 역시 서구권 작가와 기획자들 주도로 이루어진
것으로, 결국은 비서구권 작가들에 대한 제한된 인식을 각기
다른 방식으로 풀어낸 것에 지나지 않았다. 그러나 1988년 서울
올림픽과 세계현대미술제 이후 우리나라의 국제미술교류는
마치 동방의 작은 나라라는 인식, 분단국가라는 지정학적 제약에
굴하지 않겠다는 의지를 표방하는 것 마냥 자기 주도적이고
진취적으로 변화했다. 미술품 수입개방화와 1994년 세계화선언 등
세계화 분위기가 더욱 고조되면서 미술계에도 크고 작은 국제
미술행사가 생겨나고, 국내로 유입되는 해외전시 수도 큰 폭으로
증가하였다. 이 가운데 1990년 '한지'를 소재로 한 서울국제
미술제는 서구권 작가들의 열띤 작업과 경쟁의 장으로 국내외의
주목을 받았다. 1995년 광주비엔날레 창립과 같은 해 베니스
비엔날레 한국관 신설 등은 서울 올림픽 이후 지속적으로 확장세를
지켜온 국제미술교류의 성과를 보여주는 것이었다. 국립현대
미술관 국제미술 컬렉션도 이전에 비해 기증작의 수는 줄었지만,
의욕적인 수집활동을 통해 현대미술사의 면면을 채우는
다채로운 작품들이 수집되었다. 1990년대 수집된 국립현대미술관
국제미술 소장품은 '미술'을 통해 울타리 너머의 세상, 창문
너머의 세계를 조망할 수 있는 빗장을 열었다는 점에서 의의가
있다.

브라이언 헌트(미국, 1947-)
가을폭포 I
1990, 한지에 먹, 아크릴릭, 오일스틱, 167×131 cm
1990년 작가 기증 (서울국제미술제 대상 수상작)

Bryan HUNT (USA, 1947-)
Autumn Falls I
1990, Acrylic, ink and oil stick on paper, 167×131 cm
Donated by the artist in 1990 (Seoul International Art Festival Grand Prize Winner)

카를 프레드릭 레우테르스베르트(스웨덴, 1934-2016)
2-3
1990, 한지에 파스텔, 크레용, 167×132cm
1991년 작가 기증

Carl Fredrik REUTERSWARD (Sweden, 1934-2016)
2-3
1990, Pastel and crayon on paper, 167×132 cm
Donated by the artist in 1991

카를 프레드릭 레우테르스베르트(스웨덴, 1934–2016)
3-4
1990, 한지에 파스텔, 크레용, 167×132cm
1991년 작가 기증

Carl Fredrik REUTERSWARD (Sweden, 1934–2016)
3-4
1990, Pastel and crayon on paper, 167×132 cm
Donated by the artist in 1991

일리아 카바코프(러시아, 1933-)
저것들은 누구의 날개인가
1990, 한지에 수채, 잉크, 목탄, 131×165cm
1991년 구입

Ilya KABAKOV (Russia, 1933-)
Elena Lovna Socova: Whose Are Those Wings *(Elena Lovna Socova: A Qui Sont Ces Ailes?)*
1990, Watercolor, ink, charcoal on paper, 131×165 cm
Purchased in 1991

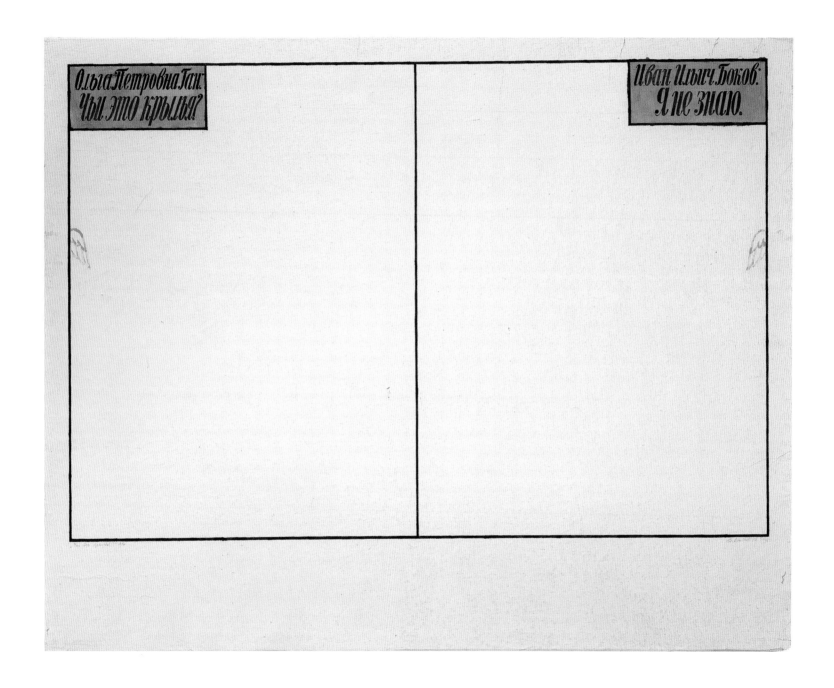

일리아 카바코프(러시아, 1933-)
저것들은 누구의 날개인가
1990, 한지에 수채, 잉크, 목탄, 131×165cm
1991년 구입

Ilya KABAKOV (Russia, 1933-)
Elena Lovna Socova: Whose Are Those Wings *(Elena Lovna Socova: A Qui Sont Ces Ailes?)*
1990, Watercolor, ink, charcoal on paper, 131×165 cm
Purchased in 1991

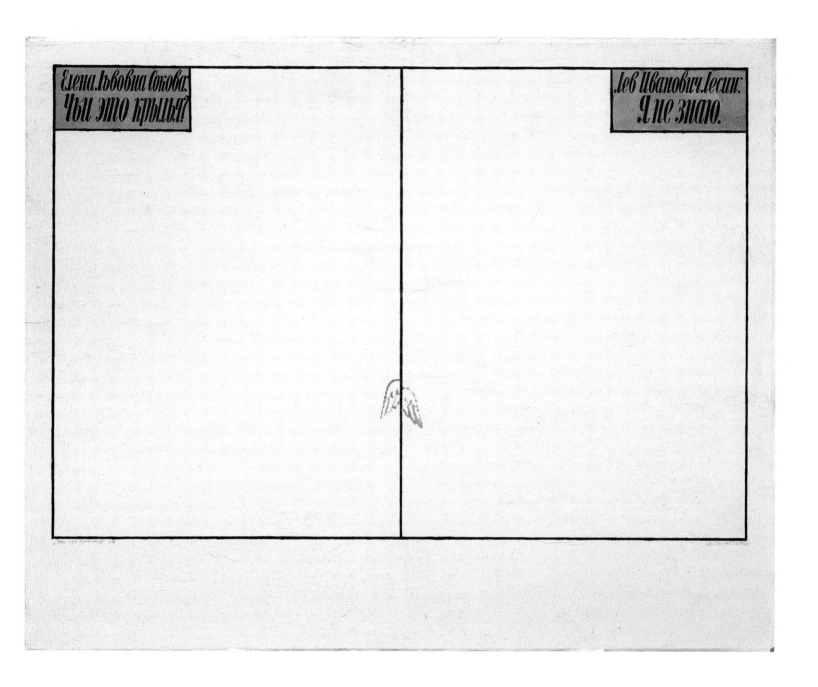

도널드 저드(미국, 1928-1994)
무제
1980, 철, 알루미늄, 아크릴수지, 239×61×69cm
1995년 구입

Donald JUDD (USA, 1928-1994)
Untitled
1980, Steel, aluminium and perspex, 239×61×69 cm
Purchased in 1995

장-미셸 바스키아(미국, 1960-1988)
무제
1982, 종이에 크레용, 수성안료, 108.5×77.5cm
1992년 구입

Jean-Michel BASQUIAT (USA, 1960-1988)
Untitled
1982, Mixed media on paper, 108.5×77.5 cm
Purchased in 1992

181

짐 다인(미국, 1935-)
색채의 전율
1990, 청동에 채색, 160.6×61.8×45.3 cm
1993년 구입
© 짐 다인 / ARS, 뉴욕 – SACK, 서울, 2021

Jim DINE (USA, 1935-)
Trembling for Color
1990, Color on bronze, 160.6×61.8×45.3 cm
Purchased in 1993
© Jim Dine / ARS, New York – SACK, Seoul, 2021

니키 드 생팔(프랑스, 1930-2002)
검은 나나(라라)
1967, 폴리에스테르에 채색, 291×172×100cm
1994년 구입

Niki De SAINT-PHALLE (France, 1930-2002)
Black Nana (Lara)
1967, Color on polyester, 291×172×100 cm
Purchased in 1994

장 피에르 레이노(프랑스, 1939-)
붉은 화분
1968, 합성수지에 채색, 195×180×180cm
1996년 구입

Jean-Pierre RAYNAUD (France, 1939-)
Pot Rouge
1968, Color on synthetic plastics, 195×180×180 cm
Purchased in 1996

앤서니 카로(영국, 1924-2013)
레몽, 시퐁
1978, 철판에 페인트, 119.5×175.5×165cm
1995년 구입

Anthony CARO (United Kingdom, 1924-2013)
Lemon, Chiffon
1978, Color on steel plate, 119.5×175.5×165 cm
Purchased in 1995

조지 시걸(미국, 1924-2000)
침대 위의 소녀 3
1973, 석고, 55×205×101 cm
1994년 구입

George SEGAL (USA, 1924-2000)
Girl on a Bed 3
1973, Plaster, 55×205×101 cm
Purchased in 1994

The Readymade Boomerang

René Block [1]
Curator, Gallerist

1990
Portfolio with prints by Dennis Adams, Barbara Bloom, K. P. Brehmer, Janet Burchill, John Cage, Tony Cragg, Rosalie Gascoigne, Richard Hamilton, Ilya Kabakov, Allan Kaprow, Bjørn Nørgaard, Nam June Paik, Sarkis, Julian Schnabel, Rosemarie Trockel, Peter Tyndall, Ken Unsworth, Ben Vautier, Boyd Webb, Lawrence Weiner and Emmett Williams.

1. The first exhibition, *Capitalist Realism* (*Kapitalistischer Realismus*, 1964), organized by René Block, featured Gerhard Richter, Zigmar Polke, Wolf Postel, and K. P. Bremer, which contained satire and humor about democratization of the market, multiplexing of images, and no-relationship between art and politics. He was the person in the scene of contemporary art in the late 20th century, which became a hot issue with Fluxus and Neodada. In addition to the 8th Biennale of Sydney in 1990, he participated as a director of the Seoul of Fluxus in 1993 in Korea, as a curator in Art Cologne, and as a director of the 4th International Istanbul Biennial, and an international judge and advisor to the 1995 Gwangju Biennale.

The print portfolio "The Readymade Boomerang" was published for the 8th Sydney Biennale of the same name in 1990. The proceeds from the sale helped finance some satellite exhibitions and the Biennale's performance program.

Starting with Marcel Duchamp, Man Ray and Francis Picabia, the exhibition entitled *The Readymade Boomerang—Certain Relations in 20th Century Art* traced the history of the readymade and the development of the object in the Sixties and Seventies and compared them with works by present-day artists. "The currents generated in this first dynamic moment are still, without doubt, flowing strongly. It is the aim of this exhibition to display something of their present vitality and so reveal the unabating centrality and recurring relevance of what arose in the visual arts of the 20th century," writes René Block in the foreword to the exhibition catalogue. In so doing, it aimed not just at the single artworks and the way in which they related to each other but rather at a question of attitude: of disrespectful humor, an inclination for working with contingency, pitiless iconoclasm and an aesthetic rather than political view of the world.

The portfolio contains prints by 21 artists. In addition to those artists who already had experience of the graphic medium, on this occasion in Rosalie Gascoigne, Ilya Kabakov and Rosemarie Trockel there were artists taking part who were using graphic techniques for the first time. In the Sydney portfolio next to classic offset prints, screen prints, stone lithography and woodcut we also find book printing on rice paper, photogravure, screen printing on galvanized steel or a rare combination of aquatint and lithograph. As in the exhibition, the portfolio brings together a multiplicity of materials and images reflecting the discourse surrounding the "original" and the encoding of meaning in the fine arts. Language plays an important part here and so is inserted in a whole range of prints as a formative element. Out of the vertical letters of *The Readymade Boomerang* John Cage developed a text on the theme of harmony to be read as it were as a score and generates a poetical pictorial effect, while Ben Vautier in his throwaway line *Am I or is Australia far away?* in a humorous way raises the issue of center and periphery. Emmett Williams, Julian Schnabel and Lawrence Weiner also work with script. Weiner who inserts words as in a sculptural process, by inserting the words 'Southern Cross', finds in *Polaris* a succinct image for life in contrasting places on the globe.

Rosalie Gascoigne stresses the significance of language as a system of legible signs and breaks up their connections by the assemblage of dismantled traffic signs. The prints by Tony Cragg and Rosemarie Trockel also follow the principle of assemblage.

Richard Hamilton is one of most innovative artists in printed graphics represented in the portfolio. *The Orangeman* (Hamilton's first print, developed using the computer paint box) deals not only with the phenomenon of focus, but also takes up a controversial political theme.

With John Cage, Ben Vautier, Emmett Williams, Allan Kaprow and Nam June Paik, the portfolio includes artists close to the international Fluxus movement, representing a temporal bridge from Duchamp to the youngest generation of artists such as Barbara Bloom, Janet Burchill and Rosemarie Trockel.

레디메이드 부메랑 포트폴리오

르네 블록[1]
전시기획자, 갤러리스트

1990

『레디메이드 부메랑 포트폴리오』(이하 '모음집')는 데니스 애덤스(Dennis Adams), 바바라 블룸(Barbara Bloom), K. P. 브레머(K. P. Brehmer), 자넷 버칠(Janet Burchill), 존 케이지(John Cage), 토니 크랙(Tony Cragg), 로잘리 개스코인(Rosalie Gascoigne), 리처드 해밀턴(Richard Hamilton), 일리야 카바코프(Ilya Kabakov), 앨런 캐프로(Allan Kaprow), 비요른 뇌르가르(Bjorn Norgaard), 백남준(Nam June Paik), 사르키스(Sarkis), 줄리언 슈나벨(Julian Schnabel), 로즈마리 트로켈(Rosemarie Trockel), 피터 틴델(Peter Tyndall), 켄 앤스워스(Ken Unsworth), 벤 보티에(Ben Vautier), 보이드 웹(Boyd Webb), 로렌스 웨이너(Lawrence Weiner) 그리고 에머트 윌리엄스(Emmett Williams)의 판화가 수록된 작품집으로 1990년 같은 제목으로 열린 제8회 시드니비엔날레 전시를 위해 제작됐다. 판매 수익금은 몇몇 연계 전시와 비엔날레의 퍼포먼스 프로그램의 재정에 지원됐다.

1. 르네 블록은 그가 첫 번째 기획한 전시 《자본주의적 사실주의자(Kapitalistischer Realismus)》(1964년)에서 시장의 민주화와 이미지의 다중화, 예술과 정치의 무관계 등에 대한 풍자와 유머를 담담하게 담았다. 이때 게르하르트 리히터, 지그마르 폴케, 볼프 포스텔, K. P. 브레머 등이 참여하였다. 그는 플럭서스, 네오다다와 같이 뜨거운 이슈가 되었던 20세기 후반 동시대미술의 현장에 함께했던 인물이다. 1990년 시드니비엔날레를 비롯하여, 1993년 국내의 플럭서스 페스티벌, 아트 퀼른의 기획, 이스탄불비엔날레 총감독, 1995년 광주비엔날레 국외 심사위원이자 자문위원으로 참여했다.

《레디메이드 부메랑―20세기 미술 내 어떤 관계(The Readymade Boomerang―Certain Relations in 20th Century Art)》라는 제목의 전시는 1960, 70년대에 마르셀 뒤샹(Marcel Duchamp), 만 레이(Man Ray) 그리고 프란시스 피카비아(Francis Picabia)로부터 시작된 레디메이드의 역사와 오브제의 발달에 관한 근원을 추적하고 이전 작가와 동시대 작가의 작품을 비교하고자 했다. 전시 서문에서 "(레디메이드) 첫 세대가 일으킨 영향력은 여전히 강력하다. 이 전시의 목적은 현재에도 수그러들지 않는 첫 세대가 지녔던 활력, 중심적 역할, 그리고 20세기 시각예술과의 관련성을 다시금 제기하고자 하는 것이다."라고 밝혔다. 그렇게 이 전시는 하나하나의 작품들이나 각각의 작품이 어떤 관계를 맺고 있는지에 주목하기 보다는, 이를테면 무례한 유머, 우발적인 성향, 무자비한 우상파괴주의 그리고 세상을 바라보는 정치적인 시각을 배제하고, 미학적 관점을 견지하는 것 등 태도의 문제를 상기시킨다.

이 모음집에는 작가 21명의 판화가 담겨있다. 이미 판화라는 매체를 접한 경험이 있는 예술가 외에도 로잘리 개스코인, 일리야 카바코프, 로즈마리 트로켈 등 판화 기법을 처음 사용하는 예술가도 참여했다. 전통적인 평판화 외에도 실크 스크린, 석판화 그리고 목판화, 심지어 얇은 쌀로 만든 중국 종이에 인쇄된 작품, 포토그라비어, 아연 도금강판 동판화와 석판화의 조합이라는 드문 예도 볼 수 있었다. 전시 주제와 마찬가지로, 이 작품 모음집은 '원본'을 둘러싼 담론을 반영하여 재료와 이미지가 지닌 다양성을 제시하였다. 여기에 속한 모든 판화에서 '언어'는 조형요소로서 중요한 역할을 갖는다. 존 케이지는 'THE READYMAID BOOMERANG'의 철자를 세로로 배열하고 각 철자를 포함한 단어를 사용해 마치 점수 기록처럼 보이면서 '조화(harmony)'라는 주제로 시적인 회화의 효과를 일으키는 텍스트로 발전시켰다. 한편, 벤 보티에는 그의 'Am I or is Australia far away?'(내가 저 멀리에 있는가? 오스트레일리아가 저 멀리 있는가?)라고 적힌 작품으로 중심부와 주변부라는 주제를 유머러스하게 표현했다.

에머트 윌리엄스, 줄리언 슈나벨, 로렌스 웨이너도 작품에 문장을 사용했다. 웨이너는 '서던크로스(Southern Cross)와 '폴라리스'(Polaris)라는 단어를 대조적으로 배치함으로써 지구에서의 상반된 삶을 극명하게 보여주고자 했다. 로잘리 개스코인은 읽기 쉬운 기호로서 언어의 의미를 강조했지만 해체된 교통신호의 아상블라주 원리로 그 연결 고리를 끊었다. 토니 크랙과 로즈마리 트로켈 역시 아상블라주 원리를 따랐다.

판화에 있어서 가장 혁신적인 아티스트 중 한 명인 리처드 해밀턴도 이 모음집에 참가했다. 컴퓨터 프로그램 페인트박스(paintbox)를 사용해서 제작한 그의 첫 번째 판화 작품 〈오렌지 당원〉(1990)은 화면의 인물에 주목하게 하는 것뿐만이 아니라 정치적 주제에 관한 논쟁을 불러일으키기도 했다. 모음집에는 국제적인 플럭서스 운동에 깊이 관여했던 존 케이지, 벤 보티에, 에머트 윌리엄스, 앨런 캐프로, 백남준과 더불어 바바라 블룸, 자넷 버칠 그리고 로즈마리 트로켈과 같은 젊은 세대 작가와 뒤샹을 이어주는 한시적인 연결점을 제시한다.

클라우스 페터 브레머(독일, 1938-1997)
손끝 사이의 느낌
1967, 종이에 판화, 식물의 씨앗, 실크스크린, 오브제 설치, 67.4×49.5cm
1991년 르네 블록 기증

Klaus Peter BREHMER (Germany, 1938-1997)
Feeling Between Fingertips
1967, Screen print on paper, mixed media, 67.4×49.5 cm
Donated by René Block in 1991

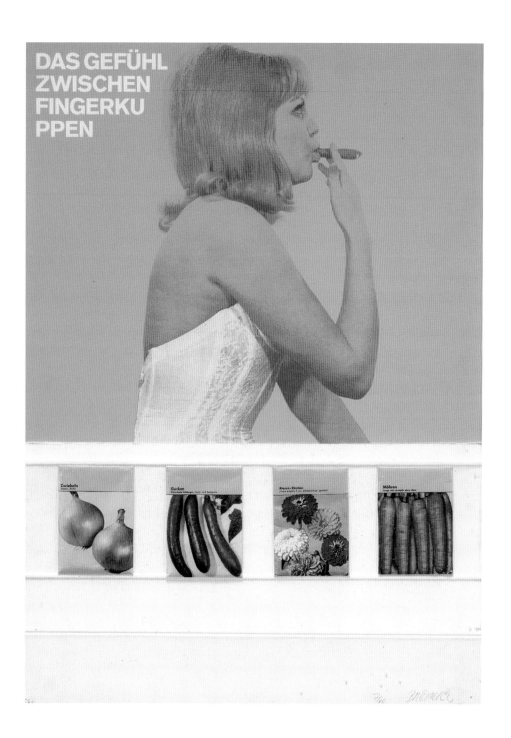

K. P. Brehmer

Since 1965, the artist K. P. Brehmer, born in Berlin in 1938, was preoccupied with the possibilities of giving the printed graphic sheet a three-dimensional form. A number of boxes and displays were created, which usually generated a world of their own by adding real things. These object graphics were created as unique pieces or in a few copies. An exception is the *Aufsteller 25, Das Gefühl zwischen Fingerkuppen …* (Display 25, The feeling between fingertips …), which was created with screen printing technique for the print portfolio *Grafik des Kapitalistischen Realismus* (Graphics of capitalist realism).

At first glance, it is an erectable advertising board with products pinned to it. The upper part is dominated by a pin-up girl smoking a cigar, while below, on a horizontally protruding surface, four real seed bags for vegetables are lined up.

The title of the work clearly indicates that the focus here is not on the enjoyment of tobacco, but on the tactile sensation that can be triggered by a roundish, long object. In addition to the cigar, the carrots and cucumbers depicted on the sachets also exhibit this shape.

The image of the woman as a sexual object of desire as well as the advertisement itself—for which advertisement for ordinary vegetables for one's own garden ever works with erotic symbols—are taken ad absurdum. In this graphic, K. P. Brehmer exposes the manipulative character of real advertising through an absurd alienation and ironic exaggeration.

K. P. 브레머, 〈손 끝 사이의 느낌〉, 1967

1938년 베를린에서 태어난 K. P. 브레머는 1965년 이래로 판화에 3차원적 조형성을 구현할 수 있는 가능성에 몰두했다. 다수의 상자와 설치 작업을 만들었는데, 여기에 실재하는 사물을 접목시켜 그만의 새로운 세계를 구축했다. 보통은 판화와 오브제가 결합된 형태를 개별 작품으로서 몇 개의 복제본만 만들었다. 그러나 이 작품은 〈자본주의 리얼리즘 판화(Grafik des Kapitalisti-schen Realimus)〉 포트폴리오의 일부분으로 실크 스크린으로 제작되었다.

얼핏 보면 작품은 제품이 꽂혀 있는 입간판처럼 보인다. 간판의 상단을 시가를 피우고 있는 핀업걸이 지배하고 있다면, 하단은 채소 씨앗 봉투가 앞으로 튀어나온 채 수평적으로 나열되어 있다.

작품의 제목은 여기서 작가가 주목하는 것이 시가의 즐거움이 아닌 동그랗고 기다란 오브제가 자극하는 촉각이란 것을 명확히 보여준다. 또한 봉투 위에 인쇄된 당근과 오이도 같은 모양을 보여준다. 여기서 씨앗 봉투의 평범한 채소 이미지가 성적인 상징처럼 읽히는 것과 광고에 등장하는 여성 이미지가 성적 욕망의 대상으로 읽히는 것은 모두 부조리한 현상이다. K. P. 브레머는 부조리한 인간 소외와 반어법적인 과장을 통해 실제 광고가 가진 교묘한 조작적 성격을 폭로한다.

게르하르트 리히터(독일, 1932-)
지그마르 폴케(독일, 1941-2010)
전환
1968, 종이에 흑백 인쇄, 46.5×67.5cm
1991년 르네 블록 기증

Gerhard RICHTER (Germany, 1932-)
Sigmar POLKE (Germany, 1941-2010)
Conversion
1968, Print on paper, 46.5×67.5 cm
Donated by René Block in 1991

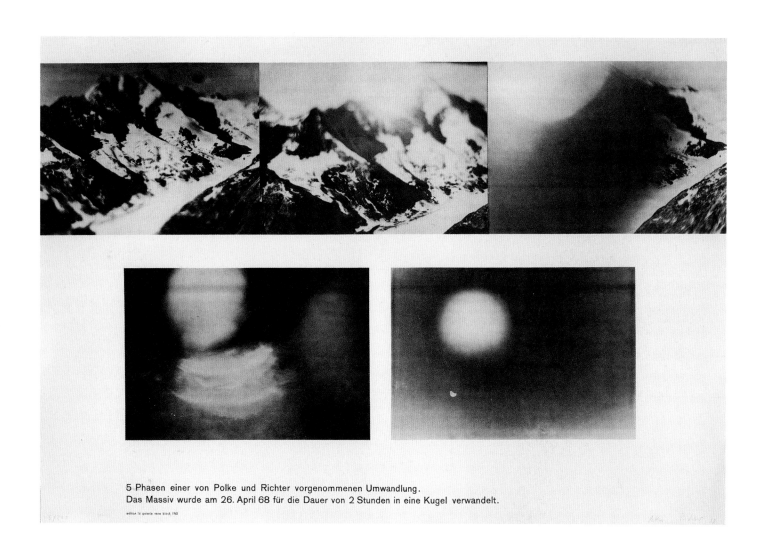

5 Phasen einer von Polke und Richter vorgenommenen Umwandlung.
Das Massiv wurde am 26. April 68 für die Dauer von 2 Stunden in eine Kugel verwandelt.

Sigmar Polke / Gerhard Richter

In addition to K. P. Brehmer, Konrad Lueg, KH Hödicke, Wolf Vostell, Gerhard Richter and Sigmar Polke had also contributed to the portfolio *Grafik des Kapitalistischen Realismus* (Graphics of capitalist realism) from 1967. The screen print *Hotel Diana* shows Richter and his artist friend Polke in a hotel room. Both of them are lying there lazily and foolishly on the bed. They flirt with not having to be serious. This kind of ironic deconstruction of the myth of the artist also manifests itself a few months later in their first and only joint work *Umwandlung* (Transformation).

This offset print shows five photographs manipulated by the artists of a mountain range that turned into a sphere for two hours. This event, namely a suspension of the laws of nature brought about by the artists, is pseudo-scientifically documented by the text placed below the photographs.

It was important to me to donate these extraordinary works by K. P. Brehmer, Sigmar Polke and Gerhard Richter to MMCA as a reminder of the 1991 exhibition *Umwandlungen / Transformations.*

2021
René Block (Curator, Gallerist)

지그마르 폴케 / 게르하르 리히터, 〈전환〉, 1968

K. P. 브레머와 더불어 콘라드 루그(Konrad Lueg), K. H. 회디케(K. H. Hödicke), 볼프 보스텔(Wolf Vostell), 게르하르 리히터(Gerhard Richter) 그리고 지그마르 폴케(Sigmar Polke) 역시 1967년부터 〈자본주의 리얼리즘 판화(Grafik des Kapitalistischen Realimus)〉 포트폴리오 제작에 참여하였다. 〈호텔 다이애나(Hotel Diana)〉는 친구 사이인 리히터와 폴케가 호텔 방에 누워있는 것을 보여주는 스크린 프린트 작품이다. 두 사람은 멍한 자세로 나른하게 침대에 누워있다. 그들에게서 진지함이란 찾아볼 수 없다. 두 사람은 그저 재미삼아 시시덕거리고 있었던 것이다. '작가 신화'의 해체에 대한 그들의 역설적인 시각이 몇 달 후 둘의 유일한 공동 작업인 이 작품, 〈전환〉에서도 드러난다.

이 평판 석판화는 두 사람이 두 시간 동안 촬영한 것으로, 산맥이 구형(球形)으로 변한 것처럼 찍힌 다섯 장의 사진을 보여준다. 두 작가의 조작에 의해 마치 자연의 법칙이 정지된 것 같은 순간으로 연출되었다. 사진 밑에 달린 설명은 이 사진을 가짜 과학 다큐멘터리 사진처럼 보이게 한다. 《테크놀로지의 예술적 전환》(1991. 3. 1-4. 14) 전시를 기념하며 K. P. 브레머의 작품과 함께, 지그마르 폴케 그리고 게르하르 리히터의 이 독특한 공동작품을 국립현대미술관에 기증하는 것은 나에게도 의미있는 일이었다.

2021년
르네 블록(전시기획자, 갤러리스트)

일리아 카바코프(러시아, 1933-)
사과
1990, 종이에 석판, 실크스크린, 39.5×59.5cm
1991년 구입

Ilya KABAKOV (Russia, 1933-)
Apple
1990, Lithograph and screen print on paper, 39.5×59.5 cm
Purchased in 1991

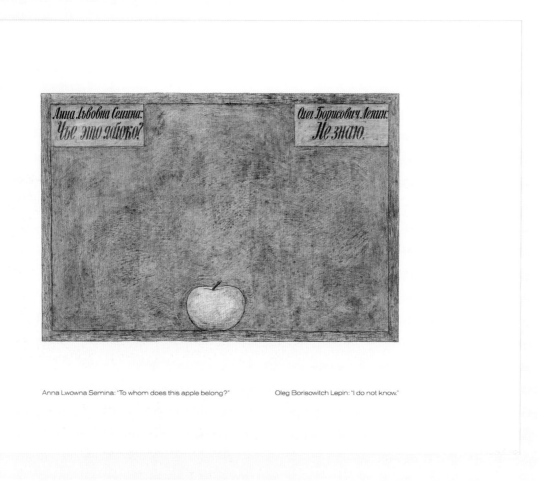

Anna Lwowna Semina: "To whom does this apple belong?"　　　　Oleg Borisowitch Lepin: "I do not know."

토니 크랙(영국, 1949-)
무제
1990, 종이에 석판, 66×57 cm
1991년 구입

Tony CRAGG (United Kingdom, 1949-)
Untitled
1990, Lithograph on paper, 66×57 cm
Purchased in 1991

바버라 블룸(미국, 1951-)
재는 재로 다이아몬드는 다이아몬드로 먼지는 먼지로
1990, 종이에 석판, 98×68cm
1991년 구입

Barbara BLOOM (USA, 1951-)
Ashes to Ashes Diamonds to Diamonds Dust to Dust
1990, Lithograph on paper, 98×68 cm
Purchased in 1991

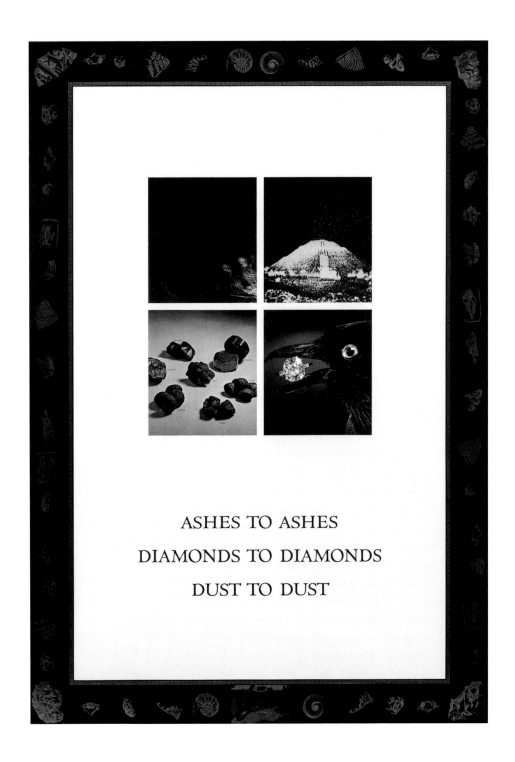

백남준 (미국, 1932–2006)
무제
1990, 종이에 석판, 98×68 cm
1991년 구입

Nam June PAIK (USA, 1932–2006)
Untitled
1990, Lithograph on paper, 98×68 cm
Purchased in 1991

로렌스 웨이너(미국, 1942-2021)
북극성
1990, 종이에 석판, 92×62.5cm
1991년 구입

Lawrence WEINER (USA, 1942-2021)
Polaris
1990, Lithograph on paper, 92×62.5 cm
Purchased in 1991

클라우스 페터 브레머(독일, 1938-1997)
몬드리안에 앞서
1990, 한지에 목판, 38.7×30cm
1991년 구입

Klaus Peter BREHMER (Germany, 1938-1997)
Prior to Mondrian
1990, Woodcut on paper, 38.7×30 cm
Purchased in 1991

보이드 웹(영국, 1947-)
껍질
1990, 종이에 석판, 63.5×88.5cm
1991년 구입

Boyd WEBB (United Kingdom, 1947-)
Cortex
1990, Lithograph on paper, 63.5×88.5 cm
Purchased in 1991

로제마리 트로켈(독일, 1952-)
카잔루크의 장미
1990, 종이에 그라비야 인쇄, 47.5×39cm
1991년 구입

Rosemarie TROCKEL (Germany, 1952-)
Rose of Kasanlak (Rose Von Kasanlak)
1990, Gravure print on paper, 47.5×39 cm
Purchased in 1991

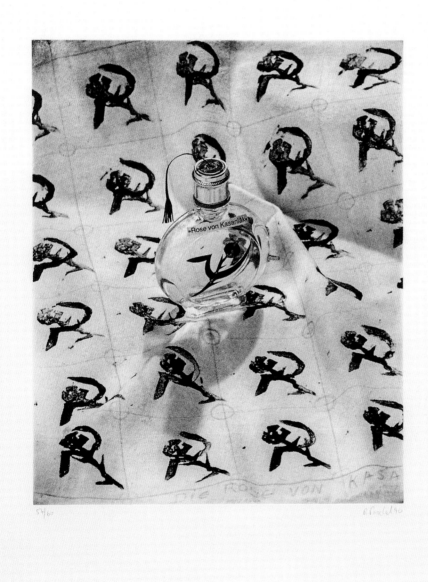

존 케이지(미국, 1912-1992)
메소스틱
1989, 종이에 실크스크린, 70×100cm
1991년 구입

John CAGE (USA, 1912-1992)
Methostic
1989, Screen print on paper, 70×100 cm
Purchased in 1991

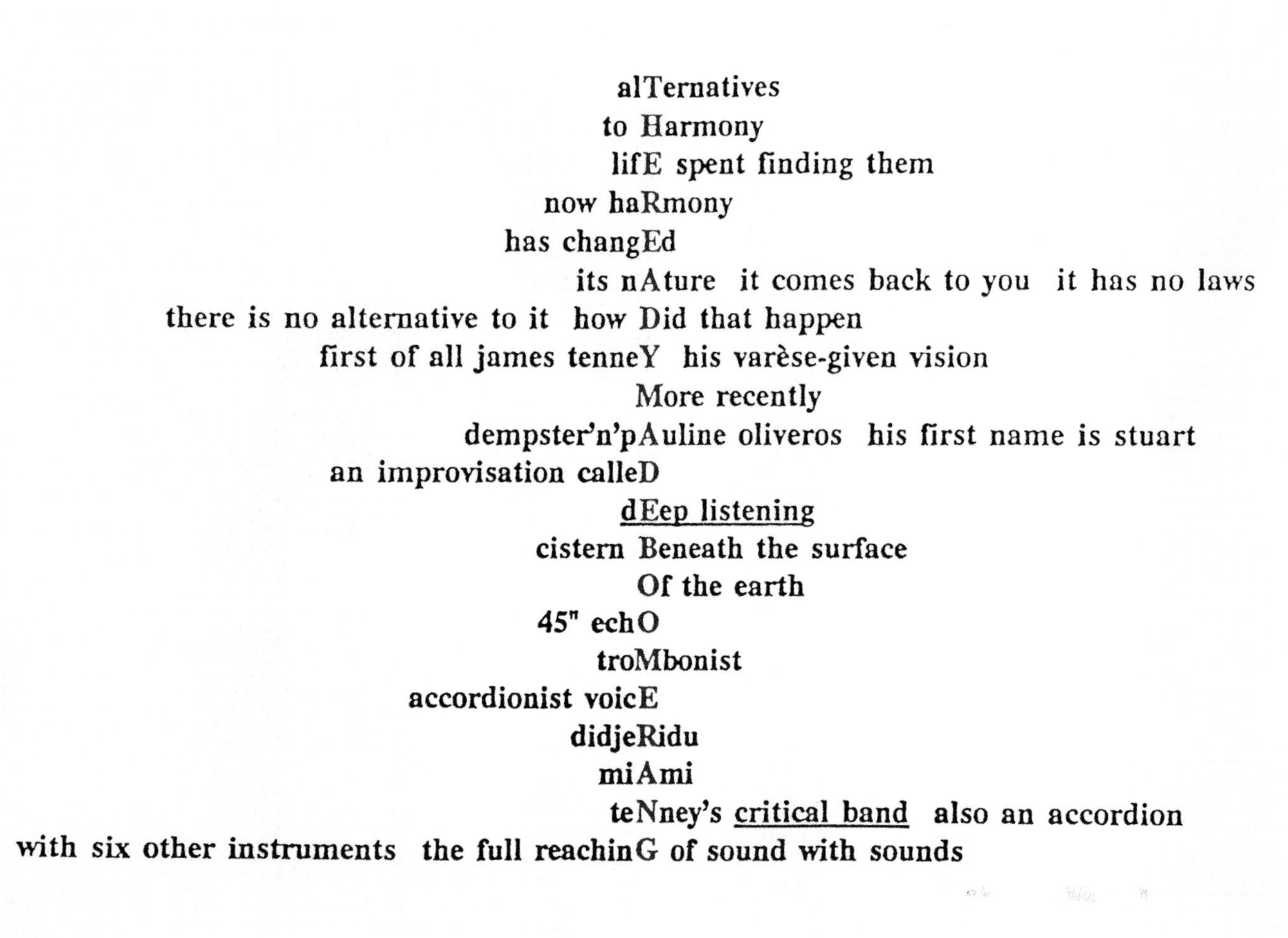

                        alTernatives
                        to Harmony
                        lifE spent finding them
                  now haRmony
               has changEd
                        its nAture it comes back to you it has no laws
      there is no alternative to it how Did that happen
            first of all james tenneY his varèse-given vision
                     More recently
                  dempster'n'pAuline oliveros his first name is stuart
         an improvisation calleD
                        dEep listening
                  cistern Beneath the surface
                     Of the earth
            45" echO
                  troMbonist
         accordionist voicE
                     didjeRidu
                  miAmi
                     teNney's critical band also an accordion
   with six other instruments the full reachinG of sound with sounds

앨런 캐프로(미국, 1927-2006)
마당
1990, 종이에 석판, 73×56cm
1991년 구입

Allan KAPROW (USA, 1927-2006)
Yard
1990, Lithograph on paper, 73×56 cm
Purchased in 1991

벤 보티에(프랑스, 1935-)
내가 저 멀리에 있는가? 오스트레일리아가 저 멀리 있는가?
1990, 종이에 실크스크린, 70×100cm
1991년 구입

Ben VAUTIER (France, 1935-)
Am I or Is Australia Far Away?
1990, Screen print on paper, 70×100 cm
Purchased in 1991

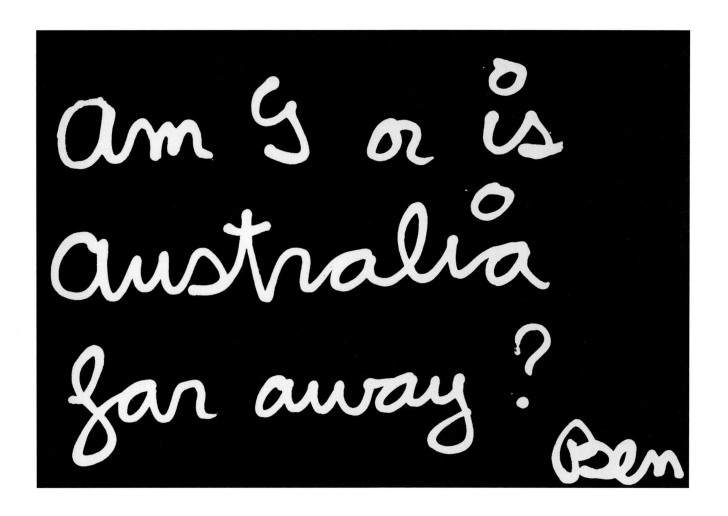

피터 틴댈(오스트레일리아, 1951-)
어떤 사람이 작품을 본다 / 누군가가 무언인가를 본다
1990, 종이에 실크스크린, 100×70cm
1991년 구입

Peter TYNDALL (Australia, 1951-)
A Person Looks at a Work of Art / Someone Looks at something
1990, Screen print on paper, 100×70 cm
Purchased in 1991

리처드 해밀턴(영국, 1922-2011)
오렌지당원
1990, 종이에 석판, 85×42.5cm
1991년 구입

Richard HAMILTON (United Kingdom, 1922-2011)
Member of Orange Party
1990, Lithograph on paper, 85×42.5 cm
Purchased in 1991

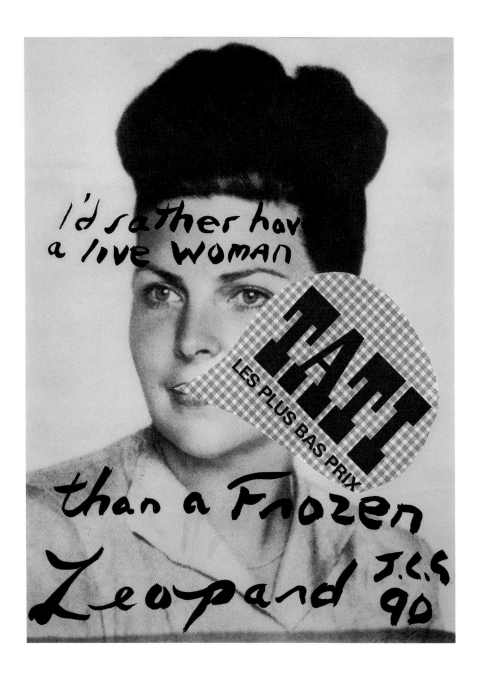

클로드 비알라(프랑스, 1936-)
무제
1982, 캔버스에 아크릴릭, 284×215cm
1986년 구입

Claude VIALLAT (France, 1936-)
Untitled
1982, Acrylic on canvas, 284×215 cm
Purchased in 1986

클로드 비알라(프랑스, 1936-)
무제
1982, 캔버스에 아크릴릭, 289×218cm
1986년 구입

Claude VIALLAT (France, 1936-)
Untitled
1982, Acrylic on canvas, 289×218 cm
Purchased in 1986

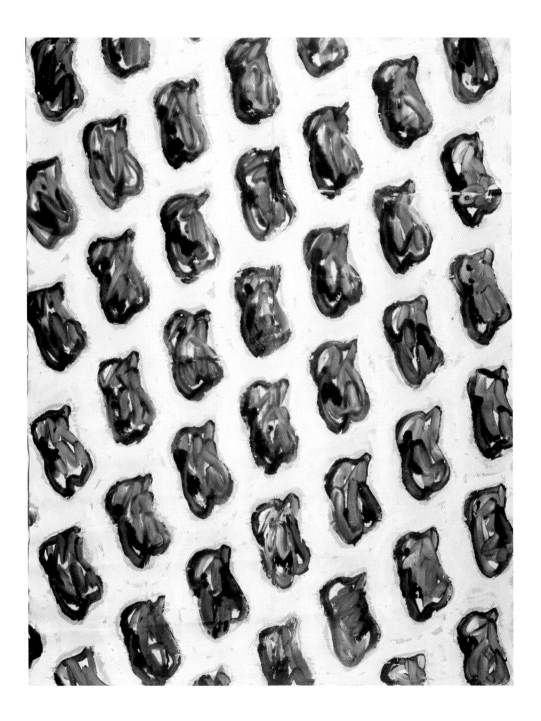

피에르 뷔라글리오(프랑스, 1939-)
집합
1988, 담배갑 포장지, 채색된 천 콜라주, 104×119cm
1989년 구입

Pierre BURAGLIO (France, 1939-)
Assemblage
1988, Mixed media, 104×119 cm
Purchased in 1989

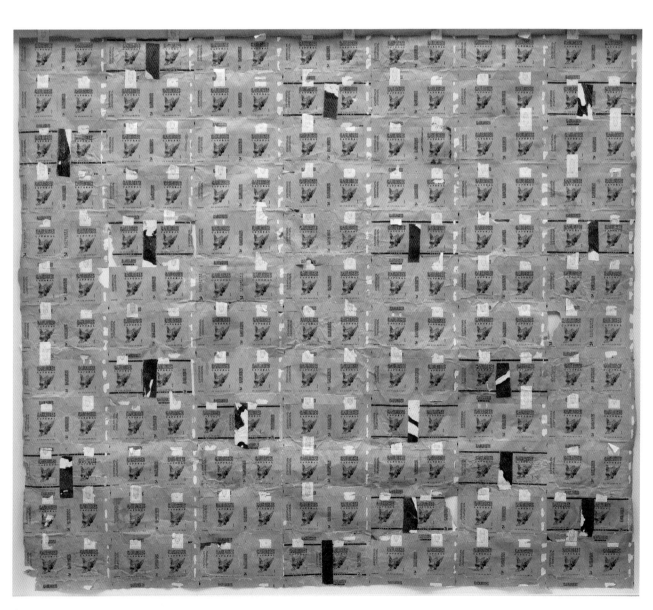

피에르 뷔라글리오(프랑스, 1939-)
창틀
1981, 나무틀, 유리, 수성도료(부분채색), 65×80cm
1989년 구입

Pierre BURAGLIO (France, 1939-)
Window Frame
1981, Mixed media, 65×80 cm
Purchased in 1989

피에르 뷔라글리오(프랑스, 1939-)
창틀
1988, 나무틀, 유리, 수성도료(부분채색), 147×50cm
1989년 구입

창틀
1988, 나무틀, 유리, 수성도료(부분채색), 193×50cm
1989년 구입

Pierre BURAGLIO (France, 1939-)
Window Frame
1988, Mixed media, 147×50 cm
Purchased in 1989

Window Frame
1988, Mixed media, 193×50 cm
Purchased in 1989

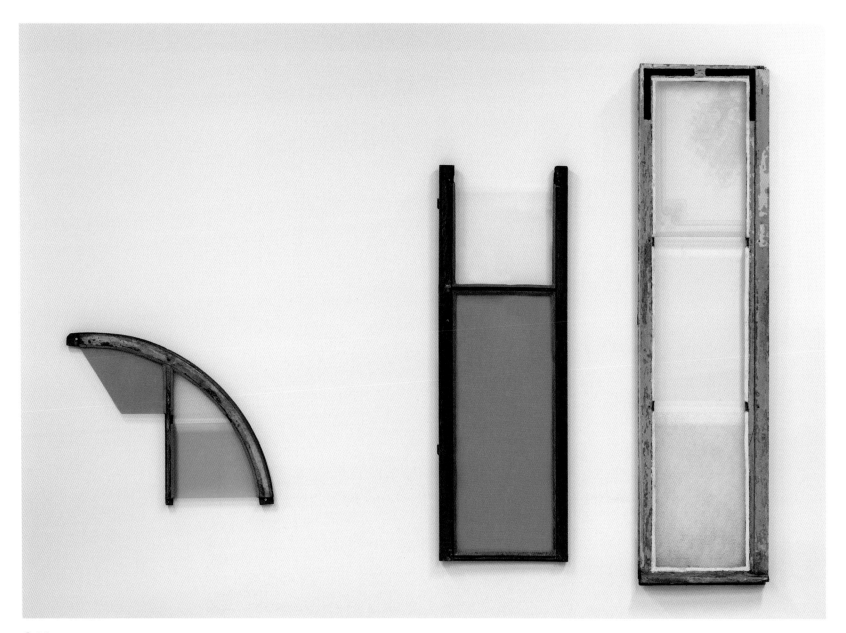

게오르그 바젤리츠(독일, 1938-)
동양여자
1987, 캔버스에 유채, 250×200cm
1989년 구입
© 게오르크 바젤리츠 2022

Georg BASELITZ (Germany, 1938-)
The Oriental Woman (Die Orientalin)
1987, Oil on canvas, 250×200 cm
Purchased in 1989
© Georg Baselitz 2022

213

마르쿠스 뤼페르츠(독일, 1941-)
철학자의 기억
1985, 캔버스에 유채, 162×130cm
1989년 구입

Markus LUPERTZ (Germany, 1941-)
Memory of Philosopher
1985, Oil on canvas, 162×130 cm
Purchased in 1989

A. R. 펭크(독일, 1939-2017)
체계화 IV
1982, 캔버스에 아크릴릭, 150×250cm
1989년 구입

A.R. PENCK (Germany, 1939-2017)
Systematization IV
1982, Acrylic on canvas, 150×250 cm
Purchased in 1989

마트코 트레보티치(크로아티아, 1935-)
노란색의 세로선
1988, 하드보드에 아크릴릭, 유채, 150.2×170.5cm
1990년 구입

Matko TREBOTIC (Croatia, 1935-)
Yellow Vertical Line
1988, Acrylic and oil on hardboard, 150.2×170.5 cm
Purchased in 1990

216

밈모 팔라디노(이탈리아, 1948-)
태양신
1986, 나무판에 마포천, 면천조각, 목탄, 지점토, 채색, 260×260cm
1995년 구입

Mimmo PALADINO (Italy, 1948-)
Baal
1986, Mixed media on panel, 260×260 cm
Purchased in 1995

엔초 쿠키(이탈리아, 1949-)
손
1993, 철판, 400×300cm
1993년 구입

Enzo CUCCHI (Italy, 1949-)
Hands
1993, Steel plate, 400×300 cm
Purchased in 1993

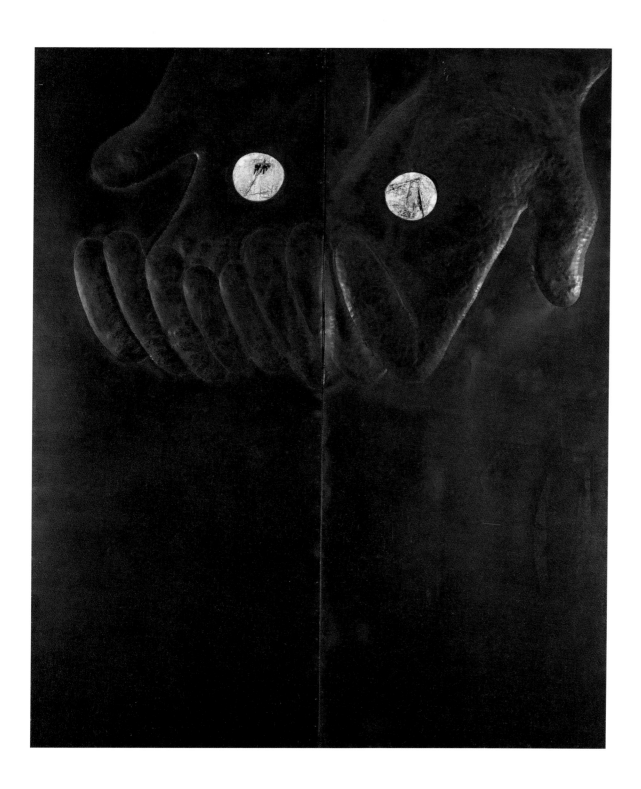

조나단 보로프스키(미국, 1942-)
망치질하는 사람
1991, 혼합재료, 354×167.5×12cm
1993년 구입

Jonathan BOROFSKY (USA, 1942-)
Hammering Man
1991, Mixed media, 354×167.5×12 cm
Purchased in 1993

토니 벌란트(미국, 1941–)
작가와 모델 #34
1991, 나무판에 철판 콜라주, 197×153cm
1993년 구입

Tony BERLANT (USA, 1941–)
Artist and Model #34
1991, Steel plate collage on wood panel, 197×153 cm
Purchased in 1993

래디 존 딜(미국, 1943-)
무제
1989, 나무판에 유성도료, 시멘트, 153×244×18 cm
1989년 구입

Laddie John DILL (USA, 1943-)
Untitled
1989, Paint and cement on panel, 153×244×18 cm
Purchased in 1989

마이클 마이클리디스(키프로스, 1923-2015)
조셉 앨버스에의 경의 No.10
1989, 나무틀에 면천(흰색, 검정색, 빨간색), 81×81×14 cm
1990년 구입

Michael MICHAELEDES (Cyprus, 1923-2015)
Homage to Josef Albers No.10
1989, Fabric on wood, 81×81×14 cm
Purchased in 1990

빅토르 바사렐리(프랑스, 1906-1997)
게자
1983, 캔버스에 아크릴릭, 121.7×120.5 cm
1990년 구입

Victor VASARELY (France, 1906-1997)
GEZA
1983, Acrylic on canvas, 121.7×120.5 cm
Purchased in 1990

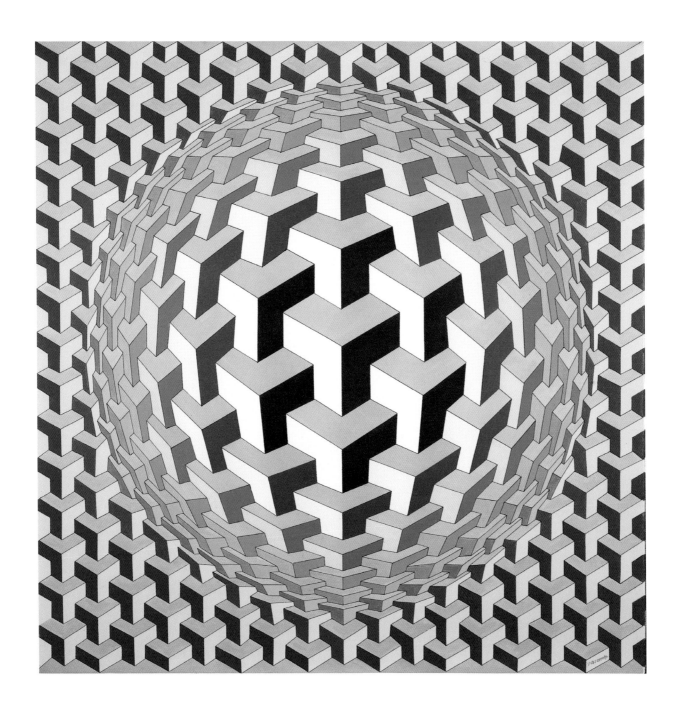

피터 핼리(미국, 1953-)
타임코드
2001, 캔버스에 아크릴릭, 데이글로아크릴, 롤라텍스, 161.5×127cm
2000년 (사)현대미술관회 기증

Peter HALLEY (USA, 1953-)
Timecode
2001, Arcrylic, Day-gol Arcrilyc, Roll-a-Tex on canvas, 161.5×127 cm
Donated by Membership Society for MMCA in 2000

국립현대미술관 국제미술소장품 현황
MMCA Global Art Collection Report 1980-2000

국립현대미술관에서는 아시아(19개국),
아메리카(12개국), 유럽(26개국),
오세아니아(1개국)으로 총 58개국, 448명의
해외 작가 작품을 소장하고 있다.

MMCA Global Art Collection has total
of 448 foreign artists in 58 countries, which
includes Asia (19 countries), America
(12 countries), Europe (26 countries), and
Oceania (1 country).

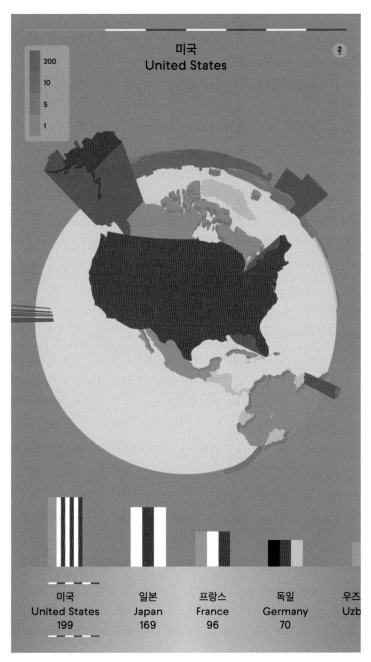

국가별 소장품 현황
Global Art Collection by country

1971년 700만원에서 시작된 소장품 수집 예산이, 1986년에는 과천관 신축과 야외조각공원 조성으로 10억에 이르렀다. 1990년대에는 10억 이하였던 수집 예산이 2002년에는 25억까지 늘었고, 2005년에는 45억에 이르렀다.

The Collection budget of MMCA, which started at 7 million won in 1971, reached 1 billion won due to the construction of MMCA, Gwacheon with outdoor sculpture garden in 1986.

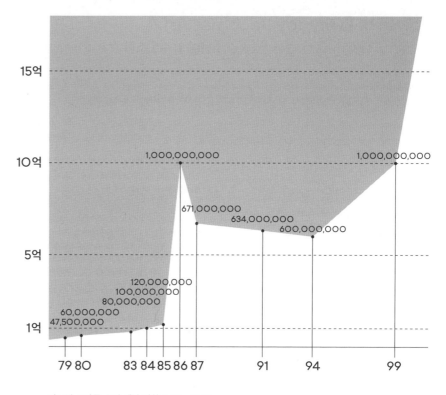

연도별 소장품 수집 예산 변화 1980-2000
The Collection Budget by year 1980-2000

연도별 해외미술품 수집량은 1988년 세계현대미술제와 같이 기증작품이 많았던 특정 계기를 제외하고는 점차 줄어드는 추세에 있다.

The amount of overseas art collections by year has decreased except for certain occasions when there were many donated works, such as Olympiad of Art in 1988.

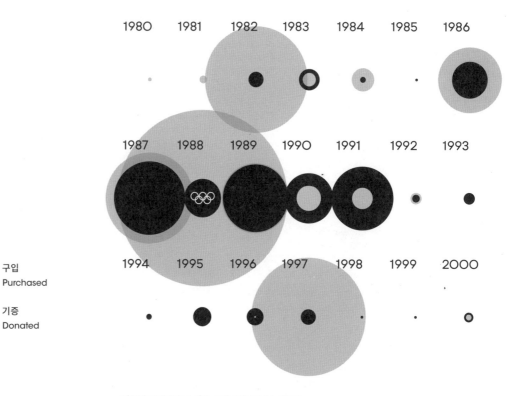

구입
Purchased

기증
Donated

연도별 국제미술 소장품 수집 변화 1980-2000
Global Art Collection by year 1980-2000

Power of Everyday Becomes Art:
From Avant-Garde Experiment to Art for Everybody

Jung Eun Young
Ph.D. in Art History, Professor at Korea National University of Education

1. In his vivid record of the art world and critical discourse in 1960s New York, art historian Irving Sandler noted that there was already a criticism against the gestural painting language of the Abstract Expressionists in the late 1950s. He described that the resisting force against the movement's transformation into a 'new academy' was rising. Irving Sandler, *American Art of the 1960s* (New York: Harper & Row, 1988), 2–3.

2. *Silence* and *A Year From Monday* contains Cage's major lectures and manuscripts from the 1940s to the 1960s. Across his remarks on experimental music, avant-garde art, Eastern philosophy, Zen Buddhism, media, and scientific theories, readers can catch a glimpse into the artist's broad philosophical thinking and transboundary practice. *Silence* (Hanover, NH: Wesleyan University Press, 1961); Cage, *A Year From Monday* (Hanover, NH: Wesleyan University Press, 1969). 'The aesthetic of indifference' is a term used by art historian Moira Roth to describe the new attitudes of New York-based artists in the 1950s and 1960s. Ross compared the fulcrum, which supports the 'axis' of indifferent aesthetics characterized by shrewd intelligence and acceptance close to passivity, to Duchamp and the lever placed on the fulcrum to Cage. Moira Roth, "The Aesthetic of Indifference," in *Difference/Indifference: Musings on Postmodernism, Marcel Duchamp and John Cage* (Amsterdam: G+B Arts International, 1998), 33–47.

3. *4:33* and *Stage #1* are both closely related to Robert Rauschenberg. Cage has revealed that his 'Song of Silence' was inspired by Rauschenberg's 'White Paintings.' In *Stage Works #1*, *White Painting* hung on an old-fashioned electronic recorder on which Ediff Piaf's album was playing. Cage, *Silence*, 98–104.

From the 1980s to the end of the 1990s, the National Museum of Modern and Contemporary Art, Korea, amassed a significant collection of artworks from overseas. Under the banner of internationalization and globalization, MMCA was committed to building a collection that reflects the course of Modern and contemporary art. And they hold significance because it is an index of historical evidence, not just a compilation of creative works by artists. This is why *Highlights of MMCA Global Art Collection from the 1980s–1990s: To the World through Art* comes across as an exhibition that contemporary art enthusiasts must have been waiting for. A close look at the works presented in this exhibition can tell the audience, implicitly and directly, how the landscape of contemporary art changed after World War II and what attempts and plans existed underneath this dynamic change. In order to understand the course and background of the artistic experimentations during this period, this essay will introduce the trends and theoretical discourses in contemporary art during the late 20th century. After World War II, New York rapidly emerged as the center of the art world. From there, experimentations of avant-garde art opened out to everyday life, intersecting with popular culture and the industrial system. By discussing this, this essay will examine what contemporary artists have done when the boundary between life and art blurs and raises a more substantial ontological question.

I. Avant-Garde Heads toward the World: John Cage and Neo-Dada

It was not a painter or sculptor but an avant-garde musician John Cage (1912–1992), who suggested a new direction for experimentation and expansion for young artists in New York in the late 1950s. More than a decade after the end of World War II, the second-generation New York School artists, including those so-called Neo-Dada, considered the 'heroic and noble' Abstract Expressionist painting as the idiom of the older generation, a 'new academy' to get over.[1] While the ideological Cold War was still in progress, the United States entered a post-capitalist system that emphasized material abundance and consumption. The late 1950s suffered from the aftermath of maniac McCarthyism; it was a preface to the volatile 1960s filled with human rights issues and anti-war movements. At this period, Cage's aesthetics of everyday life became a driving force that introduced avant-garde experiments to the world. His aesthetic was influenced by a wide range of discipline and ideas, from Marcel Duchamp (1887–1968)'s aesthetics of indifference in Readymade to Zen Buddhism's Dono on the wisdom of everyday life, McLuhanian stance on media, and the innovative works of Buckminster Fuller.[2]

Cage's 'prepared piano' and aleatory music, which he devised in 1938, are strong examples of his avant-garde experiments. Nevertheless, *4:33* (1952) premiered in Woodstock, New York in 1952, and *Theater Piece #1* performed at Black Mountain College in Asheville, North Carolina in the same year had a more significant influence on the avant-garde movement of the time. *4:33*, often called a 'silent piece,' consists of three movements without actual piano performance but the accidental sound of the surrounding during its running time. But this piece is by no means silent. There is a conventional prejudice that a concert hall should accept only music as a meaningful sound and consider all non-artistic sounds as noises. It is the hierarchy of sound that separates art and daily life. When such convention is challenged, like in Cage's *4:33*, all sounds, including noise, can be meaningful. Another work *Stage Works #1* consists of lectures and dances, poetry readings, and piano performances. Often called an 'event,' this non-hierarchical, accidental piece is suggestive of the everyday moment in which various actions and events coincide without a specific composition or narrative.[3]

일상의 힘, 미술이 되다:
전위적 실험에서 모든 이의 예술로

정은영
미술사학 박사, 한국교원대학교 교수

1. 1960년대 뉴욕의 생생한 미술계 상황과 비평 담론을 기록한 미술사학자 어빙 샌들러(Irving Sandler)는 이미 1950년대 말에 추상표현주의적인 제스처 회화가 하나의 '새로운 아카데미(a new academy)'로 변모했음을 비판하는 움직임이 점진적으로 증가하고 있었다고 기술한 바 있다. Irving Sandler, *American Art of the 1960s* (New York: Harper & Row, 1988), 2-3.

2. 1940년대부터 1960년대에 이르는 케이지의 주요 강연과 원고를 수록한 『침묵』과 『월요일로부터 1년 후』를 통해 실험 음악과 전위 미술, 동양 사상과 선불교, 매체와 과학 이론을 가로지르는 케이지의 폭넓은 철학적 사고와 탈경계적 실천을 엿볼 수 있다. John Cage, *Silence* (Hanover, NH: Wesleyan University Press, 1961); Cage, *A Year From Monday* (Hanover, NH: Wesleyan University Press, 1969). '무관심의 미학(the aesthetic of indifference)'은 미술사학자 모이라 로스(Moira Roth)가 1950년대와 1960년대 뉴욕 미술가들의 새로운 미적 태도를 지칭하기 위해 사용한 용어다. 로스는 차가운 지성과 수동성에 가까운 수용을 특징으로 하는 무관심적 미학이라는 축의 받침에 해당하는 지렛목(fulcrum)을 뒤샹으로, 그 지렛목 위에 놓인 지렛대(lever)를 케이지로 비유한 바 있다. Moira Roth, "The Aesthetic of Indifference," in *Difference/Indifference: Musings on Postmodernism, Marcel Duchamp and John Cage* (Amsterdam: G+B Arts International, 1998), 33-47.

3. 〈4분 33초〉와 〈무대 작품 #1〉은 모두 로버트 라우센버그와 긴밀하게 연결된 작품이다. 케이지는 자신의 '침묵의 곡'이 라우센버그의 〈백색 회화〉에 영감을 받은 것임을 밝힌 바 있다. 실제로 〈무대 작품 #1〉에서 에디프 피아프의 음반이 플레이되는 구식 전축 위에 걸려 있던 작품이 바로 〈백색 회화〉였다. John Cage, *Silence*, 98-104.

1980년대부터 1990년대 말까지 국제화와 세계화의 기치 아래 국립현대미술관이 소장하게 된 해외 미술작품들은 현대미술의 흐름을 반영한 컬렉션을 구축하려는 기관의 의지를 보여준다. 이 기간의 소장품들은 예술가 개인의 창조적 산물이라는 개별 작품의 수준을 넘어 현대미술의 동향을 보여주는 물리적 증거라는 역사적 지표로서 그 중요성을 지닌다. 현대미술에 관심과 애정을 지닌 관람자에게 《미술로, 세계로》 전시가 더없이 반갑게 다가오는 이유다. 이번 전시에 소개된 소장품들을 면밀히 살펴보면 제2차 세계대전 이후 현대미술의 지형이 어떻게 변화해갔는지, 그 역동적인 변화의 기저에 어떤 시도와 기획이 존재했었는지를 직간접적으로 확인할 수 있다. 이에 본고는 전시된 작품을 통해 현대미술의 주요 흐름을 파악하고 다양한 예술적 실험의 역사적 지평을 이해할 수 있도록 20세기 후반 현대미술의 추이와 이론적 쟁점을 소개하고자 한다. 특히 제2차 세계대전 이후 세계미술의 중심으로 급부상한 미국의 뉴욕을 중심으로 전후 전위예술의 실험이 일상적 삶으로 확장되면서 대중문화나 산업체계와 교차되는 과정을 논의하고, 삶과 예술의 경계가 흐려진 후 더욱 강하게 제기되는 존재론적 물음을 현대미술이 어떤 방식으로 접근하는지를 살펴보고자 한다.

I. 전위 예술, 세상 밖으로 향하다: 존 케이지와 네오다다

1950년대 후반 뉴욕의 젊은 미술가들에게 새로운 실험과 확장의 방향을 제시했던 인물은 화가나 조각가가 아닌 전위음악가 존 케이지(John Cage, 1912-1992)였다. 제2차 세계대전이 끝난 후 10여년이 지난 뉴욕에서 소위 네오다다(Neo-Dada)라 불리던 이들을 포함한 뉴욕 화파(New York School)의 2세대 예술가들에게 '영웅적이고 숭고한' 추상표현주의 회화는 도전해야 할 기성세대의 어법이나 극복해야 할 '새로운 아카데미'로 여겨졌다.[1] 당시 미국은 이데올로기적인 냉전이 지속되는 상황에서 물질적인 풍요와 소비를 내세운 후기자본주의 체제로 진입하고 있었다. 특히 광적인 매카시즘의 후폭풍이 계속되던 1950년대 말엽은 인권 문제와 반전 운동이 폭발한 1960년대를 예고하는 서막과도 같은 시기였다. 마르셀 뒤샹(Marcel Duchamp, 1887-1968)의 레디메이드에 함축된 '무관심의 미학'과 선(禪)불교의 돈오(頓悟)에 담긴 평범함 속의 깨달음, 마셜 맥클루언(Marshal McLuhan)의 미디어 사상과 버크민스터 풀러(Buckminster Fuller)의 혁신적인 상상력에 이르기까지, 광범위한 영역을 가로지르며 다양한 사상을 흡수한 케이지의 '일상의 미학'은 이 시기의 전위적 실험을 세상 밖으로 이끌어내는 추동력이 되었다.[2]

케이지의 전위적 실험은 일찍이 1938년에 고안한 '조작된 피아노(prepared piano)'나 우연성의 음악(aleatory music)을 통해 이미 강하게 드러났지만, 당대의 전위미술에 직접적인 영향을 미친 작업으로는 무엇보다 1952년에 뉴욕 주 우드스탁에서 초연된 〈4분 33초〉와 같은 해 노스캐롤라이나 주 애쉬빌의 블랙마운틴칼리지(Black Mountain College)에서 이루어진 〈무대 작품 #1(Theater Piece #1)〉을 들 수 있다. 주지하듯이, 〈4분 33초〉는 비록 3악장으로 구성되어 있긴 하지만 실제 피아노 연주 없이 오직 주어진 환경의 우연한 소리와 일정한 지속으로만 이루어져 있어 종종 '침묵의 곡(silent piece)'이라 불리기도 한다. 하지만 이 곡은 결코 아무 소리가 없는 '고요한' 곡이 아니다. 연주회장에서 기존의 음악만을 유의미한 소리로 받아들이고 그 이외의 비예술적인 소리는 사라져야 할 소음으로 간주하는 기존의 선입견, 즉 예술과 일상을 위계적으로 분리하는 전통적인 편견을 없애고 나면, 소음을 포함한 일상의 모든 사운드가 의미 있는 소리로 다가올 수 있기 때문이다. 흔히 '이벤트'라 불리기도 하는 〈무대 작품 #1〉 역시 강의와 무용, 시 낭독과 피아노 연주, 음반 플레이와 텅 빈 캔버스까지 일정한 구성이나 내러티브 없이 여러 행위와 사건들이 동시에 진행되는 비위계적이고 우연적인 일상의 상황을 제시한 것이었다.[3]

4. The non-lexical term "methostic" in the title is a neologism that combines 'methodic' and 'methystic.' In this poem, Cage mentions experimental performances such as James Tenney's *Critical Band* (1988) and Pauline Oliveros and Stuart Dempster's *Deep Listening* (1989). In particular, Deep Listening (1989) has an intoxicating and immersive effect on the listener.

5. Cage mentioned that he was very interested in poetry early on in that it allowed him to "introduce musical elements (time, sound) into the world of writing." See Cage, *Silence*. Cage seems to induce the audience to read the poem aloud and feel the voice returning in rich resonance.

6. Paul Schimmel, who served as the curator of the Museum of Modern Art in LA (MOCA, LA), pointed out that art using action and performance in the 1950s is widely found in avant-garde works in the United States, Europe, and Asia and until the 1970s. Such activities include Pollock's action painting and Kaprow's Happenings, Fluxus group's events, Fontana's Spatialism paintings, Yves Klein's anthropometry work, and Gutai Group's collective performance. Paul Schimmel, "Leap into the Void: Performance and the Object," in Kristine Stiles et al., *Out of Actions: Between Performance and the Object, 1949–1979* (New York: Thames and Hudson, 1998), 17–119.

The Readymade Boomerang portfolio (1990) exhibited in *Highlights of MMCA Global Art Collection from the 1980s–1990s: To the World through Art* demonstrates that Cage's everyday aesthetics based on Duchamp's Readymade influenced the work of many artists for a long time. The Readymade Boomerang portfolio was produced by Berlin-based curator and art dealer René Block to fund the satellite exhibitions and performance programs of the 8th Sydney Biennale in 1990. This portfolio contains prints by 21 artists, some emerging and others who had subscribed to artistic movements such as neo-dada, Fluxus, Pop Art, and Conceptualism. Among the compilation of ironic and witty contents made with borrowed texts, prints, ordinary objects, and photos, the most eye-catching is Cage's poem *Methostic*, which borrowed the form of a calligram [1].[4] Cage's lifelong interest was finding an alternative to harmony, and he realized that there is none since there is no rule. Through *Methostic*, Cage implies that harmony of sound constantly comes back in various forms beyond its rule or alternative. The poem is read like a pre-Buddhist monologue and has 'THE READYMADE BOOMERANG' vertically typed in red.[5] It is a tribute to the enduring aesthetics of Duchamp's Readymade in the late 20th century, like a boomerang thrown far and coming back.

Robert Rauschenberg (1925–2008) [2] and his partner Jasper Johns (1930–) are often most frequently mentioned as Neo-Dada artists directly influenced by Duchamp-Cage aesthetics. But those that must not be left out in this discourse are Allan Kaprow (1927–2006), Claes Oldenburg (1929–), and George Brecht (1926–2008), La Monte Young (1935–), and Jim Dine (1935–). They went beyond the scope of painting and sculpture to include assemblage, environment, installation, and performance and experimented with happening, event, and performance in the late 1950s. They all took the Experimental Music Composition course offered by Cage at the New School for Social Research in New York between spring 1956 and summer 1960.[6]

[1]
존 케이지, 〈메소스틱〉, 1989, 종이에 실크스크린, 70 × 100 cm
John CAGE, *Methostic*, 1989, Screen print on paper, 70 × 100 cm

4. 사전에 존재하지 않는 'methostic'이라는
제목은 'methodic(방법적인)'과 'methystic
(도취시키는)'을 합성한 신조어로 보인다.
이 시에서 케이지는 제임스 테니(James Tenney)의
Critical Band(1988)를 비롯하여 폴린 올리베로스
(Pauline Oliveros)와 스튜어트 뎀스터(Stuart
Dempster)의 *Deep Listening*(1989) 등
실험적인 연주곡을 언급하고 있는데, 특히 *Deep
Listening*은 듣는 이를 소리 자체에 빠지게 하며
도취시키는 특징을 지니고 있다.

5. 케이지는 "문자의 세계에 음악적 요소(시간,
소리)를 도입"할 수 있도록 해준다는 점에서
일찍이 시에 대해 많은 관심을 가져왔다고 언급한 바
있다. Cage, *Silence* 참고. 케이지는 관람자가
이 시를 소리 내어 읽으며 그 음성이 풍부한 공명
속에서 되돌아오는 것을 느끼도록 유도하는
듯하다.

6. LA 현대미술관(MOCA, LA)의 큐레이터를
역임했던 폴 쉬멜(Paul Schimmel)이 지적하듯이,
1950년대에 행위와 퍼포먼스를 사용한
예술은 폴록의 액션 페인팅이나 캐프로의 해프닝 및
플럭서스 그룹의 이벤트뿐 아니라 폰타나의
공간주의 회화, 이브 클랭의 인간측정기 작업,
구타이 그룹의 집단 포퍼먼스 등 미국과 유럽 및
아시아의 전위적인 작업에서 널리 발견되며,
1970년대까지 지속적으로 이어진다. Paul
Schimmel, "Leap into the Void: Performance
and the Object," in Kristine Stiles et al.,
*Out of Actions: Between Performance and
the Object, 1949-1979* (New York: Thames
and Hudson, 1998), 17-119.

《미술로, 세계로》에 전시된 〈레디메이드 부메랑〉(1990)
판화 포트폴리오는 뒤샹의 레디메이드에 기반을 둔
케이지의 일상의 미학이 이후 오랫동안 많은 예술가들의
창작과 실험에 지속되었음을 보여준다. 1990년 제8회
시드니비엔날레의 연계 전시와 퍼포먼스 프로그램을
후원하기 위해 베를린 기반 큐레이터이자 아트 딜러인
르네 블록(René Block)이 주도하여 제작 판매한
이 포트폴리오는 총 21인의 네오다다, 플럭서스, 팝아트,
개념미술 작가 및 당시의 신진 예술가들의 판화를 포함하고
있다. 텍스트와 인쇄물, 평범한 물건과 사진 등을
차용하여 아이러니와 위트가 넘치는 내용으로 구성한
포트폴리오 중 무엇보다 눈길을 끄는 것은 칼리그람 형식을
차용한 케이지의 시 〈메소스틱(Methostic)〉이다[1].[4]
화음에 대한 대안을 찾아 일생을 보냈지만 결국 어떤
법칙도 존재하지 않기에 그에 대한 어떤 대안도 있을 수
없는 바, 소리의 하모니는 법칙이나 대안을 넘어선
다양한 양상으로 끊임없이 되돌아온다는 내용을 암시하고
있다. 선불교적인 독백과도 같은 시의 중앙에는 붉은
색으로 타이핑된 'THE READYMADE BOOMERANG'이
세로로 길게 이어져 있다.[5] 멀리 던져졌다가 다시금
던진 곳으로 되돌아오는 부메랑처럼 20세기 후반의 예술
전반에 지속적으로 되돌아오는 뒤샹의 레디메이드
미학에 바치는 헌사라 할 수 있다.

뒤샹-케이지 미학에 직접적인 영향을 받은 대표적인
네오다다 예술가로 흔히 로버트 라우센버그(Robert
Rauschenberg, 1925-2008)[2]와 그의 파트너였던
재스퍼 존스(Jasper Johns, 1930-)가 거론되지만,
이들 외에도 1950년대 후반에 회화나 조각의 범위를 넘어
아상블라주, 환경, 설치, 퍼포먼스 등을 진행한 앨런
캐프로(Allan Kaprow, 1927-2006), 클래스 올덴버그
(Claes Oldenburg, 1929-), 조지 브레히트(George
Brecht, 1926-2008), 라 몬테 영(La Monte Young,
1935-), 짐 다인(Jim Dine, 1935-) 등을 빼놓을 수
없다. 해프닝, 이벤트, 퍼포먼스를 실험했던 이들 대부분은
케이지가 1956년 봄부터 1960년 여름 사이에 뉴욕의
사회연구 뉴스쿨(New School for Social Research)에서
개설했던 '실험음악 작곡' 강좌를 들었던 이들이었다.[6]

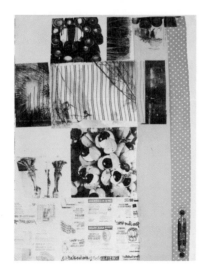

[2]
로버트 라우센버그, 〈팀〉, 1978, 종이에 사진 전사 및 직물 콜라주, 77.5×59cm
Robert RAUSCHENBERG, *Teem*, 1978, Mixed media, 77.5×59 cm

7. Allan Kaprow, "Formalism: Flogging a Dead Horse" (1974), in *Essays on the Blurring of Art and Life*, ed. Jeff Kelley (Berkeley: University of California Press, 1993), 60.

8. Allan Kaprow, "The Legacy of Jackson Pollock," *Art News* 57, No. 6 (October 1958), 57. Cape Rowe. In this article, Kaprow declared that escaping from a single, flat, rectangular screen, that is, completely giving up painting, is Pollock's legacy.

Notably, Kaprow, the founder of Happening, utilized Cage's experimental lessons to expand the scope of a painting by looking into the behavioral quality inherent in the painting practice of Jackson Pollock (1912–1956). Kaprow's print *Yard* (1990) [3] in the Readymade Boomerang portfolio pays homage to the 'Environmentals' of the same name that had been shown at the backyard of Martha Jackson Gallery in 1961. In the backyard filled with used tires, Kaprow allowed the viewers to climb or move them, creating a playful environment for natural interaction between the work and the audience [4]. He expanded everyday behavior and space into Happening and environmental installation, stressing that Cage's idea on how music and noise are one was a lesson that life and art are one as well.[7] In his 1958 article from *Art News*, "The Legacy of Jackson Pollock," Kaprow wrote, "the young artist of today need no longer say "I am a painter" or "a poet" or "a dancer." He is simply an "artist." All of life will be open to him. He will discover out of the ordinary things the meaning of ordinariness." It was a declaration of the end of Formalism, a movement that emphasized the aesthetic purity of visual art and the distinction between the discipline's mediums.[8]

Formalism, which dominated American art criticism in the 1940s and 1950s, weakened further around 1960. The important work of experimental and young artists was already happening at the intersection of daily life and art, not in the inherent realm of each medium. Duchamp-Cage's everyday aesthetics showed that the boundary between life and art could blur or disappear at any time, and it remained important even for the incredibly "American" art of Pop Art and Minimalism.

II. Art of Everyday:
Pop Art and the Shadow of Consumerism

While Cage was expanding his Readymade aesthetics into daily life by encouraging performances and events beyond the forms of art in the United States, there was Joseph Beuys (1921–1986) in Germany. He was making symbolic sculptures and performances based on the concept of 'artist as a spiritual medium,' declaring that everyone is an artist. Unlike Duchamp, who maintained shrewd intelligence and indifferent irony, Beuys criticized the materialistic culture of post-1960s capitalism and advocated sociopolitical participation. He presented ritual-inspired performances using materials that symbolize healing or spirituality, such as fat and felt, dead rabbits and blackboards, pianos, and cane.

[3]
앨런 캐프로, 〈마당〉, 1990, 종이에 석판, 73×56cm
Allan KAPROW, *Yard*, 1990, Lithograph on paper, 73×56 cm

7. Allan Kaprow, "Formalism: Flogging a Dead Horse" (1974), in *Essays on the Blurring of Art and Life*, ed. Jeff Kelley (Berkeley: University of California Press, 1993), 60.

8. Allan Kaprow, "The Legacy of Jackson Pollock," *Art News* 57, No. 6 (October 1958), 57. 캐프로는 이 글에서 단일하고 평평한 사각형의 화면을 벗어나는 것, 즉 회화를 완전히 포기하는 것이야말로 폴록의 유산임을 밝히고 있다.

해프닝의 창시자인 캐프로는 그 중 대표적인 인물로 잭슨 폴록(Jackson Pollock, 1912-1956)의 회화에 내재한 행위성에 주목하고 이를 회화 영역 너머로 확장하는 데에 케이지의 실험적 교훈을 적용했다. 〈레디메이드 부메랑〉에 포함된 캐프로의 판화 〈마당(Yard)〉(1990)[3]은 1961년 마사 잭슨 갤러리(Martha Jackson Gallery)의 뒷마당에 설치했던 동명의 환경작업(Environments)을 기념한 작품이다. 캐프로는 〈마당〉의 관람자들이 중고 타이어로 가득 채워진 뒷마당에서 타이어에 올라타거나 타이어를 이리저리 옮기며 일종의 놀이 환경에서처럼 자유롭게 상호작용하도록 하였다[4]. 일상적인 행위와 공간을 해프닝과 환경설치로 확장한 캐프로는 "음악적인 소리와 소음은 결국 하나"라는 케이지의 가르침이야말로 "삶과 예술 역시 하나"임을 설파한 것이었다고 강조한 바 있다.[7] 특히 1958년 『아트뉴스』에 기고한 「잭슨 폴록의 유산」에서 그는 "오늘날 젊은 작가들은 더 이상 '나는 화가다' 또는 '나는 시인이다' 또는 '나는 무용가다'라고 말할 필요가 없다. 그들은 이제 '예술가'로 충분하다. 삶 전체가 그들에게 열려 있다. 그들은 평범한 것에서 평범함의 의미를 발견할 것이다."라고 주장하며, 매체의 구분과 예술의 순수성을 강조하던 형식주의의 종언을 선언했다.[8]

1940-50년대 미국의 미술비평을 지배하던 형식주의적 모더니즘은 1960년을 전후로 한층 더 약화되기 시작했고, 실험적인 젊은 예술가들의 주요 작업은 이미 각 매체의 순수한 고유 영역에서가 아니라 일상과 예술이 교차하는 혼성적인 현장에서 이루어지고 있었다. 삶과 예술의 경계는 언제든 흐려지거나 사라질 수 있음을 보여준 뒤샹-케이지의 일상의 미학은 팝아트와 미니멀리즘이라는 지극히 '미국적인' 미술의 기저에도 여전히 중요하게 자리잡고 있었다.

II. 일상의 미술: 팝아트와 소비사회의 그림자

미국에서 케이지가 뒤샹의 레디메이드 미학을 일상으로 확장하며 조형예술의 경계를 넘어선 퍼포먼스와 이벤트를 독려하고 있을 때, 독일에서는 요제프 보이스(Joseph Beuys, 1921-1986)가 영매로서의 예술가 개념을 바탕으로 사회의 '모든 사람이 예술가'임을 외치며 상징적인 조각과 퍼포먼스를 전개하고 있었다. 차가운 지성과 무관심적인 아이러니를 견지했던 뒤샹과 달리, 유기적인 재료와 사회정치적 참여를 내세운 보이스는 1960년대 이후 자본주의의 물질문명을 비판하며 지방과 펠트, 죽은 토끼와 칠판, 피아노와 지팡이 등 치유나 영성(靈性)을 상징하는 재료와 소재를 사용한 제의적인 퍼포먼스를 이어갔다.

[4]
중고 타이어로 채워진 〈마당〉에 아들과 함께 있는 캐프로
Allan Kaprow and his son in the original *Yard*

9. Caroline Tisdall, *Joseph Beuys* (New York: Guggenheim Museum of Art, 1979), 17. Beuys' recount on the crash landing of a Luftwaffe plane in 1943 and his resuscitation with the help of the Tartars was widely known in the United States through the Guggenheim exhibition catalog in 1979. However, it had been questioned of authenticity and incited criticism of the self-mystification. Despite the controversies, Beuys continued to strengthen his image as a spiritual medium. In a performance called *I Like America, America Likes Me*, He had 50 copies of the Wall Street Journal delivered to him every day, stacked them in two rows, wrapped himself in a felt blanket, and communicated with a coyote with a shepherd's wand. This performance was held at René Block's gallery in New York in 1974.

10. Victoria Walters, "Joseph Beuys and EURASIA," *Tate Papers* no. 31, 2019. https://www.tate.org.uk/research/publications/tate-papers/31/joseph-beuys-eurasia (Retrieved 30 November 2021)

11. Irving Sandler notes that New York's Pop Art began with Oldenburg's solo exhibition *The Store*, held in December 1961 in Lower Manhattan, and Dine's solo exhibition at Martha Jackson Gallery in January 1962. He writes that solo exhibitions of major Pop Art artists have been held one after another since then. Irving Sandler, *American Art of the 1960s*, 143–144.

12. Pop Art was started in 1952 by the Independent Group, a group of young artists at the Institute of Contemporary Art in London. It dealt with rich consumer goods and popular culture introduced from the post-war United States, as shown in the collage works of Eduardo Paolozzi (1924–2005) and Richard Hamilton (1922–2011). *This Is Tomorrow*, held by the Independent Group at the Whitechapel Gallery in London in 1956, exhibited American product advertisements, sci-fi films, and popular culture in the form of holistic installation, simultaneously criticizing and admiring materialism.

13. Jonathan Fineberg, *Art Since 1940: Strategies of Being*, Second Edition (Englewood Cliffs: Prentice Hall, 2000), 246.

14. Lucy Lippard, *Pop Art* (New York: Frederick A. Praeger, 1966), 174–175.

As is well known, Cage and Beuys are connected through the Fluxus movement, and Nam June Paik (1932–2006) was the key figure who played an active role at this crosspoint. Paik's *Highland I* [5] is a color print of a photo collage and drawing on an old 18th-century map that pays tribute to Beuys. Centered around the Black Sea, this old and colored map meticulously depicts the Crimea Peninsula and the surrounding areas. Beuys, a former Luftwaffe, was rescued and revived by the Tartar nomads in the Crimea Peninsula during World War II. In Paik's map, Tartar tribes are marked across the peninsula, and a black-and-white photograph of Beuys is affixed next to a drawing of a vehicle in soaring red flames.[9] The torn-edged photo of Beuys is from the artist's performance *Sibirische Symphonie, 1. Satz* at the Dusseldorf Academy of Arts in 1963. This performance was a part of Beuys' Eurasia project to imagine Europe and Asia as a whole and revive the cultural nomads who once crossed Europe, Siberia, Mongolia, China, and Northeast Asia.[10] *Highland I* implies that Beuys and Paik are cultural nomads and artistic collaborators, each representing Europe and Asia respectively, and at the same time, have a bond with the nomads in history that traversed vast continents.

Meanwhile, in the United States, some of the Happening and performance artists who abandoned the canvas and went to the stage under the influence of Cage began to switch to work with some formative and fixed forms while maintaining the subject matter of everyday objects. Notable artists include Oldenburg and Dine, who soon joined a big wave called Pop Art [6].[11] Pop art began in 1952 as a "British Pop" by the Independent Group formed by young artists at the Institute of Contemporary Art in London.[12] Nevertheless, since it was heavily influenced by post-war popular culture in its creation, the movement flourished in the United States, the home of post-capitalist consumerism. As a result, while the Independent Group maintained a somewhat critical stance on American consumer culture and embraced some degree of radical politics, American Pop Art artists who grew up in consumer society and worked with it were generally considered apolitical.[13]

In fact, early American Pop Art was understood or compared to the playful and poetic Nouveau réalisme from France rather than ironic and political British Pop. This was because of the 1962 exhibition *The New Realists* at Sydney Janis Gallery, which is said to be the cornerstone of the movement. An extensive range of artists had been selected to participate in this exhibition, including New-York-based Pop Art artists such as Andy Warhol (1928–1987), Roy Lichtenstein (1923–1997), James Rosenquist (1933–2017), and George Segal (1924–2000); popular performer-turned-sculptors such as aforementioned Oldenburg and Dine; even the Nouveau réalisme artists such as Yves Klein (1928–1962), Arman (1928–2005), and Jean Tinguely (1925–1991). Lucy Lippard later pointed out that the works by Nouveau réalisme artists from Paris seemed relatively plain, overly elaborate, or even surrealistic next to the intensely colorful and stylistically impersonal works of Pop Art artists from New York. Consequently, this exhibition revealed the different viewpoints and inquiries on forms, rather than similarities, that these two groups had.[14]

[5]
백남준, 〈고지대 I〉, 1988, 컬러 인쇄물 위에 연필, 50×59 cm
Nam June PAIK, *Highland I*, 1988, Pencil on color print, 50×59 cm

9. Caroline Tisdall, *Joseph Beuys* (New York: Guggenheim Museum of Art, 1979), 17. 1943년 독일 공군기의 불시착과 타르타르 족의 도움으로 소생한 일화에 대한 보이스의 자전적인 회고는 1979년 구겐하임 전시도록을 통해 미국 내에 널리 알려졌지만, 이후 사건의 신빙성에 대한 의문이 제기되기도 하고 예술가의 자기 신비화라는 비판이 이어지기도 했다. 하지만 보이스는 1974년 르네 블록의 초청으로 블록의 뉴욕 갤러리에서 행한 〈나는 미국을 좋아하고 미국은 나를 좋아한다〉라는 퍼포먼스에서 매일 50부에 달하는 월스트리트저널을 배달시켜 두 줄로 쌓아놓고 동시에 펠트 담요로 자신을 감싼 채 양치기 지팡이로 코요테와 소통하는 등 자본주의에 대한 비판을 표명하며 영매로서의 예술가 이미지를 강화해 나갔다.

10. Victoria Walters, "Joseph Beuys and EURASIA," *Tate Papers* no. 31, 2019. https://www.tate.org.uk/research/publications/tate-papers/31/joseph-beuys-eurasia (2021년 11월 30일 검색)

11. 어빙 샌들러는 1961년 12월 로우 맨해튼에서 실제 상점을 얻어 개최한 올덴버그의 개인전 《스토어(The Store)》 및 1962년 1월 마사 잭슨 갤러리에서 열린 다인의 개인전과 더불어 뉴욕의 팝아트가 개시되었다고 언급하고 있으며, 그 후로 주요 팝아트 작가들의 개인전이 연이어 개최되었다고 쓰고 있다. Irving Sandler, *American Art of the 1960s*, 143-144.

12. 1952년 런던의 현대미술원(Institute of Contemporary Arts)의 젊은 예술가들이 결성한 인디펜던트 그룹에 의해 시작된 팝아트는 당시 에두아르도 파올로치(Eduardo Paolozzi, 1924-2005)나 리처드 해밀턴(Richard Hamilton, 1922-2011)의 콜라주에서 드러나듯이 전후 미국으로부터 유입된 풍요로운 소비재와 대중문화를 주요 내용으로 다루고 있다. 특히 인디펜던트 그룹이 1956년 런던의 화이트채플 갤러리에서 개최한 《이것이 내일이다(This Is Tomorrow)》는 미국의 제품 광고, SF 영화, 대중문화를 총체적인 설치형식으로 전시하며 물질주의에 대한 비판과 동경을 동시에 담고 있었다.

13. Jonathan Fineberg, *Art Since 1940: Strategies of Being*, Second Edition (Englewood Cliffs: Prentice Hall, 2000), 246.

14. Lucy Lippard, *Pop Art* (New York: Frederick A. Praeger, 1966), 174-175.

주지하듯이 케이지와 보이스는 플럭서스를 접점으로 서로 이어지며, 이 접점에서 활약하던 핵심 인물이 다름 아닌 백남준(1932-2006)이었다. 백남준의 〈고지대 I〉[5]은 18세기의 고지도에 드로잉과 사진 콜라주를 가한 작품을 컬러 프린트한 것으로, 보이스에게 직접적인 경의를 표한 작품이다. 흑해를 중심으로 크리미아 반도를 비롯한 주변 지역이 상세히 묘사되어 있는 컬러 고지도에는, 제2차 세계대전 중 독일 공군이었던 보이스가 크리미아 반도에서 추락한 후 타르타르 유목민에게 구출되어 부활과 소생을 경험했다는 자전적인 일화를 상기시키듯, 반도 전역에 타르타르 족이 표시되어 있고, 붉은 불길이 치솟는 듯한 운반 기구 드로잉 옆에 보이스의 흑백 사진이 붙어 있다.[9] 모서리가 찢겨진 이 사진은 1963년 뒤셀도르프 예술아카데미에서 보이스가 진행한 퍼포먼스 〈시베리아 심포니 1악장(Sibirische Symphonie, 1. Satz)〉을 찍은 기록 사진의 일부다. 이 퍼포먼스는 유럽과 아시아를 하나의 총체로 상상하며 유럽, 시베리아, 몽고, 중국, 동북아에 이르는 거대한 대륙을 가로지르는 문화적 유목민을 부활시키려는 보이스의 '유라시아(Eurasia)' 프로젝트의 일환으로 행해졌던 것이다.[10] 〈고지대 I〉은 보이스와 백남준이 각각 유럽과 아시아를 상징하는 문화적 유목민이자 예술적 협업자이며 동시에 거대한 대륙을 가로지르던 역사 속의 유목민과 유대감을 지닌 존재임을 암시한다.

[6]
짐 다인, 〈색채의 전율〉, 1990, 청동에 채색, 160.6×61.8×45.3cm
Jim DINE, *Trembling for Color*, 1990, Color on bronze, 160.6×61.8×45.3 cm

한편 미국에서는 케이지의 영향을 받아 캔버스를 버리고 무대로 나아갔던 해프닝이나 퍼포먼스 예술가들 일부가 일상 사물의 소재를 그대로 유지하면서 일정 부분 조형적인 형식과 고정된 형태를 갖춘 작업으로 전환하기 시작했다. 대표적인 작가로 올덴버그와 다인을 들 수 있는데, 이들은 곧이어 팝아트라 불리는 커다란 흐름에 합류하게 된다[6].[11] 역사적으로 팝아트는 1952년 런던 현대미술원(Institute of Contemporary Arts)의 젊은 예술가들이 결성한 인디펜던트 그룹(Independent Group)에 의해 '브리티시 팝'으로 시작했지만,[12] 명실공히 전후 대중문화가 탄생시킨 팝아트는 후기자본주의 소비사회의 본고장인 미국에서 번성했다. 이로 인해 인디펜던트 그룹이 미국의 소비문화에 대해 다소 비판적 거리를 유지하며 어느 정도 전위적인 정치성을 배태하고 있었던 반면, 소비사회 속에서 성장하고 그와 더불어 활동했던 미국의 팝아트 작가들은 전반적으로 비정치적이었다는 평가를 받기도 한다.[13]

실제로 미국의 초기 팝아트는 아이러니하고 정치적인 브리티시 팝보다는 오히려 유희적이고 시적인 프랑스의 누보 레알리즘(Nouveau Réalisme)과 연결하여 이해되거나 비교되기도 했다. 이는 미국 팝아트의 공식적인 시작으로 일컬어지는 1962년 시드니 재니스 갤러리(Sidney Janis Gallery)의 《새로운 리얼리스트(The New Realists)》 전시 때문이었다. 이 전시에는 앤디 워홀(Andy Warhol, 1928-1987), 로이 리히텐슈타인(Roy Lichtenstein, 1923-1997), 제임스 로젠퀴스트(James Rosenquist, 1933-2017), 조지 시걸(George Segal, 1924-2000) 등 뉴욕의 주요 팝아트 화가들은 물론, 앞서 언급한 올덴버그와 다인 등 퍼포먼스에서 대중적인 오브제나 조각으로 전환한 예술가들, 그리고 이브 클랭(Yves Klein, 1928-1962), 아르망(Arman, 1928-2005), 장 팅글리(Jean Tinguely, 1925-1991) 등 프랑스의 누보 레알리즘 작가들까지 광범위하게 참여했다. 그러나 루시 리파드(Lucy Lippard)가 당시의 전시에 대해 지적한 바와 같이, 강렬한 원색과 비개인적인 스타일로 일상의 현실을 있는 그대로 옮겨 놓은 뉴욕의 팝아트 곁에서 파리의 누보 레알리즘은 상대적으로 밋밋하거나 반대로 지나치게 공들인 것처럼 보였고 간혹 초현실주의적인 느낌이 강하게 느껴질 정도여서, 양자는 분명 공통적인 유사성보다는 서로 상이한 태도와 조형성을 드러냈다.[14]

15. Andy Warhol and Pat Hackett, *Popism: The Warhol's '60s* (New York: Harcourt Brace Jovanovich, 1980), 3.

16. Andy Warhol in interviews by G. R. Swenson, "What Is Pop Art?", *Art News* 62 (November 1963), 26; reprinted in Steven Henry Madoff, ed., *Pop Art: A Critical History* (Berkeley: University of California Press, 1997), 103. For the social context of Warhol's Pop Art, refer to Hal Foster, "Death in America," *October* 75 (Winter 1996), 37–60; Thomas Crow, "Saturday Disasters: Trace and Reference in Early Warhol," *Modern Art and the Common Culture* (New Haven and London: Yale University Press, 1996), See 49–48.

17. Gretchen Berg, "Andy: My True Story," Los Angeles Free Press (March 17, 1967), 3; Kynaston McShine, ed. *Andy Warhol: A Retrospective* (New York: Museum of Modern Art, 1989), Recited from 457.

American Pop Art exposed what consumer culture truly was, highlighting the dark shadows cast by the light of abundance. As Warhol notes, "artists in the Pop Art movement created images that immediately caught their eye as they walked down the streets of Broadway: cartoons, picnic tables, men's trousers, celebrities, shower curtains, refrigerators, and Coca-Cola bottles. These are the products of the great modern society, in which the Abstract Expressionists tried very hard not to pay attention." [15] However, there was an increasing monolith, passive consumption, pervasive inequality, and anonymous human relations behind the materially affluent society. And Pop Art was a testimony to both the abundance and poverty of such material culture. In his shrewd observation on American society at the time, Warhol commented, "Russia is doing it under government. It's happening here [in America] all by itself without being under a strict government … Everybody looks alike and acts alike, and we're getting more and more that way." [16] After switching from a commercial designer to a fine artist in 1960, Warhol revealed the dark shadow of the United States in the 1960s by discussing social deaths and disasters with subjects like car accidents, execution by electric chairs, human rights protests, and violence suppression from 1962. Included in *Highlights of MMCA Global Art Collection from the 1980s–1990s: To the World through Art* is Warhol's *Self-Portrait* (1985), a silkscreen work made two years before his death. "Nothing exists behind it"— it is a confession of an artist who became a mirror of the hollowness of American society. [7] [17]

In the 1970s, Minimalism expanded to language, behavior, and land, showing a radical move to fundamentally dismantle the traditional art concept. Meanwhile, Warhol or Liechtenstein's Pop Art seemed to have remained relatively in the realm of the canvas. However, the movement that utilized popular culture and consumerism remained influential, evidently by their successors. There was a revival of expressionistic image painting started by Julian Schnabel (1951–) and Robert Longo (1953–) around 1980. Graffiti-influenced artists such as Keith Haring (1958–1990) and Jean-Michel Basquiat (1960–1988) [8] were active in the New York scene. Neo-Pop artists such as Jeff Koons (1955–) and Haim Steinbach (1944–) developed kitsch aesthetics.

[7]
앤디 워홀, 〈자화상〉, 1985, 캔버스에 포토 실크스크린, 100 × 100 cm
Andy WARHOL, *Self-Portrait*, 1985, Screen print on canvas, 100 × 100 cm

238

15. Andy Warhol and Pat Hackett, *Popism: The Warhol's '60s* (New York: Harcourt Brace Jovanovich, 1980), 3.

16. Andy Warhol in interviews by G. R. Swenson, "What Is Pop Art?", *Art News* 62, November 1963, 26., reprinted in Steven Henry Madoff, ed., *Pop Art: A Critical History* (Berkeley: University of California Press, 1997), 103. 워홀의 팝아트가 지닌 사회 맥락적 의미에 대해서는 Hal Foster, "Death in America," *October* 75 (Winter 1996): 37–60., Thomas Crow, "Saturday Disasters: Trace and Reference in Early Warhol," *Modern Art and the Common Culture* (New Haven and London: Yale University Press, 1996), 49–48. 참조.

17. Gretchen Berg, "Andy: My True Story," *Los Angeles Free Press*, March 17, 1967, 3., Kynaston McShine, ed., *Andy Warhol: A Retrospective* (New York: Museum of Modern Art, 1989), 457. 재인용.

특히 미국의 팝아트는 소비사회의 실체를 있는 그대로 보여줌으로써 풍요로움의 빛이 만들어내는 어두운 그림자를 더욱 적나라하게 가시화했다. 워홀이 언급하듯이, "팝아트 작가들은 브로드웨이 거리를 걷다보면 곧바로 눈에 들어오는 것들—만화, 피크닉 테이블, 남성 바지, 유명 연예인, 샤워 커튼, 냉장고, 코카콜라 병—을 이미지로 만들었다. 이런 것들은 추상표현주의자들이 눈길을 주지 않으려고 엄청 노력했던 위대한 현대사회의 산물들이다."15 하지만 물질적으로 '풍요로운 사회(affluent society)'의 이면에는 점증하는 획일화와 수동적인 소비, 저변화된 불평등과 익명적인 인간관계 등 어두운 현실이 자리잡고 있었고, 팝아트는 그러한 물질문화의 풍요와 빈곤을 동시에 증언하고 있었다. "러시아가 정부 주도하에 그렇게 [모든 사람들이 똑같이 생각하도록] 만들고 있다면, 여기에서는 엄격한 정부 없이도 저절로 그런 일이 일어나고 있다. 모든 사람이 비슷하게 생겼고 비슷하게 행동하며, 점점 더 그렇게 되어가고 있다."라는 워홀의 언급에서 당시 미국 사회에 대한 그의 날카로운 시각을 확인할 수 있다.16 1960년에 상업디자이너에서 순수미술가로 전환한 그는 이미 1962년 이후 자동차 사고와 사형집행용 전기의자, 인권 시위와 폭력 진압 등 사회적 죽음과 재난을 집중적으로 다루며 1960년대 미국의 어두운 그림자를 가감 없이 드러냈다. 《미술로, 세계로》에 소개된 워홀의 〈자화상〉(1985)은 그가 세상을 떠나기 2년 전에 제작한 실크스크린 작품으로, '나의 표면 뒤에는 아무것도 존재하지 않는다' 라고 고백하며 스스로 공허한 미국 사회의 거울이 되었던 워홀을 만나볼 수 있다[7].17

1970년대에는 미니멀리즘이 언어, 행위, 대지로 확장되며 전통적인 미술작품 개념을 근본적으로 해체하는 급진적인 양상을 보인데 반해, 워홀이나 리히텐슈타인의 팝아트는 상대적으로 캔버스의 영역에 머물러 있는 듯한 인상을 주기도 했다. 하지만 1980년 전후로 줄리언 슈나벨(Julian Schnabel, 1951–)이나 로버트 롱고 (Robert Longo, 1953–) 등에 의해 시작된 표현주의적인 이미지 페인팅의 부활과 키스 해링(Keith Haring, 1958– 1990)이나 장-미셸 바스키아(Jean-Michel Basquiat, 1960–1988)[8]와 같은 뉴욕 그라피티 화가들의 활동, 그리고 제프 쿤스(Jeff Koons, 1955–)나 하임 스타인바흐(Haim Steinbach, 1944–) 등 네오팝의 키치 미학에서 드러나듯이, 대중문화와 소비사회를 문화적 자양분으로 삼았던 팝아트의 힘은 여전히 건재하게 남아 있었다.

[8]
장-미셸 바스키아, 〈무제〉, 1982, 종이에 크레용, 수성안료, 108.5×77.5cm
Jean-Michel BASQUIAT, *Untitled*, 1982, Mixed media on paper, 108.5×77.5 cm

III. From Special Object to Expanded Field: Human—Intermediate of Nature and Society

The Responsive Eye, held at the Museum of Modern and Contemporary Art (MoMA) in February 1965, is often referred to as an exhibition that introduced Op Art to the world, fronted by Victor de Vasarely (1906–1997) [9] and Bridget Riley (1931–). However, this exhibition also showcased works of artists investigating geometric abstraction and tactile visuality, the former by Joseph Albers (1888–1976), Ad Reinhardt (1913–1967), Ellsworth Kelley (1923–2015), and the latter by Robert Irwin (1928–) and Günther Uecker (1930–).[18] Op Art quickly drew the attention of the New York art scene by replacing Pop Art's pop-culture and everyday-influenced images with stimulating, fantastical, and kinetic ones with repetitive and geometric patterns.

However, Op Art was limited to patterns on a flat surface compared to Minimalism. Minimalism was first introduced via *Primary Structures* at the New York Museum of Jewish Art in April of the following year. It was based on a wide range of theories and art historical influence, ranging from the body subject emphasized by Merleau-Ponty's Phenomenology of Perception to Object and Space Perception of Gestalt psychology, Russian Constructivist art, and Brancusi's sculpture. It showed three-dimensional space rather than a flat surface, a moving body that transcends visual subjecthood, and an actual object rather than a compositional painting.

Artists considered to be key figures in the Minimalism movement are Donald Judd (1928–1994), Dan Flavin (1933–1996), Robert Morris (1931–2018), Carl Andre (1935–), and Sol LeWitt (1928–2007). Having held major solo exhibitions between 1963 and 1965, they presented works with outstanding systems and immediate objecthood, combining non-relational unity that removed the internal structure and introducing modules as the basic unit.[19] After that, these artists utilized the production method that minimized the artist's subjective intervention. They used items like mass-produced fluorescent lamps or steel plates and arranged structures specially manufactured in a small factory according to mathematical permutations. For example, Judd's *Untitled* [10], often called a 'stack,' is a stack of cubes of the same size and material on top of each other. It has materiality devoid of human-centered form, a three-dimensional space that does not suffer from the problem of deception, which he emphasized in "Specific Objects" in 1965. However, the immediacy of Judd's objects is self-evident as it is complex; it has a clear structure but crosses the boundaries of the existing Formalist categories. His 'stack' is a stack of cubes hanging on the wall like a painting but looking close to a sculpture in its shape. At the same time, it seems to have a shelf-like function that exists only in itself—a unique object "not a painting or sculpture."[20]

Minimalism emphasized the actual space, the process of phenomenological experience, and the complexity and conceptuality inherent in self-evident and straightforward structures. It also created a variety of movements called Post-Minimalism. Post-minimalism, coined by critic Robert Pincus-Witten, refers to work that started from minimal structures of Conceptual Art, Process Art, and Land Art but went beyond and dismantled them to move toward an 'expanded chapter.'[21] For example, Sol LeWitt's practice went toward the direction of Conceptual Art because the artist was interested in the continuum and the mechanical performance of concepts. Morris emphasized physicality and 'semi-form' and went for Process Art. Robert Smithson (1938–1973) and Walter de Maria (1935–), who paid attention to mineralogy, thermodynamics, geology, and metrology, leaned toward Land Art, exhibiting mirror chambers and steel structures in shows like *Primary Structure*.

18. William C. Seitz, *The Responsive Eye* (New York: The Museum of Modern Art, 1965).

19. Art historian James Meyer, a distinguished researcher on Minimalism, argues that the different forms and preferences of these key artists in the movements are worthy of paying attention to. Meyer emphasized that, based on fundamental heterogeneity, Minimalism is not a consistent movement but a "field of proximity and clash, similarities and difference." James Meyer, *Minimalism: Art and Polemics in the Sixties* (New Haven and London: Yale University Press, 2001), 3–9.

20. Donald Judd, "Specific Objects," *Arts Yearbook* 8 (1985), 74–82.

21. Robert Pincus-Witten, "The Seventies," *Eye to Eye: Twenty Years of Art Criticism* (Ann Arbor: UMI Research Press, 1984), 123–139. Pincus-Witten first devised 'Post-Minimalism' in 1968 in reference to the works of LeWitt and Morris and Mel Bockner, Dan Graham, Eva Hesse, Bruce Nauman, Richard Serra, and Robert Smithson. Art historian Rosalind Krauss used the term 'extended field' to explain the situation in which Minimalism's "self-evident structure" expands to place-specific installation and land art in the antagonistic relationship between architecture and nature from the Structuralist's perspective. Rosalind Krauss, "Sculpture in the Expanded Field," *October* 8 (Spring 1979), 30–44.

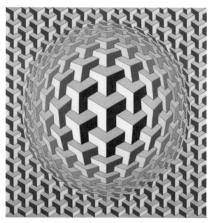

[9]
빅토르 바사렐리, 〈게자〉, 1983, 캔버스에 아크릴릭, 121.7×120.5cm
Victor VASARELY, *GEZA*, 1983, Acrylic on canvas, 121.7×120.5 cm

III. 특수한 사물에서 확장된 장으로:
인간 ─ 자연과 사회의 중간자

1965년 2월 뉴욕 현대미술관(MoMA)에서 열린 《반응하는 눈(The Responsive Eye)》은 빅토르 바사렐리(Victor de Vasarely, 1906–1997)[9], 브리지트 라일리(Bridget Riley, 1931–) 등으로 대표되는 옵아트(Op Art)의 등장을 알린 역사적 전시로 언급되지만, 요제프 알버스(Josef Albers, 1888–1976), 애드 라인하르트(Ad Reinhardt, 1913–1967), 엘스워스 켈리(Ellsworth Kelley, 1923–2015) 등의 기하학적 추상과 로버트 어윈(Robert Irwin, 1928–), 귄터 워커(Günther Uecker, 1930–) 등 촉각적 시각성을 다루는 다양한 작품을 총망라한 전시였다.[18] 팝아트의 대중문화 도상이나 일상적인 이미지를 없애고 대신 반복적인 패턴과 기하학적 구성으로 시신경을 직접 자극하며 환영적인 운동감을 자아내는 옵아트는 곧바로 뉴욕 미술계의 관심을 집중시켰다.

하지만 이듬해 4월 뉴욕 유대미술관(Jewish Museum)의 《프라이머리 스트럭처(Primary Structures)》 전시를 통해 전격 소개된 미니멀리즘(Minimalism)에 비하면 옵아트의 시각적 자극은 상대적으로 평면의 패턴에 국한된 것이었다. 메를로-퐁티의 지각의 현상학이 강조하는 몸주체, 게슈탈트 심리학의 사물과 공간 지각, 러시아 구축주의 미술과 브랑쿠시의 조각 등 다양한 이론과 예술사를 기반으로 한 미니멀 아트는 환영을 만들어내는 평면이 아닌 3차원의 공간을, 시각적 주체를 넘어선 움직이는 몸주체를, 구성적인 회화가 아닌 즉물적인 사물을 내세웠다.

18. William C. Seitz, *The Responsive Eye* (New York: The Museum of Modern Art, 1965).

19. 미니멀리즘에 대한 대표적인 연구자인 미술사학자 제임스 마이어는 이들 핵심 작가들의 상이한 형식과 서로 다른 지향에 주목해야 한다고 주장하며, 미니멀리즘이 하나의 일관된 운동이 아니라 근본적인 이질성을 바탕으로 한 '인접과 출동, 근접성과 차이의 장(field)'임을 강조한다. James Meyer, *Minimalism: Art and Polemics in the Sixties* (New Haven and London: Yale University Press, 2001), 3–9.

20. Donald Judd, "Specific Objects," *Arts Yearbook* 8 (1985), 74–82.

21. Robert Pincus-Witten, "The Seventies," *Eye to Eye: Twenty Years of Art Criticism* (Ann Arbor: UMI Research Press, 1984), 123–139. 핀커스-위텐은 1968년에 '포스트-미니멀리즘'을 처음 고안했으며, 르윗, 모리스를 포함해 멜 보크너, 댄 그레이엄, 에바 헤세, 브루스 나우만, 리처드 세라, 로버트 스미슨 등을 지칭하는 용어로 사용했다. 한편, '확장된 장'이란 미술사학자 로잘린드 크라우스가 1970년대 이후 미니멀리즘의 '자명한 구조'가 건축과 자연의 대립적 관계 속에서 장소특정적 설치와 대지미술로 확장되는 상황을 구조주의적으로 설명하며 사용한 개념이다. Rosalind Krauss, "Sculpture in the Expanded Field," *October* 8 (Spring 1979): 30–44.

미니멀리즘의 핵심 작가로 손꼽히는 도널드 저드(Donald Judd, 1928–1994), 댄 플래빈(Dan Flavin, 1933–1996), 로버트 모리스(Robert Morris, 1931–2018), 칼 안드레(Carl Andre, 1935–), 솔 르윗(Sol LeWitt, 1928–2007)은 이미 1963년부터 1965년 사이에 내적인 구성이 제거된 비관계적 단일성과 기본 단위인 모듈을 조합한 체계적 즉물성이 두드러진 구조물을 선보이며 주요 개인전을 개최했다.[19] 이후에도 이들은 대량생산된 형광등이나 철판을 그대로 사용하고 소규모 공장에서 특수 제작한 구조물을 수학적 순열에 따라 배치하는 등 작가의 주관적인 개입을 최소화하는 제작 방식을 이어갔다. 동일한 크기와 재료의 입방체가 층층이 쌓여 있어 흔히 '스택(stack)'이라 불리는 저드의 〈무제(Untitled)〉[10]는 일찍이 1965년에 그가 「특수한 사물들(Specific Objects)」에서 강조한 바 있는 미니멀리즘의 특징, 즉 환영의 문제가 사라진 3차원 공간, 인간중심적인 형태를 찾아볼 수 없는 사물의 즉물성을 지니고 있다. 하지만 저드의 사물이 지닌 즉물성은 명료한 구조를 지니고 있어 자명하면서도 기존의 형식주의적 범주들의 사이에 걸쳐 있어 복합적이다. 그의 '스택'은 회화처럼 벽에 걸려 있지만 조각에 가깝고, 조각처럼 보이지만 제품의 모습을 취하고 있으며, 선반 같은 기능을 지닌 듯하지만 오직 그 자체로 존재하는 입방체들의 연속체로서, 말 그대로 "회화도 조각도 아닌" 특수한 사물이다.[20]

미니멀리즘이 강조한 실제적인 공간과 현상학적 체험의 과정, 단순하고 자명한 구조물에 내재된 복합성과 개념성은 이른바 '포스트-미니멀리즘(Post-Minimalism)'이라 불리는 다양한 흐름을 만들어냈다. 비평가 로버트 핀커스-위텐(Robert Pincus-Witten)이 명명한 '포스트-미니멀리즘'은 개념미술, 과정미술, 대지미술 등 미니멀 구조물에서 출발하되 그것을 극복하고 해체하여 '확장된 장'으로 나아간 작업을 지칭하는 것이었다.[21] 예컨대, 연속체와 개념의 기계적 수행에 관심을 둔 솔 르윗은 개념미술로, 신체성과 '반-형식'을 중시한 모리스는 과정미술로, 그리고 《프라이머리 스트럭처》에 거울상 챔버와 철골 구조물을 전시하며 광물학, 열역학, 지질학, 측정학에 주목했던 로버트 스미슨(Robert Smithson, 1938–1973)과 월터 드 마리아(Walter de Maria, b. 1935)는 대지미술로 나아갔다.

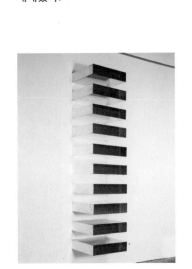

[10]
도널드 저드, 〈무제〉, 1980, 철, 알루미늄, 아크릴수지, 239×61×69 cm
Donald JUDD, *Untitled*, 1980, Steel, aluminium and perspex, 239×61×69 cm

22. The environment-oriented works of Christo and Jeanne-Claude went through a preparation process that takes from several years to decades, but most of them are installed for 1–3 weeks before being demolished. Since there was no revenue from the sale of works or admission fees, they depended on selling Christo's drawings, collages, and packaging objects to finance the realization of the project.

23. John Beardsley, *Earthworks and Beyond; Contemporary Art in the Landscape* (New York: Abbeville Press, 1998), 41–57.

In particular, Land Art, which literally brought contemporary art into a vast field, continued to unfold and persist in a broad range of environments encompassing the land, nature, civilization, and society even after Smithson's shortened life. Christo Javacheff (1935–2020) made *Valley Curtain* [11] in 1972 as a sketch for a work that installed a huge orange curtain in a valley between mountain peaks in Colorado.[22] As a member of the Nouveau réalisme movement around 1960, Christo worked on enwrapping everyday objects. Later, together with his wife Jeanne-Claude (1935–2009), he expanded the scale of projects to public buildings and the larger context of nature and integrated the social process itself into part of his practice, elevating land art to a new level. Christo created preparatory drawings while imagining the final installation, and they match surprisingly accurately with the realized projects due to his excellent description and skill. Unfortunately, *Valley Curtain* was demolished after being installed for a short time of 28 hours due to strong winds.

Meanwhile, Land Art was practiced in the UK on a much smaller and intimate scale than its US counterpart. A notable example is Andy Goldsworthy (1956–), who made ephemeral sculptures out of petals, fallen leaves, stones, and branches while wandering through sparsely populated forests or plateaus.[23] His drawing [12] in *Highlights of MMCA Global Art Collection from the 1980s–1990s: To the World through Art* is a frottage work produced by collecting natural objects such as rock plates, arranging them in a circle rubbing graphite and oil sticks with paper on it. The unique surface created by the material interaction and process has a different indexical flair from that of a documentary photograph.

The 1990s began with the fall of the Berlin Wall at the end of the 1980s. The dissolution of the Soviet Union followed. The last decade of the 20th century, when post-historical consciousness such as 'the end of history' or 'the end of art' prevailed, was also a period of accelerating global connection with the advent of the Internet and the World Wide Web. Now that 20 years have passed since we entered the 21st century, it is meaningful in many ways to look back on the past century with an exhibition like *Highlights of MMCA Global Art Collection from the 1980s–1990s: To the World through Art*. Since the 1960s, avant-garde experiments have spread beyond the boundaries of art and permeated into the world of ordinary life. Everyday art in sync with popular culture and industrial society has emerged and expanded to the land and nature. Although we live in a future-like present where technological innovation turns imagination into reality, we still exist as an intermediary between nature and society. There is a lot to think about whether human beings could persist as a constant creator like the working image [13] of Jonathan Borofsky (1942–) or the content and well-off beings within a geometric-circuit-perfect network of Peter Halley (1953–)[14].

[11]
크리스토 야바체프, 〈계곡장막〉, 1972, 종이에 흑연, 천, 색연필, 아크릴릭, 지도 인쇄물, 71×56cm
Christo JAVACHEFF, *A Valley Curtain,* 1972, Mixed media, 71×56cm

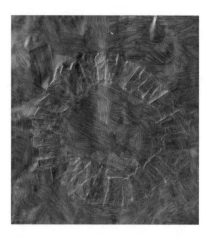

[12]
앤디 골즈워시, 〈무제(흑)〉, 1989, 종이에 흑연, 크레용, 오일스틱, 엠보싱, 158×146cm
Andy GOLDSWORTHY, *Untitled (Black),* 1989, Crayon, oilstick on paper, 158×146cm

특히 현대미술을 진정한 의미의 '확장된 장'으로 끌어낸 대지미술은 짧은 생애를 마친 스미슨 이후에도 대지와 자연, 문명과 사회를 포괄하는 폭넓은 환경에서 펼쳐지며 지속되었다. 크리스토(Christo Javacheff, 1935-2020)의 〈계곡 장막(Valley Curtain)〉(1972)[11]은 1972년 콜로라도 주 산봉우리 사이의 계곡에 거대한 오렌지 색 장막을 설치한 초기 대지미술 작업의 스케치 작품이다.[22] 1960년 경 누보 레알리즘 그룹의 일원으로 일상 사물을 포장하는 작업을 했던 그는 이후 아내인 잔-클로드(Jeanne-Claude, 1935-2009)와 함께 공공건물과 대자연으로 프로젝트의 스케일을 확장하고 사회적 과정 자체를 작업의 일부로 들여옴으로써 대지미술을 새로운 차원으로 끌어올렸다. 작업을 준비하는 과정에서 최종 설치 모습을 상상하며 제작하는 그의 드로잉은 뛰어난 묘사력과 기량으로 인해 이후 실현된 프로젝트와 놀랍도록 정확하게 일치하는데, 안타깝게도 실제 〈계곡 장막〉은 강풍으로 인해 28시간이라는 짧은 시간 동안 설치된 후 철거되었다.

한편 영국의 대지미술은 미국에 비해 그 규모나 스케일이 작고 공공 프로젝트보다는 사적인 행위의 흔적인 경우가 많다. 인적이 드문 숲이나 고원을 방랑자처럼 떠돌아다니면서 꽃잎이나 낙엽, 돌이나 나뭇가지로 일시적인 조각을 만들고 사진 기록을 남기는 앤디 골즈워시(Andy Goldsworthy, 1956-)가 대표적이다.[23] 《미술로, 세계로》에 전시된 그의 드로잉[12]은 암석 판들로 추정되는 자연물을 모아 원형으로 배치한 후 그 위에 종이를 대고 흑연과 오일스틱을 문질러 제작한 프로타주(frottage) 작품으로, 행위와 재료의 상호작용이 만들어낸 독특한 표면으로 인해 기록 사진과는 또 다른 지표적 특성을 지니고 있다.

1980년대의 끝자락에 베를린 장벽이 무너졌고, 곧이어 소비에트 연방이 해체되면서 1990년대가 시작되었다. '역사의 종언'이나 '예술의 종말'과 같은 탈역사적 의식이 팽배했던 20세기의 마지막 10년은 동시에 인터넷과 월드와이드웹이 출현하며 전 지구적인 연결이 점차 가속화되는 시기이기도 했다. 21세기에 접어든지 어느덧 20여년이 지난 지금, 《미술로, 세계로》 전시를 보며 지난 세기의 뒷모습을 되돌아보는 것은 여러 모로 의미 있는 일이다. 1960년대 이후 전위적인 실험이 예술의 경계를 넘어 평범한 생활 세계로 뻗어 나갔고, 대중문화나 산업사회와 호흡을 같이 하는 일상의 미술이 출현해 대지와 자연으로 확장되었다. 과학기술의 혁신이 상상을 현실로 바꾸고 있는 미래 같은 현재에 살고 있지만, 우리는 여전히 자연과 사회의 중간자로 존재한다. 사이-존재인 인간이 조나단 보로프스키(Jonathan Borofsky, 1942-)의 노동하는 형상[13]처럼 끊임없이 무엇인가를 만들며 창조하는 존재로 살아남을 수 있을 것이지, 혹은 피터 핼리(Peter Halley, 1953-)의 기하학적 회로[14]처럼 완벽하게 폐쇄된 네트워크 속에서 부유하는 존재로 살아가게 될 것인지, 전시를 둘러보며 다시금 생각해본다.

22. 크리스토와 잔-클로드 부부의 환경미술 작업은 짧게는 수년 길게는 수십 년에 걸친 준비 과정을 거치지만 대부분 1-3주 정도 설치된 후 철거된다. 작품 판매나 입장료 수익이 전혀 없기 때문에, 이들은 프로젝트 실현을 위한 일체의 재정을 크리스토가 만든 드로잉, 콜라주, 포장 오브제 등의 판매 수익에 의존한다.

23. John Beardsley, *Earthworks and Beyond; Contemporary Art in the Landscape* (New York: Abbeville Press, 1998), 41-57.

[13]
조나단 보로프스키, 〈망치질하는 사람〉, 1991, 혼합재료, 354×167.5×12cm
Jonathan BOROFSKY, *Hammering Man*, 1991, Mixed media, 354×167.5×12cm

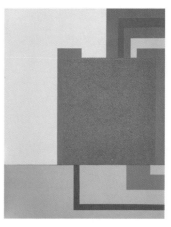

[14]
피터 핼리, 타임코드, 2001, 캔버스에 아크릴릭, 데이글로아크릴, 롤라텍스, 161.5×127cm
Peter HALLEY, *Timecode*, 2001, Arcrylic, Day-glo Arcrilyc, Roll-a-Tex on canvas, 161.5×127cm

Contemporary Art in France after the 1960s

Han Seunghye
Art History, Ewha Womans University

1. Pierre Restany, "La réalité dépasse la fiction" *1960: Les Nouveaux Réalistes,* (Paris: MAM, 1986), 267.

2. Gérard Durozoi, *Le Journal de l'art des années 60,* (Paris: Hazan, 2008), 29.

3. This exhibition was held from May 17 to June 10, 1961, at Galerie J, located in the sixth arrondissement of Paris.

4. Pierre Restany, "À 40° au-dessus de Dada," *1960: Les Nouveaux Réalistes,* (Paris: MAM, 1986), 267.

If one were asked to demonstrate their knowledge of the French painters (artists, writers), they would probably come up with the names of Impressionists such as Édouard Manet (1832–1883) or Claude Monet (1840–1926). Marcel Duchamp (1887–1968), who turned a toilet fountain into a work of art, could also be mentioned by those interested in art history. Such guess is closely related to how French art is positioned in Western art history. French art had an unprecedented heyday from the end of the 19th century when Impressionist painters led contemporary art until the first half of the 20th century when the Dadaism and Surrealism movements flourished. However, their status as a commander of Western art dwindled after World War II, and the United States, emerging as a powerhouse in the 60s, took the lead. Even after that, French artists continued to make colorful contributions to art history with the sensibility and subject matter for the new era. This essay attempts to discuss what is relatively less known to us: the history of art in France from the 1960s to the 1980s.

Bold Foreclosure of Reality: Nouveau Réalisme[1]

In the preface for an exhibition held in April of 1960 at the Galerie Apollinaire in Milan, French critic Pierre Restany (1930–2003) declared that the era of 'long monopoly' by traditional paintings and sculptures has come to an end.[2] Artists supported by Lestani at the time were bringing various objects into their practice, ranging from household goods to garbage, automobiles, and giant machines. In the preface for *À 40° au-dessus de DADA*, an exhibition in the following year, Restany substantialized the aesthetics that Nouveau Réalisme had put forward in comparison to the anti-artistic trend led by the Dadaists.[3] Dadaism was an art movement that emerged when all values, including Western European history, philosophy, and culture, collapsed onto the pile of ashes from World War I. Artists such as Tristan Tsara (1896–1963) and Francis Picabia (1879–1953) ridiculed the long-standing tradition of Western art, bringing accidental, shocking, and vain elements to their practices to challenge the conventions and expectations. Among them, Marcel Duchamp devised the concept of Readymade by elevating secular and quotidian objects to the realm of sophisticated artworks. Such effort had been deemed the most "anti-artistic gesture" done within the creative domain of an artist. However, Restany argued that such anti-art movements have failed, expressing that the concept of Readymade had now become an integral component of the "survey of new expressions," not the "extreme of negation or controversy."[4]

1960년대 이후의 프랑스 현대미술

한승혜
이화여자대학교 미술사학

1. Pierre Restany, "La réalité dépasse la fiction" *1960: Les Nouveaux Réalistes*, (Paris: MAM, 1986), 267.

2. Gérard Durozoi, *Le Journal de l'art des années 60*, (Paris: Hazan, 2008), 29.

3. 이 전시회는 파리 6구에 위치했던 제이갤러리(Galerie J)에서 1961년 5월 17일부터 6월 10일까지 개최되었다.

4. Pierre Restany, "À 40° au-dessus de Dada," *1960: Les Nouveaux Réalistes*, (Paris: MAM, 1986), 267.

만약 프랑스 화가(예술가, 작가)들 중에서 아는 사람이 있는가라는 질문을 받는다면, 아마도 대부분은 에두아르 마네(Édouard Manet, 1832-1883)나 클로드 모네(Claude Monet, 1840-1926)와 같은 인상파 화가를 떠올리거나, 그중에서 미술사에 관심을 갖고 있던 이라면 변기를 예술로 둔갑시킨 마르셀 뒤샹(Marcel Duchamp, 1887-1968)을 언급할 수도 있을 것이다. 이러한 추측은 서양 미술사에서 프랑스 미술이 차지해왔던 나름의 위치와도 관련이 있다. 인상파 화가들이 현대 미술을 주도했던 19세기 말부터 다다이즘과 초현실주의 운동이 활발히 전개되었던 20세기 전반기까지, 프랑스 미술은 유래없는 전성기를 구가하였다. 하지만 2차 세계대전 이후 절정의 시기는 내리막에 접어들었고, 1960년대에 이르러 강국으로 부상한 미국이 서구 미술의 주도권을 쥐게 된다. 그러나 1960년대 이후에도 프랑스 예술가들은 새로운 시대가 요구하는 감각과 주제 의식을 바탕으로 그들의 미술사를 다채롭게 장식하였다. 이 글은 상대적으로 우리에게 덜 알려진 1960년대부터 1980년대까지의 프랑스 미술사에 대해 이야기해 보고자 한다.

"현실의 직접적인 차압": 누보 레알리즘(Nouveau Réalisme)[1]

프랑스 비평가 피에르 레스타니(Pierre Restany, 1930-2003)는 1960년 4월, 밀라노의 아폴리네르 갤러리(galerie Apollinaire)에서 열렸던 전시의 서문에서, 전통적인 회화와 조각이 누렸던 "오랜 독점"의 시대가 막을 내리는 순간이 다가왔음을 선언했다.[2] 당시 레스타니가 지지했던 예술가들은 각종 생활용품부터 쓰레기, 자동차, 거대한 기계에 이르기까지 다양한 오브제들을 예술의 맥락에 들어오고 있었다. 이듬해인 1961년 레스타니는 《다다보다 40도 위에서(À 40° au-dessus de DADA)》라는 전시의 서문을 통해 다다이즘을 필두로 하는 반예술적 흐름에 견주어 누보 레알리즘이 내세웠던 미학을 구체화한다.[3] 다다이즘은 1차 세계대전의 발발로 인해 서구 유럽의 역사와 철학, 문화 등 모든 것이 잿더미 위에 무너졌던 시기에 등장한 예술운동이었다. 트리스탄 차라(Tristan Tzara, 1896-1963)나 프란시스 피카비아(Francis Picabia, 1879-1953)와 같은 일련의 예술가들은 유구한 서구 미술의 전통을 조롱하며 외견상 회의적인 태도로, 미술에 우연적이고, 충격적이며, 허무맹랑한 요소들을 끌어들여 보는 이들을 당혹게 만들었다. 그중 마르셀 뒤샹은 어디에서나 볼 수 있는 세속적인 사물들을 고고한 미술작품이라 칭하며 '레디메이드(ready-made)'라는 예술개념을 탄생시켰고, 레디메이드는 예술가의 창조적 행위 안에서 할 수 있는 최대한의 "반예술적 제스처"로 여겨졌다. 그러나 레스타니는 그 같은 반예술적 예술 운동들이 실패해왔다고 평가하면서, 누보 레알리즘 작가들에게 레디메이드는 이제 더 이상 "부정이나 논쟁의 극치"가 아닌 "새로운 표현의 총람"을 구성하는 중요한 요소가 되었음을 표명했다.[4]

5. Since 1961, César (1921–1998) has been working with "foreclosure". In the case of Arman (1928–2005), he began collecting and accumulating objects thrown away in the garbage dump from 1959 and began to crush or cut them from 1961.

6. Hervé Gauville, *L'Art depuis 1945 (groupes et mouvements)*, (Paris: Hazan, 2007), 252.

7. Otto Hahn, "Martial Raysse ou la beauté comme invention et délire" *Art International*, vol. X/6, (1966), 80.

8. Pierre Restany, *60/90. Trente ans de Nouveau Réalisme*, (Paris: Éditions de la Différence, 1990), 76.

In fact, Nouveau Réalisme artists had utilized the concept of Readymade on some level by compressing colored tin cans to produce works close to abstract sculptures [1] or by performing the art of breaking or exploding musical instruments or old furniture.[5] Jacques Villeglé (1926–), Raymond Hains (1926–2005), Mimmo Rotella (1918–2006), and François Dufrêne (1930–1982), who had already been active as a group since 1949, took posters off of the walls from all over the city and exhibited them. Villeglé and Hains became interested in forming new characters and color compositions by layering and tearing up the posters, while an Italian artist Mimmo Rotella worked with film posters to explore his interest in actors' faces or bodily gestures.[6] In the case of Martial Raysse (1936–), the artist grafted images borrowed from popular magazines with real-life objects. [2] Women in swimsuits, "visual clichés" of popular culture [7], have played a role in Raysse's work since 1960. By juxtaposing them with objects such as beach hats, Raysee's work blurs the distinction between reality and fantasy. His works inquire how reflective images in popular magazines are of the reality of ordinary people, hinting that the images representing the consumerism of the time might even be more realistic than the actual reality, hence, Simulacre.

French society around the 1960s underwent a rapid transformation via consumerism during a period of economic recovery, the so-called '30 Years of Glory'. The introduction of consumer-oriented culture and the development of mass media from the United States have unprecedentedly changed the lives of French people. Nouveau Réalisme was a response to such social change; to borrow the expression of Restani, it was "a poetic recycling of urban, industrial, and advertising reality." [8] The work of the Nouveau Réalisme artists as a group was officially concluded in 1963. Still, to this day, each artist continues to work to reveal the richness, and its other side, of the society transformed by consumerism.

[1]
세자르 발다치니, 〈압축(만치니) II〉, 1993, 채색된 압축 양철통, 155×65×65cm
César BALDACCINI, *Mancini II*, 1993, Mixed media, 155×65×65 cm

5. 세자르(César, 1921-1998)는 1961년부터 기계를 이용하는 압착의 방식을 택하여 작업했다. 아르망(Arman, 1928-2005)의 경우, 1959년부터 쓰레기장에 버려진 물건을 수집하여 축적(accumulation)하는 작업을 시작했고, 1961년부터는 사물을 부수거나 절단하는 작업을 병행하였다.

6. Hervé Gauville, *L'Art depuis 1945 (groupes et mouvements)*, (Paris: Hazan, 2007), 252.

7. Otto Hahn, "Martial Raysse ou la beauté comme invention et délire," *Art International*, vol. X/6 (1966): 80.

8. Pierre Restany, *60/90. Trente ans de Nouveau Réalisme*, (Paris: Éditions de la Différence, 1990), 76.

실제로 누보 레알리즘 작가들은 채색한 양철통을 압착(compression)하여 추상조각에 가까운 작품을 제작[1]하거나, 악기나 고가구를 부수거나 폭파하는 행위 예술을 보여줌으로써 또 다른 차원에서 레디메이드를 활용하였다.5 1949년부터 이미 그룹으로 활동하고 있던 자크 빌글레(Jacques Villeglé, 1926-)와 레이몽 앵스(Raymond Hains, 1926-2005), 밈모 로텔라(Mimmo Rotella, 1918-2006), 프랑수아 뒤프렌(François Dufrêne, 1930-1982)은 도시 곳곳에 나붙어있는 포스터를 그대로 떼어와 전시하는 작업을 진행했다. 빌글레나 앵스는 여러 겹으로 붙어있는 포스터들을 찢는 방식을 통해, 새롭게 관계를 맺게 되는 문자나 색채에 관심을 갖고 작업했다면, 이탈리아 태생의 로텔라의 경우, 주로 영화 포스터를 선택하여 배우들의 얼굴이나 제스처를 활용한 작업을 보여주었다.6 또한 막시알 레이스(Martial Raysse, 1936-)는 대중잡지로부터 차용한 이미지들을 실제 사물들과 접목하는 작업을 보여주었다[2]. 1960년부터 그의 작품에 등장하는 수영복 차림의 여인들은 대중문화의 "시각적 클리셰"이면서도,7 해변용 모자와 같은 실제 오브제와 결합됨으로써 관람자들로 하여금 현실과 가상을 교란시키는 역할을 했다. 레이스의 작품들은 대중잡지에 등장하는 이미지들이 과연 평범한 이들의 삶과 얼마만큼 닮았는지를 묻고 있으며, 당대 소비사회를 대변하는 이미지들이 실제 현실보다 더욱 현실 같은 이미지, 즉 하나의 '시뮬라크르(simulacre)'임을 말하고 있다.

1960년대 전후의 프랑스 사회는 이른바 '영광의 30년(Trente Glorieuses)'이라 불리는 경제적 회복기를 거치면서 급격하게 소비사회로 나아가는 시기였다. 미국으로부터 유입된 소비문화와 대중매체의 발달이라는 거대한 흐름은 프랑스인들의 삶을 이전과 비교할 수 없을 정도로 새롭게 바꾸어놓았다. 누보 레알리즘은 그러한 사회적 변화를 담고 있다는 점에서 레스타니의 표현처럼 "도시와 산업, 광고적 현실의 시적 재활용"이었다.8 그룹으로서의 작가들의 활동은 1963년에 공식적으로 마무리가 되지만, 오늘날까지도 누보 레알리즘 작가들은 소비사회의 풍요로움과 그 이면을 보여주는 작업을 이어나가고 있다.

[2]
막시알 레이스, 〈지난 여름 갑자기〉, 1963, 채색된 사진과 오브제, 106×227×58cm, 퐁피두 센터, 파리.
Martial Raysse, *Soudain l'été dernier*, 1963, Color on photo and objects, 106×227×58 cm, Centre Pompidou, Paris.

Art in Action: Nouvelle Figuration

In France, the term 'Nouvelle Figuration' was first used by Jean-Louis Ferrier (1926–2002) in the magazine called *Temps modernes* in 1959.[9] Nouvelle Figuration paintings arose with an entirely different form from that of Figurative Expressionism or Socialist Realism from the 1950s.[10] Nouvelle Figuration artists incorporated images from the mass media such as photography, cartoons, magazines, and movies into their work, featuring distinctive outlines, flatness, and artificial colors on graphic-like screens. *La Figuration Narrative dans Art Contemporain*, curated by Gérald Gassiot-Talabot (1929–2002) and held in Paris and Prague in 1965, showcased works incorporating patterns and the methods of screen division in film, serial comics, and photo novels. Among them, a scandalous work *Vivre et laisser mourir ou la fin tragique de Marcel Duchamp* (1965) [3] by Gilles Aillaud (1928–2005), Eduardo Arroyo (1937–2018), and Antonio Recalcati (1938–) depicts Duchamp, the most hailed French artist of the time, as its subject matter, as in the Nouveau Realism Manifesto.[11] Across the eight panels of the work, they featured the depiction of Duchamp's works along with scenes of torturing and even murdering the artist who was still alive at the time. They criticized Duchamp for making art conceptual and esoteric, thereby inexorably obscuring the status of an artist. Aillaud, Arroyo, and Recalcati were more interested in taking a step closer to the viewers by reintroducing an anecdotal structure that anyone can easily understand.

Nouvelle Figuration artists became more radical with the outbreak of the 68 Revolution at the end of the 1960s. At that time, an impending fundamental social change in France was imminent as the strong nationalism based on de Gaulleism and the values of a new generation collided. Going with the current at the time, the Nouvelle Figuration artists raised the flag of opposition to the authoritarianism prevailing throughout society. Including *Salle rouge pour le Vietnam* which was against the Vietnam War that sparked the 68 Revolution[12], they organized exhibitions condemning violence by the public authority and racism. One of their exhibitions deals with the coal mine accident in the dram that killed 16 miners.[13] With *Gabrielle Russier, Qui tue?* (1970–71) and *Vérités sur un fait divers: Gabrielle Russier* (1970), they spoke about a scandal between a teacher and a high school student at the time to spark up a discussion on social morality and system's violence against individuals.

9. Jean-Luc Chalumeau, *La Nouvelle Figuration*, (Paris: Cercle d'art, c. 2003), 17.

10. Popular expressions for figurative art at the time include 'Figuration Fantastique', 'Réalistes Poétiques', and 'Misérabilisme'. Their forms can be characterized as expressive and grotesque.

11. Gassiot-Talabot recalled, "when the painting was displayed, it truly caused an explosion of anger and even a nerve attack. People tried to tear the painting, cursed us, and unexpected slanders were written in the guest book." Francis Parent, Raymond Perrot, Le Salon de la Jeune peinture: Une Histoire, 1950–1983, (Paris: Jeune Peinture, 1983), 46. There were opinions that the sadistic acts toward Duchamp were rather excessive even within the Nouvelle Figuration group. Jacques Monory (1924–2018), Peter Klasen (1935–), Jan Voss (1936–) expressed opposition, while Hervé Télémaque (1937–) filed a petition. Refer to Jean Luc Chalumeau, ibid., (Paris: Cercle d'art, c. 2003), See 26, 32.

12. Exhibition titled *Aspects of Racism* was particularly successful and even toured other provinces. However, the exhibition was forced to close by the municipal prosecutor's office in the city of Brive. The pretext for the closure was that Paolo Baratella (1935–)'s paintings were rather sensational, which resulted in Baratella's arrest and an order to destroy the work. Refer to Jean Luc Chalumea, ibid., (Paris: Cercle d'art, 2003), 80.

13. On February 4, 1970, an investigation for the accident at Fouquières-les-Lens found that the safety of the miners was neglected for the sake of profit. Centering on Gérard Fromanger (1939–2021), a number of Nouvelle Figuration artists participated in this exhibition and later published *L'album de la veuve d'un mineur*. Refer to Jean Luc Chalumeau, ibid., (Paris: Cercle d'art, 2003), See 91.

[3]
질 아이요, 에두아르도 아로요, 안토니오 레칼카티, 〈살기와 죽도록 내버려 두기 혹은 마르셀 뒤샹의 비극적 최후〉, 1965, 캔버스에 아크릴, 163×992cm(8점으로 구성된 폴립티크: 각 162×114cm, 163×130cm), 국립 소피아 왕비 예술센터, 마드리드.
Gilles Aillaud, Eduardo Arroyo, Antonio Recalcati, *Vivre et laisser mourir ou la fin tragique de Marcel Duchamp*, 1965, Acrylic on canvas, 163×992 cm, Museo Nacional Centro de Arte Reina Sofía, Madrid.

행동하는 미술: 신구상(Nouvelle Figuration)

'신구상'이라는 용어는 1959년 『현대(Temps modernes)』라는 잡지에서 장 루이 페리에(Jean-Louis Ferrier, 1926-2002)에 의해 프랑스에서는 처음으로 사용되었다.[9] 신구상 회화는 1950년대에 존재했던 표현주의적인 구상 미술이나 사회주의 리얼리즘과는 전혀 다른 조형성을 보이며 등장하였다.[10] 신구상 작가들은 사진과 만화, 잡지, 영화 등의 대중매체로부터 수용한 이미지들을 작업에 도입하여, 뚜렷한 윤곽선과 평면성, 인조적인 색채 등이 특징인 그래픽과 같은 화면을 구사하였다. 1965년 파리와 프라하에서 개최된 《현대미술에서의 서술적 구상(La Figuration Narrative dans l'art contemporain)》전은 제라드 가시오 탈라보(Gérald Gassiot-Talabot, 1929-2002)에 의해 기획된 전시로서, 출품된 작품들은 영화에서 볼 수 있는 화면 분할이나, 연재만화, 사진소설 등의 전개 방식을 수용한 예들을 볼 수 있었다. 그중에서도 질 아이요(Gilles Aillaud, 1928-2005)와 에두아르도 아로요(Eduardo Arroyo, 1937-2018), 안토니오 레칼카티(Antonio Recalcati, 1938-)의 공동 작품인 〈살기와 죽도록 내버려 두기 혹은 마르셀 뒤샹의 비극적 최후(Vivre et laisser mourir ou la fin tragique de Marcel Duchamp)〉(1965)[3]는 앞서 살펴본 누보 레알리즘의 선언문에서와 마찬가지로, 당시까지 생존해 있던 프랑스 미술의 거장인 뒤샹을 소재로 삼으면서 큰 스캔들을 일으켰다.[11] 세 예술가는 뒤샹의 대표작을 그린 화면들과 함께, 뒤샹에게 고문을 가하고, 심지어 살인을 저지르는 장면들을 8개의 패널에 묘사하였다. 그들은 뒤샹이 예술을 삶과 동떨어진 개념적이고 어려운 것으로 만들었고, 이를 통해 예술가의 지위를 한없이 높여 놓았다고 비판했다. 그에 반해 세 예술가는 누구나 쉽게 이해할 수 있는 일화적인 구조를 회화에 재도입함으로써 관람자들에게 한 걸음 더 가까이 다가가고자 하는 의지를 드러냈다.

이러한 신구상 작가들의 작업 태도는 1960년대 말에 68혁명이 일어나면서 더욱 과격한 성격을 띠게 된다. 그 당시 프랑스에서는 드골주의를 기반으로 하는 강력한 국가주의와 새로운 세대의 가치관이 충돌하면서 급진적으로 사회적 변혁이 요구되고 있었다. 신구상 작가들은 그러한 변혁의 움직임에 힘입어 사회 전반에 팽배해있던 권위주의에 반발의 깃발을 들어 올렸다. 그들은 68혁명을 촉발시켰던 베트남 전쟁에 반대하는 《베트남을 위한 붉은 방(Salle rouge pour le Vietnam)》전을 시작으로, 공권력의 폭력성을 규탄하는 전시, 인종 차별에 반대하는 전시 등을 개최했다.[12] 또한 16명의 광부의 사망을 불러왔던 탄광 사고를 규탄하는 전시회를 비롯하여,[13] 《가브리엘 뤼시에, 누가 죽였나?(Gabrielle Russier, Qui tue ?)》(1970-71)전이나 《서로 다른 사실에 대한 진실들: 가브리엘 뤼시에(Vérités sur un fait divers: Gabrielle Russier)》(1970)전은 당시에 이슈가 되었던 교사와 학생의 스캔들을 주제로 하여, 사회제도와 윤리체계가 개인에게 가할 수 있는 폭력성에 대해 고발하였다.

9. Jean-Luc Chalumeau, La Nouvelle Figuration, (Paris: Cercle d'art, c. 2003), 17.

10. 당대에 유행했던 구상미술을 일컫는 표현들은 다음과 같다: '환상적 구상(Figuration Fantastique)', '시적 사실주의자들(Réalistes Poétiques)', '참상주의(Misérabilisme)'. 이들은 대부분 표현적이고 그로테스크한 조형적 특징을 공유하였다.

11. 탈라보는 "그 그림이 전시되었을 때, 진정으로 분노의 폭발이 일어났고 신경 발작을 일으켰으며, 사람들은 그림을 찢으려 하고, 우리에게 욕을 하고, 방명록에는 상상도 할 수 없는 비방들이 쓰였다."고 회고하였다. Francis Parent, Raymond Perrot, Le Salon de la Jeune peinture: Une Histoire, 1950-1983, (Paris: Jeune Peinture, 1983), 46. 한편 신구상 작가들 내부에서도 뒤샹에 대한 가학적 묘사가 지나쳤다는 의견이 나왔다. 자크 모노리(Jacques Monory, 1924-2018)와 피터 클라센(Peter Klasen, 1935-), 얀 보스(Jan Voss, 1936-)가 반대의 뜻을 밝혔으며, 에르베 텔레마크(Hervé Télémaque, 1937-)는 탄원서를 제출하기도 하였다. Jean Luc Chalumeau, 같은 책, 26, 32. 참조.

12. 특히 《인종주의의 양상들(Aspects of Racism)》전은 크게 성공하여 지방에서 순회 전시를 하였는데, 그 중 브리브(Brive)라는 도시에서는 지방 검사국에 의해 전시가 폐쇄 조치되는 일을 겪기도 했다. 폐쇄의 구실은 파올로 바라텔라(Paolo Baratella, 1935-)의 그림이 다소 선정적이라는 것이었고, 이로 인해 바라텔라는 체포된 후 받은 재판에서 그림을 파기하라는 판결을 받았다. Jean Luc Chalumeau, 같은 책, 80.

13. 1970년 2월 4일, 푸퀴에르 레 랑스(Fouquières-les-Lens)에서 일어난 이 탄광 사고는 수익을 위해 광부들의 안전이 무시되었다는 조사 결과가 나왔다. 제라드 프로망제(Gérard Fromanger, 1939-2021)를 중심으로 다수의 신구상 작가들이 이 전시에 참여하였고, 몇몇은 『한 광부의 미망인을 위한 작품집(L'album de la veuve d'un mineur)』을 출판하기도 했다. Jean Luc Chalumeau, 같은 책, 91. 참조.

14. Jean Luc Chalumeau, ibid., (Paris: Cercle d'art, 2003), 87.

15. Jean Luc Chalumeau, ibid., (Paris: Cercle d'art, 2007), 54.

16. Bertini in his early days taught himself to pursue Informel abstraction. He moved to Paris in 1951 and, with the help of Talabo, participated in the Nouvelle Figuration movement. His collage work began in 1960. Jean-Paul Ameline, *Figuration Narrative, Paris 1960–1970*, (Paris: Éditions du Center Pompidou/RMN), 2008, 337.

17. Their place of birth played an important role in their settlement around Southern France. Except for Marc Devade (1943–1983) from Paris, Viallat and André-Pierre Arnal (1939–) were from Nîmes, Louis Kahn from Beaulieu-sur-Mer, Dezeuze from Alès, Vincent Bioulès (1938–) from Montpellier, and Dola from Nice.

18. Participants of this exhibition include Viallat, Dezeuze, Patrick Saytour (1935–), André Valensi (1947–1999), and Bernard Pagès, (1940–).

19. Supports/Surfaces artists described these places as 'neutral' because they considered them to be outside the control of art institutions and their systematic influences. O'Neill, Rosemary, "'Été 70: The Plein-air Exhibitions of Supports/Surfaces'" in *Journal of Curatorial Studies* 1: 3, (2012), 350.

After promptly retorting to political events and social issues in the 1960s and 1970s, most Nouvelle Figuration artists returned to their own studios in the 1980s. Notably, Peter Klasen from Germany had continuously exposed the latent risks in the industrial society through his practice. He participated in *Mythologies Quotidiennes* (1964), the first group exhibition of Nouvelle Figuration artists held at the Paris Museum of Modern Art. His work *Wagon Citerne Gris/Bache* (1984) [4] is a hyper-realistic depiction of a tank car and a tarp made with a mixture of compressed air and paints using an aérographe.[14] This painting method resulted in a glossy finish similar to photography, allowing the viewers to confront the work with a sense of encountering a real tank car and the danger of industrial society it signifies. In an interview, Klasen said that "the painting is an act that is conscious of the danger posed by technological advances."[15] Additionally, *Sulfurated Venus* (1983) [5] by Italian artist Gianni Bertini (1922–2010) is a solid example of his oeuvre that combines the popular representation of female bodies in mass media with disparate images.[16]

Dismantling Traditional Painting: Supports/Surfaces

Supports/Surfaces is an avant-garde group that emerged mainly in southern France at the end of the 1960s, with notable figures such as Claude Viallat (1936–), Louis Cane (1943–), and Noël Dolla (1945–), and Daniel Dezeuze (1942–). The reason why these artists decided to base in southern France, not Paris, where the attention of the art world was focused, was, above all, related to their intention to break away from the Paris-centered art world.[17] In the summer of 1970, artists who were almost unknown at that time presented 12 pieces of installation works in an exhibition titled *Intérieur/Extérieur*.[18] They installed works in relatively obscure and deserted places; ranging from grass on the outskirts of Nice, a southern French city, to a small fishing village in Villefranche-sur-Mer, an abandoned rocky mountain in Aubais, a quiet beach in Maguelone, as well as public spaces such as streets, squares, and even a quiet bookstore.[19] These installations raised inquiries on how art reflects natural or social places and how the audience responds to works of art without prior knowledge, commercial publicity, or judgment of critics. In fact, the installations eventually became a playground for local children. [6]

[4]
피터 클라센, 〈회색 탱크차/방수포〉, 1984, 캔버스에 유채, 크레용, 162×130cm
Peter KLASEN, *Wagon Citerne Gris/Bache*, 1984, Acrylic on canvas, 162×130 cm

14. Jean Luc Chalumeau, 같은 책, 87.

15. Jean Luc Chalumeau, 같은 책, 54.

16. 베르티니는 작업 초기 독학으로 앵포르멜 추상을 추구하였다. 그러다 1951년에 파리로 이주하여, 탈라보의 도움으로 신구상 운동에 참여하였다. 콜라주 작업은 1960년부터 시작하였다. Jean-Paul Ameline, *Figuration Narrative, Paris 1960–1970*, (Paris: Éditions du Centre Pompidou/RMN, 2008), 337.

17. 이들이 남프랑스를 중심으로 활동했던 또 다른 이유로 그들의 출생지도 큰 역할을 하였다. 파리 출신이었던 마크 드바드(Marc Devade, 1943–1983)를 제외하고, 비알라와 앙드레 피에르 아르날(André-Pierre Arnal, 1939–)은 님므(Nîmes), 루이 칸은 보리유-쉬르-메르(Beaulieu-sur-Mer), 드죄즈는 아를(Alès), 뱅상 비울레스(Vincent Bioulès, 1938–)는 몽펠리에(Montpellier), 돌라는 니스(Nice) 출신으로, 주요 작가들이 모두 남프랑스 출신이었다.

18. 이 전시회에는 비알라, 드죄즈, 파트릭 세투르(Patrick Saytour, 1935–), 앙드레 발랑시(André Valensi, 1947–1999), 베르나르 파제스(Bernard Pagès, 1940–) 등이 참여했다.

19. 쉬포르 쉬르파스 작가들은 이 장소들이 예술 기관과 그 시스템의 제어로부터 벗어난 공간이라 생각했기 때문에 그 장소들을 '중립적'이라 표현했다. O'Neill, Rosemary, "'Été 70: The Plein-air Exhibitions of Supports-Surfaces'" *Journal of Curatorial Studies* 1: 3 (2012): 350.

이렇듯 1960–70년대에 정치적 사건이나 사회적 이슈에 즉각적으로 반응했던 신구상 작가들은 1980년대에 이르러서는 대부분 각자의 작업실로 돌아가 개인적인 작업을 이어나간다. 1964년 파리 시립 현대미술관에서 열렸던 신구상 작가들의 첫 그룹전인 《일상의 신화(Mythologies Quotidiennes)》전을 비롯해 다수의 전시에 참여했던 독일 출신의 피터 클라센은 1980년대 이후에도 위험이 잠재해 있는 산업 사회의 단면을 폭로하는 작업을 보여준다. 클라센의 작품 〈회색 탱크차/방수포〉(1984)[4]는 탱크차와 방수포의 일부를 극사실적으로 묘사하고 있는데, 그는 주로 압착시킨 공기와 물감을 혼합하고, 그 혼합물을 분무기(aérographe)를 이용해 뿜어내는 방식을 통해 그림의 표면에 윤기가 나도록 작업하였다.[14] 이러한 방식은 그가 재현하는 이미지들이 실제와 거의 유사한 사진처럼 보이도록 만들었으며, 관람자들은 그의 작품 앞에서 탱크차와 마주하는 느낌을 받게 되고, 더 나아가 산업 사회에 산재해 있는 위험 요소들에 대해 다시금 인지하는 기회를 얻게 되었다. 클라센은 한 대담에서 "나에게 그림을 그리는 일은… 기술적 진보에 의해 야기되는 위험에 대해 의식하는 행위이다"라고 말한 바 있다.[15] 한편, 이탈리아 태생의 신구상 작가인 지안니 베르티니(Gianni Bertini, 1922–2010)의 작품인 〈유황 처리된 비너스(Sulfurated Venus)〉(1983)[5]는, 대중매체에 흔히 등장하는 여성의 신체 이미지와 함께 이질적인 이미지들을 병치하는 그의 작업 세계를 잘 보여준다.[16]

전통 회화의 해체: 쉬포르 쉬르파스 (Supports/Surfaces)

쉬포르 쉬르파스는 1960년대 말에 남프랑스를 중심으로 등장했던 전위그룹으로, 클로드 비알라(Claude Viallat, 1936–)와 루이 칸(Louis Cane, 1943–), 노엘 돌라(Noël Dolla, 1945–), 다니엘 드죄즈(Daniel Dezeuze, 1942–) 등이 주요 작가로 활동하였다. 이 작가들이 미술계의 관심이 집중되어 있던 파리가 아닌 남프랑스를 근거지로 정하게 된 계기는 무엇보다 파리 중심의 미술계로부터 탈피하고자 했던 의도와 관련이 있었다.[17] 1970년 여름, 무명이나 다름없던 작가들은 《실내/실외(Intérieur/Extérieur)》라는 제목의 전시회를 통해 12점의 설치 작업을 선보였다.[18] 작가들은 프랑스 남부 도시인 니스의 변두리 풀숲부터 빌프랑쉬-쉬르-메르(Villefranche-sur-Mer)의 작은 어촌마을, 오베(Aubais)의 버려진 돌산 그리고 마귈롱(Maguelone)의 한적한 해변에 이르기까지 인적이 드문 장소에 작품을 설치했으며, 그 근방의 도로와 광장, 작은 서점과 같은 공공장소에도 작품을 전시했다.[19] 이 설치 작업들은 예술이 어떠한 방식으로 자연 혹은 사회적 장소들과 조응하는지에 관해 질문을 던졌고, 사전지식이나 상업적인 홍보, 비평가의 판단이 부재하는 상황에서 관람자들이 예술작품에 어떻게 반응하는지에 대해서도 실험할 수 있었다. 실제로 작가들의 설치 작업은 동네 아이들이 놀이터가 되었다[6].

[5]
잔니 베르티니, 〈유황 처리된 비너스〉, 1983, 면천에 사진 꼴라주, 잉크, 아크릴, 유채, 162×117cm
Gianni BERTINI, Sulfurated Venus, 1983, Photo collage, ink, acrylic and oil on cotton fabric, 162×117cm

[6]
오베에 설치되었던 클로드 비알라의 작품과 동네 아이들의 모습
Artwork by Claude VIALLAT installed in Aubais, and children

20. The first group exhibition of Supports/ Surfaces artists, *Support-Surface*, was held at the ARC in September 1970 with the support of the Paris Museum of Modern Art. The show was jointly curated by Pierre Gaudibert (1928–2006) and Viallat. In its current (plural) form, the group's name was ironically coined in April 1971, when the group split into two factions and opened different exhibitions. Hervé Gauville, *ibid.*, (Paris: Hazan, 2007), 166.

The name 'Supports/Surfaces' was initially proposed by Bioulès as the group's first exhibition title and was later solidified as their moniker. At that time, the term was singular, unlike how it is in plural. [20] In the French language, 'Support' means the wooden structure of the canvas, and 'surface' means the fabric stretched on the support. The artists of Supports/Surfaces attempted to demystify the traditional meaning of painting perpetuated by the previous generation. They instead focused on highlighting the actual material of the medium, such as canvas cloth or wooden supports. For example, some paid attention to the canvas fabric itself separated from the support, focusing on the original properties of the fabric and transforming it in an original way. Namely, Louis Cane made 'toiles découpées' out of large painted canvas similar to Color-field Abstract works [7] or 'toiles tamponnées' by painting with stamps. In the case of Noël Dolla and Patrick Saytour, the former presented a series of dipped-in-dye works by absorbing liquid in fabric, while the latter focused on burning, folding, and cutting out the dyed fabric. [8]

Claude Viallat played a central role in Supports/ Surfaces movement. Viallat maximized the physical properties of canvas fabrics by creating a huge net made of enlarged warp and weft, the most fundamental elements of the material. [6] Later, he attempted to challenge the convention of painting by discovering mediums of various kinds that could replace canvas cloth, such as tablecloths, curtains, and tent tarps. Viallat's *Untitled* (1982) [9] from the early 1980s is made with mesh backed by a layer of paper, which can be understood as another metaphor for warp and weft. Certain aspects in this work seem to be in the shape of kidney beans or pallette. (I consider these shapes to elicit the empty spaces of the stretched net, yet it is highly likely that they are not indicative or representative of any particular object.) Today, these forms are still considered his signature.

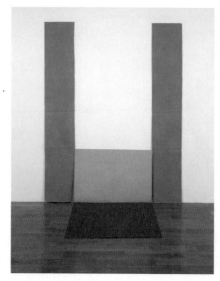

[7]
루이 칸, 〈잘린 캔버스〉, 1971, 캔버스에 유채, 240×189×98cm
(벽 부분: 240×189cm, 바닥 부분: 98×107cm), 퐁피두 센터, 파리.
Louis Cane, *toile découpée*, 1971, Oil on canvas,
240×189×98 cm, Centre Pompidou, Paris.

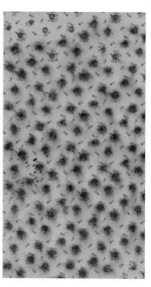

[8]
파트릭 세투르, 〈태우기〉, 1967, 기름칠한 천에 연소, 82×45cm,
쎄이슨 & 베네티에르 갤러리
Patrick Saytour, *Brûlage*, 1967, Burnt fabric, 82×45 cm,
Ceysson & Bénétière, Paris.

20. 쉬포르 쉬르파스의 첫 번째 그룹 전시회인 《쉬포르 쉬르파스(Support-Surface)》전은 1970년 9월 파리 시립 현대미술관의 지원을 받아 ARC에서 개최되었다. 이 전시회는 피에르 고디베르(Pierre Gaudibert, 1928–2006)와 비알라가 공동 기획했다. 한편, 현재의 복수형의 명칭은 공교롭게도 1971년 4월 그룹이 두 파로 분열되어 각각 다른 전시를 열게 되었던 시기에 확정된다. Hervé Gauville, 같은 책, 166.

'쉬포르 쉬르파스'라는 명칭은 작가 중 한 명인 비울레스가 그들의 첫 번째 그룹전의 제목으로 제안한 것이 그룹의 이름으로 굳어진 것으로, 당시에는 현재의 복수형이 아닌 단수형의 이름이 사용되었다.[20] 프랑스어인 '쉬포르(support)'는 캔버스의 지지대를 의미하고, '쉬르파스(surface)'는 캔버스의 표면을 뜻했다. 쉬포르 쉬르파스 작가들은 전통적인 의미의 '회화'를 해체하기 위하여 예술가들이 캔버스 위에 재현해왔던 환영을 걷어내고, 그 환영에 의해 가려져있던 실제 사물들인 캔버스 천이나 나무 지지대 등을 가시화하는 작업을 시도했다. 가령, 지지대와 분리된 캔버스 천 자체를 주목한 작가들은 천이라는 직물이 지니는 본래 성질에 집중하여, 각자가 고안한 방식으로 천에 변형을 가하는 작업을 보여주었다. 예컨대, 루이 칸은 채색한 거대한 캔버스로 색면 추상과 같은 작업들(toiles découpées)[7]을 제작하였고, 캔버스에 반복적으로 도장을 찍는 패턴 작업들(toiles tamponnées)을 시도하기도 했다. 또한 노엘 돌라는 천이 액체를 흡수하는 성질을 이용하여 염료에 담그는 일련의 작업들을 선보였고, 세투르는 염색된 천을 태우거나 접은 후 오리는 작업에 몰두하였다[8].

쉬포르 쉬르파스에서 중심적인 역할을 했던 비알라의 경우, 직물의 가장 근본적인 요소라 할 수 있는 날실과 씨실을 크게 확장한 형태인 거대한 그물을 통해 캔버스 천이 지니는 물성을 극대화하였다[6]. 이후에는 캔버스 천을 대체할 수 있는 전혀 다른 재질의 매체들을 발굴하여 회화의 가능성에 도전하였는데, 이를테면 식탁보나 커튼, 텐트의 방수포 등을 활용한 작업을 보여주었다. 1980년대 초의 비알라의 작품 〈무제〉(1982)[9]에서는 날실과 씨실의 또 다른 은유라 할 수 있는 망사를 종이 뒤에 덧댄 작업을 볼 수 있다. 또한 〈무제〉(1982)[10]에서 사선으로 병렬된 일정한 형태들은 강낭콩이나 팔레트의 형상이라 여겨지기도 한다. (필자는 이 형태가 늘어진 그물의 날실과 씨실의 빈 공간을 묘사한 것 같아 보이기도 하나, 실제로는 그 어떤 대상도 지시하거나 재현하지 않았을 가능성이 높다.) 이 형태들은 오늘날까지도 그의 시그니처로 여겨진다.

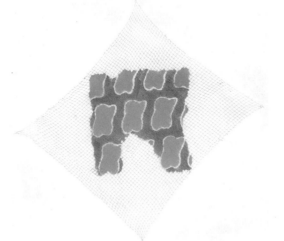

[9]
클로드 비알라, 〈무제〉, 1982, 망사에 종이, 아크릴릭, 289×218cm
Claude VIALLAT, *Untitled*, 1982, Acrylic and paper on netting thread, 288×280 cm

[10]
클로드 비알라, 〈무제〉, 1982, 캔버스에 아크릴릭, 284×215cm
Claude VIALLAT, *Untitled*, 1982, Acrylic on canvas, 284×215 cm

21. The exhibition *Finir en beauté* held in June 1981 was when the Figuration Libre artists garnered attention from the Paris scene. Bernard Lamarche-Vadel (1949–2000), a critic and editor of *Artistes*, organized and even provided his home as the venue for the exhibition. Four of the eight artists who participated in this project were mentioned above. Refer to Hervé Gauville, *L'Art depuis 1945 (groupes et mouvements)*, (Paris: Hazan, 2007), 90. On the other hand, the term 'Figuration Libre' was coined by Ben Vautier (1935–) after visiting the exhibition of Combas and Di Rosa in Nice in the summer of the same year. Catherine Flohic, *Eighty: Les Peintres en France dans les années 80*, no. 27, (Paris: Eighty magazine, 1989), 63.

22. Hervé Perdriolle, *Figuration libre: une initiation à la culture mass-médias*, (Éditions Axe-Sud, 1985), 4.

23. Hervé Gauville, ibid., (Paris: Hazan, 2007), 92.

24. Catherine Flohic, *Eighty: Les Peintres en France dans les années 80*, no. 17, (Paris: Eighty magazine), 1987, 62.

Viewers who expected the world reproduced in the frame realized that the aura of painting was nothing but an illusion created by convention as they confronted canvas fabric itself or rectangular wooden supports in the same context. Artists of the Supports/Surfaces movement created a completely different type of painting through ceaseless analysis of each physical component that constituted the medium. They took a step further and questioned the exhibition space, which contributed to the mythification of the discipline. To reject the conventional method of hanging works on the wall according to the viewer's eye level, they let their works hang from the ceiling or lay on the floor. The aforementioned exhibition *Intérieur/Extérieur* can also be understood as a part of their avant-garde experiment, an attempt to suggest a new distribution network for art away from art museums and galleries. Afterward, the Supports/Surfaces movement artists split into two groups: Paris-based artists who wished to combine their work with political ideology and Southern France-based artists who wanted to continue analyzing the pure nature of painting as a medium. The group officially disbanded after their last group exhibition in June 1971.

Back to Figuration: Figuration Libre

The Supports/Surfaces movement was similar to Conceptual art, Minimalism, and Land art in that they challenged the institutions and rejected the mythification of painting. Their analytical and intellectual attitudes were challenged and inspired the revived interest in figuration art in the 1980s. In the early 1980s, some of the young artists in their early 20s at the time such as Rémi Blanchard (1958–1993), François Boisrond (1959–), Robert Combas (1957–), and Herbé Di Rosa (1959–) stood out with their figurative works.[21] They were later were referred to as Figuration Libre artists. Figuration Libre artists were influenced mainly by popular cultures such as cartoons and rock music. They presented works seemingly opposite previous generations', using childlike and exaggerated speech and the production style reminiscent of erotic and violent lower-class culture. In the case of Boisrond, he utilized cartoon-frame-like composition to produce autobiographical works depicting personal memories or whimsical moments of daily life. [11]

Hervé Perdriolle (1954–), who curated several exhibitions for the Figuration Libre artists, wrote in *FIGURATION LIBRE: une initiation a la culture mass media* that he wanted his book to remain as an ordinary consumer product rather than a book about theory; this exemplifies the core spirit of the Figuration Libre movement.[22] The Figuration Libre artists did not consider art museums or galleries to be the only places for their art and began actively responding to commercial requests in 1982. They voluntarily produced posters for the food company Félix Potin or, in the case of Di Rosa, participated in the production of toys for a company called Starlux.[23] Di Rosa once said in an interview that "my heart flutters when I think about how modern art had been a prerogative of the elites. Rock music and classical music, paintings and cartoons, culture stepped down from the pedestal ... I want everything to be on the same level."[24]

21. 자유 구상 작가들이 파리 미술계의 주목을 받기 시작한 것은 1981년 6월에 열렸던 《멋지게 끝나다 (Finir en beauté)》라는 전시회부터이다. 이 전시회는 비평가이자, 『예술가들(Artistes)』이라는 잡지의 편집장이었던 베르나르 라마르쉬-바델 (Bernard Lamarche-Vadel, 1949-2000)의 기획 하에 개최되었으며, 바델의 집이 전시의 장소로 이용되었다. 여기에 참여했던 8명의 작가들 중 4명이 앞서 언급한 자유 구상 작가들이었다. Hervé Gauville, 위의 책, 90. 한편, '자유 구상'이라는 명칭은 같은 해 여름에 니스에서 열렸던 꽁바스와 디 로사의 전시회를 방문한 벤(Ben Vautier, 1935-)이 그들의 작품을 보고 만든 용어이다. Catherine Flohic, Eighty: Les Peintres en France dans les années 80, no. 27 (Paris: Eighty magazine, 1989), 63.

22. Hervé Perdriolle, Figuration libre: une initiation à la culture mass-medias, (Éditions Axe-Sud 1985), 4.

23. Hervé Gauville, 같은 책, 92.

24. Catherine Flohic, Eighty: Les Peintres en France dans les années 80, no. 17 (Paris: Eighty magazine, 1987), 62.

액자 틀 안의 재현된 세계를 기대했던 관람자들은 캔버스 천 자체가 하나의 작품이 되거나, 덩그러니 사각 형태의 틀만 남겨진 나무 지지대를 마주하게 되면서, 그간 회화가 지녀왔던 아우라가 관습에 의해 만들어진 허구였음을 깨닫게 되었다. 쉬포르 쉬르파스 작가들은 회화를 구성하던 각각의 사물들에 대한 끊임없는 분석을 통해 전혀 다른 새로운 유형의 회화를 탄생시켰다. 그리고 더 나아가 회화가 지녔던 신화를 만드는데 일조해온 전시 공간에 대해서도 의문을 제기하면서, 관람자의 눈높이에 맞춰 작품을 벽에 걸어놓았던 기존의 방식을 거부하고, 작품을 천장에 매달거나 바닥에 늘어뜨리는 등의 시도를 보여준다. 앞서 보았던 《실내/실외》전도 미술관이나 갤러리로부터 벗어나 미술작품의 새로운 유통망을 제시하고자 했던 쉬포르 쉬르파스 그룹의 전위적인 실험의 일환이었다고 볼 수 있다. 이후 쉬포르 쉬르파스 그룹은, 작업과 정치 이데올로기를 결합하고자 했던 파리 중심의 작가들과 회화 매체의 순수한 성질의 분석에 계속 매진하고자 했던 남프랑스 중심의 작가들로 분열되어, 1971년 6월 그룹으로서의 마지막 전시회를 끝으로 공식적으로 해체된다.

[11]
프랑수아 브와롱, 〈인간 박물관 I〉, 1980, 캔버스에 아크릴, 208×197.5cm, 퐁피두 센터, 파리.
François Boisrond, Human Museum I (Musee de l'Hommel), 1980, Acrylic on canvas, 208×197.5 cm, Centre Pompidou, Paris.

다시 구상으로: 자유 구상(Figuration Libre)

쉬포르 쉬르파스 작가들의 작업은 제도권에 도전하고, 회화의 환영주의를 거부했다는 점에서 동시대의 개념미술이나 미니멀리즘, 대지미술과 상당 부분 공유하는 지점이 있었다. 쉬포르 쉬르파스 작가들의 분석적이고 지적인 작업 태도와 그 결과물은 1980년대에 이르러 그에 반(反)하는 예술 경향으로서 구상 미술이 또다시 부상하는 계기로 작용한다. 1980년대 초, 당시 20대 초반의 젊은 작가들이었던 레미 블랑샤르(Rémi Blanchard, 1958-1993)와 프랑수아 브와롱(François Boisrond, 1959-), 로베르 꽁바스(Robert Combas, 1957-), 에르베 디 로사(Hervé Di Rosa, 1959-) 등은 구상회화를 통해 두각을 나타내기 시작하면서, 일명 '자유 구상' 작가들로 불리게 된다.[21] 이들은 주로 만화나 록 음악과 같은 대중문화로부터 영향을 받아, 서투르면서도 과장된 화법, 에로틱하고 폭력적인 저급문화를 연상시키는 연출 등을 통해 이전 세대와는 정반대라 할 수 있는 작업들을 선보였다. 예컨대, 자유 구상 작가 중 한 명인 브와롱은 만화 이미지와 같은 화면에 자신만이 알 수 있는 기억들을 묘사한 자전적인 작업이나, 개인적인 일상을 그린 작품들을 제작했다[11]. 자유 구상과 관련한 다수의 전시를 기획했던 에르베 페드리올(Hervé Perdriolle, 1954-)은 『자유 구상: 대중매체 문화의 입문서(Figuration libre: une initiation à la culture mass-medias)』에서 자신의 저서조차 하나의 이론서이기보다는 흔한 소비상품으로 남기를 바란다고 서술하고 있는데, 이는 자유 구상 작가들의 미술작품에 대한 태도를 함축하고 있다.[22] 자유 구상 작가들은 미술관이나 갤러리를 그들의 작품을 보여줄 수 있는 유일한 장소로 생각하지 않았으며, 이에 1982년부터 적극적으로 상업적인 주문에 응하기 시작한다. 그들은 자발적으로 펠릭스 포탱(Félix Potin) 식료품 회사의 광고 포스터를 제작하거나, 디 로사의 경우 스타뤽스(Starlux) 회사의 장난감 제작에 참여하였다.[23] 디 로사는 한 인터뷰에서 "현대미술은 엘리트들의 전유물이었고, 나는 그 사실에 (화가 나서) 심장이 벌렁거렸다. 록 음악과 클래식, 회화와 만화, 좌대에서 내려온 문화... 나는 모든 것들이 같은 높이에 있기를 바란다."고 술회했다.[24]

25. In 1979, a group called Transavanguardia formed in Italy under the support of critic Achille Bonito-Oliva (1939–) Like the French Figuration Libre artists, Transavanguardia also had a skeptical attitude toward Minimalism and Arte Povera. They brought forth Giorgio de Chirico (1888–1978), a master of Italian art, to the frontline in reviving the figurative paintings in their home country.

26. Interestingly, this exhibition also included artists from the Supports/Surfaces movement such as Viallat.

The rise of figurative art in the 1980s was not limited to France.[25] German artists who had already been active since the 1960s, such as Georg Baselitz (1938–), Gerhard Richter (1932–), and Sigma Polke (1941–2010), pivoted the revival of figurative art in the country in the 1980s. Baselitz, Marcus Lüpertz (1941–), [12] and A. R. Penck (1939–2017) participated in the exhibition *Die Neuen Wilden* held in Aachen in 1980, showcasing that painting has again begun to express the experiences of modern people, especially pain and anxiety.[26] After the construction of the Berlin Wall in 1961, German figurative artists found themselves in West Germany, which achieved economic stability with the US Marshall Plan. They paid attention to the alienation of Germans hidden behind material wealth and the memories of the wars swallowed up by the splendor of the mass media. From 1963, Polke expresses photographic images of mass media with halftone dots to reveal their mechanical essence. His work exposed the loopholes of such images, which led the audience to reconsider the flashy images from mass media that embroidered society of the time. In addition, Richter brought out the trauma inherent in ordinary photographs through his unique photographic painting. The different approach to artistic experimentation between France and Germany highlights the different moods of the two countries at the time. In contrast to the Figuration Libre artists in France who tried to reflect the tastes of the younger generation by actively incorporating the vulgar aspects of popular culture and discourse, the Germans dealt with heavy and severe subjects such as their bleak perspective on mass media, the Holocaust, and the wars.

Conclusion

Since the 1960s, artists in the West have grown to be incredibly conscious of the boundaries and hierarchies that have been passed down from the past. They have been challenging the homogeneous categorization of art into painting and sculpture, hierarchies between so-called high-end and low-end art, and the unquestioned authority of genius artists. Such aspects can all be found even in what we have discussed in this essay. The works of Nouveau Réalisme artists used mundane objects, worn-out posters, and old scraps of metal. Nouvelle Figuration artists implicitly and explicitly devised images of mass reproduction and helped break down the walls between traditional genres, fine art, and popular culture. In the case of Supports/Surfaces artists, they entered the lives of ordinary people with their works and narrowed the distance between art and life, gradually cultivating a more intimate relationship between artists and the audience. This essay attempted to examine the efforts and traces of French artists struggling in their distinctive way within the context of Western contemporary art. *Highlights of MMCA Global Art Collection from the 1980s–1990s: To the World through Art* at the National Museum of Modern and Contemporary Art will be an opportunity to see and appreciate their works.

[12]
마르쿠스 뤼페르츠, 〈철학자의 기억〉, 1985, 캔버스에 유채, 162×130cm
Markus LUPERTZ, *Memory of Philosopher*, 1985, Oil on canvas, 162×130 cm

25. 1979년 이탈리아에서도 비평가 아킬레 보니토 올리바(Achille Bonito-Oliva, 1939-)의 지지 하에 트랜스 아방가르드 그룹(Transavanguardia)이 등장하였으며, 이 그룹도 프랑스의 자유 구상 작가들과 마찬가지로 개념적인 경향의 미니멀리즘과 아르테 포베라에 비판적인 입장을 드러냈다. 이들은 이탈리아 미술의 거장인 조르조 데 키리코(Giorgio de Chirico, 1888-1978)를 내세우며 자국에서의 구상 회화의 부활에 힘을 쏟았다.

26. 이 전시회에는 흥미롭게도 비알라를 비롯한 쉬포르 쉬르파스 작가들도 참여했다.

한편, 1980년대의 이러한 구상미술의 부상은 비단 프랑스에만 국한된 움직임은 아니었다.[25] 독일에서는 1960년대부터 이미 활동해왔던 게오르그 바젤리츠(Georg Baselitz, 1938-)나 게르하르트 리히터(Gerhard Richter, 1932-), 지그마르 폴케(Sigmar Polke 1941-2010)와 같은 작가들을 중심으로 1980년대의 구상미술의 부흥을 이끌었다. 1980년 아헨(Aachen)이라는 도시에서 있었던 《신야수파(Die Neuen Wilden)》전에는 바젤리츠를 비롯하여 마르쿠스 뤼페르츠(Markus Lüpertz, 1941-)[12], A. R. 펭크(A. R. Penck, 1939-2017) 등이 참여하였는데, 이 전시는 회화가 다시 현대인들의 삶의 경험들, 그중에서도 고통과 불안 등을 표현하기 시작했음을 알리는 계기가 된다.[26] 독일의 구상 작가들은 1961년 베를린 장벽이 세워진 이후, 미국의 마셜 플랜의 원조를 기반으로 경제적 안정을 이룬 서독에서 활동하였다. 그러나 이들이 주목한 것은 물질적 풍요로움 뒤에 가려진 독일인들의 소외나, 대중매체의 화려함이 삼켜버린 전쟁의 기억 같은 것들이었다. 폴케의 경우, 1963년부터 대중매체의 사진 이미지를 망점으로 표현함으로써 그 기계적 본질을 드러내면서도, 그러한 이미지들이 지니는 허점을 폭로하는 작업을 보여줌으로써 당대 사회를 수놓았던 현란한 대중매체 이미지들을 재고하게 했다. 또한 리히터는 특유의 사진 회화를 통해 평범한 사진들 속에 내재해있는 트라우마를 끄집어내는 작업을 보여주었다. 개인만이 알 수 있는 내밀한 일화들이나 의도적으로 대중문화의 저속한 면을 강조하며 당대 젊은 세대의 취향을 담으려 했던 프랑스의 자유 구상 작가들과는 대조적으로, 대중매체 이미지에 대한 차가운 시선이나 유대인 학살, 전쟁과 같은 무겁고 진지한 주제를 다루었던 독일 작가들은 비슷한 시기 두 국가의 상이한 사회적 배경을 대변하고 있다.

나가며

1960년대 이후의 서구 미술가들은 과거로부터 이어져 온 다양한 경계와 위계에 문제의식을 가지고, 회화와 조각으로 구분되어왔던 장르 간의 경계나 소위 말하는 고급미술과 저급미술 사이의 위계, 천재 예술가가 지녀왔던 절대적 권위 등에 도전해왔다. 앞서 살펴보았던 프랑스 현대미술 속에서도 우리는 그러한 면면들을 발견할 수 있다. 자질구레한 물건들이나 해진 포스터, 낡은 고철 등을 이용한 누보 레알리즘의 작품들과 대량 복제된 이미지들을 직간접적으로 도입했던 구상 작가들의 작업은 전통적인 장르뿐 아니라, 순수미술과 대중문화 간의 벽을 허무는데 일조하였다. 또, 평범한 이들의 삶 속에 들어가 작품을 전시했던 쉬포르 쉬르파스 작가들은 예술과 삶의 거리를 좁히고, 예술가와 관람자가 상호 간 영향을 주고받을 수 있는 수평적인 관계로 나아가도록 하였다. 이 글은 서양 현대미술의 흐름 속에서 프랑스 미술가들이 분투해온 노력과 흔적을 살펴보고자 하였다. 이번 국립현대미술관의 소장품 전시회인 《미술로, 세계로》를 통해 앞서 살펴보았던 프랑스 현대미술의 작품들을 직접 보고 감상할 수 있는 기회가 되기를 바란다.

국립현대미술관 해외작품 소장작가 리스트
MMCA Global Art Collection Artists since established in 1969

아메리카(America)

멕시코(Mexico)

카를로스 토레스(Carlos TORRES)	1949-
호르헤 두본(Jorge DUBON)	1938-2004

미국(USA)

게리 시몬스(Gary SIMMONS)	1964-
김보현(KIM Po)	1917-2014
김원숙(KIM Wonsook)	1953-
김종성(KIMM Jongsoung)	1935-
니콜라스 스페라키스(Nicholas SPERAKIS)	1943-
니키리(Nikki S. LEE)	1970-
데니스 애덤스(Dennis ADAMS)	1948-
데니스 오펜하임(Dennis OPPENHEIM)	1938-2011
데비한(Debbie HAN)	1969-
도널드 저드(Donald JUDD)	1928-1994
랄프 깁슨(Ralph GIBSON)	1939-
래디 존 딜(Laddie John DILL)	1943-
레오나르드 그레이(Leonard J. GRAY)	1925-2019
로렌스 웨이너(Lawrence WEINER)	1942-2021
로버트 라우센버그(Robert RAUSCHENBERG)	1925-2008
로버트 이벤도르프(Robert EBENDORF)	1938-
로스 블렉크너(Ross BLECKNER)	1949-
루돌프 칼 고르만(Rudolph Carl GORMAN)	1931-2005
루이즈 부르주아(Louise BOURGEOIS)	1911-2010
리처드 아누스카이비치(Richard ANUSZKIEWICZ)	1930-2020
리처드 프랭크린(Richard FRANKLIN)	1930-
마이크 앤드 덕 스탄(Mike & Doug STARN)	1961-
마이클 헤이든(Michael HAYDEN)	1961-
마저리 시크(Marjorie SCHICK)	1941-2017
매튜 토마스(Mattew THOMAS)	연도미상(Date Unknown)
메릴린 다 실바(Marilyn DA SILVA)	1952-
민병옥(MIN Byoungok)	1941-
바바라 크루거(Barbara KRUGER)	1945-
바버라 블룸(Barbara BLOOM)	1951-
백남준(Nam June PAIK)	1932-2006
베니 카맨(Beanie KAMAN)	1954-
베티 골드(Betty GOLD)	1935-
브라이언 헌트(Bryan HUNT)	1947-
빌 비올라(Bill VIOLA)	1951-
사토루 아베(Satoru ABE)	1926-
샌디 스코글런드(Sandy SKOGLUND)	1946-
샘 채컬리언(Sam TCHAKALIAN)	1929-2004
샘 프란시스(Sam FRANCIS)	1923-1994
신디 셔먼(Cindy SHERMAN)	1954-
신현광(SHIN Hyunkwang)	1936-
아르망(Arman)	1928-2005
아이작 위트킨(Isaac WITKIN)	1936-2006
안드레스 세라노(Andres SERRANO)	1950-

애이드리언 워커 호워드(Adrienne Walker HOARD)	1946-
앤디 워홀(Andy WARHOL)	1928-1987
앨런 맥컬럼(Allan MCCOLLUM)	1944-
앨런 캐프로(Allan KAPROW)	1927-2006
에릭 오르(Eric ORR)	1939-1998
에머트 윌리엄스(Emmett WILLIAMS)	1925-2007
웨인 숀필드(Wayne SCHOENFELD)	1948-
윌리엄 데일리(William DALEY)	1925-
자크 블라스(Zach BLAS)	1981-
장-미셸 바스키아(Jean-Michel BASQUIAT)	1960-1988
재커리 폼왈트(Zachary FORMWALT)	1979-
잭 다 실바(Jack DA SILVA)	연도미상(Date Unknown)
정연희(Younhee CHUNG PAIK)	1945-
제니 홀저(Jenny HOLZER)	1950-
제임스 로젠퀴스트(James ROSENQUIST)	1933-2017
제임스 카세베르(James CASEBERE)	1953-
제프 러셀(Jeff RUSSELL)	1942-
조나단 보로프스키(Jonathan BOROFSKY)	1942-
조지 시걸(George SEGAL)	1924-2000
존 배(John PAI)	1937-
존 케이지(John CAGE)	1912-1992
존 팔(John PFAHL)	1939-2020
죠셉 피아센틴(Joseph PIASENTIN)	1950-
줄리언 슈나벨(Julian SCHNABEL)	1951-
줄스 올리츠키(Jules OLITSKI)	1922-2007
짐 다인(Jim DINE)	1935-
척 클로즈(Chuck CLOSE)	1940-2021
캐롤 서머스(Carol SUMMERS)	1925-2016
커크 맹거스(Kirk MANGUS)	1952-2013
크리스토(Christo JAVACHEFF)	1935-2020
탈 스트리터(Tal STREETER)	1934-2014
토니 마시(Tony MARSH)	1954-
토니 벌란트(Tony BERLANT)	1941-
톰 위셀만(Tom WESSELMANN)	1931-2004
톰 크럼팩(Tom KRUMPAK)	1949-
팀 프렌티스(Tim PRENTICE)	1930-
폴 개린(Paul GARRIN)	1957-
프랭크 스텔라(Frank STELLA)	1936-
프레드 펜스터(Fred FENSTER)	1934-
피터 칼라스(Peter CALLAS)	1952-
피터 핼리(Peter HALLEY)	1953-

베네수엘라(Venezuela)

헤수스 라파엘 소토(Jesus Rafael SOTO)	1923-2005

브라질(Brazil)

고영자(KOH Youngja)	1944-
프란스 크라이츠베르그(Frans KRAJBERG)	1921-2017

아르헨티나(Argentina)

미겔 앙헬 리오스(Miguel Angel RIOS)	1943-
히울라 코시세(Gyula KOSICE)	1924-2016

우루과이(Uruguay)

엘비오 마제(Elbio MAZET)	1939-

칠레(Chile)

로베르토 마타(Roberto MATTA)	1911-2002
마리오 토랄(Mario TORAL)	1934-
이반 나바로(Ivan NAVARRO)	1972-

캐나다(Canada)

소렐 이트로그(Sorel ETROG)	1933-2014
알렉산드라 해세커(Alexandra HAESEKER)	1945-

콜롬비아(Columbia)

에드가르 네그레트(Edgar NEGRET)	1920-2012
페르난도 보테로(Fernando BOTERO)	1932-

쿠바(Cuba)

아구스틴 카르데나스 알폰소(Augustin CARDENAS AIFONSO)	1927-2001

페루(Peru)

페르난도 데 시슬로(Fernando DE SZYSZLO)	1925-2017

푸에르토리코(Puerto Rico)

루이스 에르난데스 크루즈(Luis Hernandez CRUZ)	1936-

아시아(Asia)

네팔(Nepal)

람 쿠마르 판다이(Ram Kumar PANDAY)	1946-
케사브 프라사드 말라(Keshav Prasad MALLA)	1944-

레바논(Lebanon)

로저 스페이르(Roger SFEIR)	1952-
아크람 쟈타리(Akram ZAATARI)	1966-
왈리드 라드(Walid RAAD)	1967-

말레이시아(Malaysia)

롱 티엔신(Long THIEN-SHIH)	1946-

몽골(Mongolia)

문키짐 츄르티민(Munkhjin TSULTEMIN)	1953-

스리랑카(Sri Lanka)

H. A. 카루나라트네(H. A. KARUNARATNE)	1929-

싱가포르(Singapore)

탄 스위얀(TAN Swiehian)	1943-
호 추 니엔(HO Tzu Nyen)	1976-

우즈베키스탄(Uzbekistan)

신순남(Nikolai sergeevich SHIN)	1928-2006

이란(Iran)

가셈 하지쟈데(Ghasem HAJIZADEH)	1947-

이스라엘(Israel)

다니 카라반(Dani KARAVAN)	1930-2021
다비드 아다리(David ADARY)	1942-
오페 르루쉬(Ofer LELLOUCHE)	1947-

인도(India)

날리니 말라니(Nalini MALANI)	1946-
라젠드라 다완(Rajendra DHAWAN)	1936-2012
사티쉬 판찰(Satish PANCHAL)	1935-
아누팜 수드(Anupam SUD)	1944-
아키탐 나라야난(Akkitam NARAYANAN)	1939-
요게쉬 바브(Yogesh BARVE)	1989-
요겐 쵸드리(Jogen CHOWDHURY)	1939-

인도네시아(Indonesia)

압둘 자릴 피로우스(Abdul Djalil PIROUS)	1932-
티모테우스 A. 쿠스노(Timoteus A. KUSNO)	1989-

일본(Japan)

가와카미 리키조(KAWAKAMI Rikijo)	1935-
가키자키 히로시(KAKIZAKI Hiroshi)	1946-
가타야마 단(KATAYAMA Tan)	연도미상(Date Unknown)
가토 쇼린진(KATO Shorinjin)	1898-1983
고바다케 히로시(KOBADAKE Hiroshi)	1935-
고바야시 고헤이(KOBAYASHI Kohei)	1974-
고삼권(GO Samgwon)	1939-
고시야 겐이치(KOSHIYA Kenichi)	1943-
고토 마이크(KOTO Mike)	1943-
곽덕준(KWAK Duckjun)	1937-
구로사키 아키라(KUROSAKI Akira)	1937-2019
기무라 고스케(KIMURA Kosuke)	1936-
기무라 마사노부(KIMURA Masanobu)	1941-2021
나카무라 고헤이(NAKAMURA Kohei)	1951-
나카무라 교이치(NAKAMURA Kyoichi)	1949-
나카바야시 다다요시(NAKABAYASHI Tadayoshi)	1937-
노다 데쓰야(NODA Tetsuya)	1940-
노자키 요시오(NOZAKI Yoshio)	연도미상(Date Unknown)
니즈마 미노루(NIZUMA Minoru)	1930-1998
다나베 가주로(TANABE Kazuro)	1937-
다나베 미쓰아키(TANABE Mitsuaki)	1939-2015
데시가하라 히로시(TESHIGAHARA Hiroshi)	1927-2001
데즈카 아이코(TEZUKA Aiko)	1976-
도리이 노보루(TORII Noboru)	1918-2011
모토나가 사다마사(MOTONAGA Sadamasa)	1922-2011
문승근(MOON Seungkeun)	1947-1982
미나미카와 시몬(MINAMIKAWA Shimon)	1972-
바바 아키라(BABA Akira)	1932-2000
박일남(PARK Ilnam)	1957-
사사키 도오루(SASAKI Tohru)	1949-2007
사이토 요시시게(SAITO Yoshishige)	1904-2001
소마키 고이치(SOMAKI Koichi)	1952-
시미즈 렌도쿠(SHIMIZU Rentoku)	1904-1995
쓰지 히사시(TSUJI Hisashi)	1884-1974
아라이 요시노리(ARAI Yoshinori)	1949-
아이-오(Ay-O)	1931-

안도 요시시게(ANDO Yoshishige) 1888-1967
야마나카 젠(YAMANAKA Gen) 1954-
야마모토 요코(YAMAMOTO Yoko) 1952-
야자키 가쓰미(YAZAKI Katsumi) 1940-
오가와 고이치(OGAWA Koichi) 1950-
오노 다다시(ONO Tadashi) 1960-
오노사토 도시노부(ONOSATO Toshinobu) 1912-1986
오카다 마사히로(OKADA Masahiro) 1947-
오카베 마사오(OKABE Masao) 1942-
오타 사부로(OTA Saburo) 1950-
와타나베 도요시게(WATANABE Toyoshige) 1931-
요시다 호다카(YOSHIDA Hodaka) 1926-1995
요코미조 시즈카(YOKOMIZO Shizuka) 1966-
요코오 다다노리(YOKOO Tadanori) 1936-
우다 슈잔(UDA Shuzan) 1877-1945
우에다 기미오(UEDA Kimio) 연도미상(Date Unknown)
우치다 하루유키(UCHIDA Haruyuki) 1952-
이노우에 고조(INOUE Kozo) 1937-2017
이다 쇼이치(IDA Shoichi) 1941-2006
이시가키 미쓰오(ISHIGAKI Mitsuo) 1942-1991
이와시타 히로미치(IWASITA Hiromichi) 1942-
이치하라 아리노리(ICHIHARA Arinori) 1910-2010
이타타니 미치코(ITATANI Michiko) 1948-
케이 오마타(Kay OMATA) 연도미상(Date Unknown)
쿠사마 야요이(KUSAMA Yayoi) 1929-
하라 다케시(HARA Takeshi) 1942-
하세가와 쇼이치(HASEGAWA Shoichi) 1929-
후루도이 고지(FURUDOI Koji) 1947-2008
후루이케 다이스케(FURUIKE Daisuke) 1973-
후지이 히카루(FUJII Hikaru) 1976-
히라타 미노루(HIRATA Minoru) 1930-2018

중국(China)
런순청(REN Shuncheng) 1951-
류예자오(LIU Yezhao) 1910-2003
리 솽(LI Shuang) 1957-
리커란(LI Keran) 1907-1989
양지앙 그룹(Yangjiang Group) 2002
양푸둥(YANG Fudong) 1971-
위안윈성(YUAN Yunsheng) 1937-
장자오선(JIANG Zhaoshen) 1925-1996
천원링(Chen WENLING) 1969-
타오 후이(TAO Hui) 1987-
피아오 광시에(PIAO Guangxie) 1970-
황지에(HUANG Jie) 1902-1995

카자흐스탄(Kazakhstan)
김세르게이(Sergei Duhaevich KIM) 1952-

타이완(Taiwan)
니하오(Ni Hao) 1989-
랴오시우핑(LIAO Shiou-ping) 1936-
리스츠(LEE Shichi) 1938-
장쉬잔(ZHANG Xuzhan) 1988-
장자오탕(CHANG Chaotang) 1943-
처우잉(CHOU Ying) 1922-2011

태국(Thailand)
타본 코-우돔비트(Thavorn KO-UDOMVIT) 1956-
프리사 아르준카(Pricha ARJUNKA) 1936-

터키(Turkey)
사르키스(Sarkis ZABUNYAN) 1938-

파키스탄(Pakistan)
바시르 미르자(Bashir MIRZA) 1941-2000
이스마일 구르지(Ismail GULGEE) 1926-2007

필리핀(Philippines)
마누엘 발데모르(Manuel BALDEMOR) 1947-
비르질리오 아비아도(Virgilio AVIADO) 1944-
파시타 아바드(Pacita ABAD) 1946-2004

아프리카(Africa)

남아프리카 공화국(Republic of South Africa)
윌리엄 켄트리지(William KENTRIDGE) 1955-

알제리(Algeria)
모한드 아마라(Mohand AMARA) 1952-

카메룬(Cameroon)
파스칼 켄파크(Pascal KENFACK) 1950-

코트디부아르(Ivory Coast)
미셸 코조(Michel KODJO) 1935-2021
크라 엔게산(Kra N'GUESSAN) 1954-

튀니지(Tunisia)
아메드 하제리(Ahmed HAJERI) 1948-
헤디 터키(Hedi TURKI) 1922-2019

오세아니아(Oceania)

오스트레일리아(Australia)

나이젤 헬리어(Nigel HELYER)	1951-
로렌스 다우스(Lawrence DAWS)	1927-
로버트 쥬니퍼(Robert JUNIPER)	1929-2012
로잘리 가스코인(Rosaile GASCOIGNE)	1917-1999
반덕 마리카(Banduk MARIKA)	1954-2021
브룩 앤드류(Brook ANDREW)	1970-
시드니 놀란(Sidney NOLAN)	1917-1992
시드니 볼(Sydney BALL)	1933-2017
아서 보이드(Arthur BOYD)	1920-1999
안젤리카 메시티(Angelica Mesiti)	1976-
앤 톰슨(Ann THOMSON)	1933-
얀 센베르그스(Jan SENBERGS)	1939-
자네트 버칠(Janet BURCHILL)	1955-
제니 왓슨(Jenny WATSON)	1951-
존 닉슨(John NIXON)	1949-
존 영(John YOUNG)	1956-
존 올센(John OLSEN)	1928-
찰리 소포(Charlie SOFO)	1983-
켄 언스워드(Ken UNSWORTH)	1931-
팀 스토리어(Tim STORRIER)	1949-
피터 틴댈(Peter TYNDALL)	1951-

유럽(Europe)

그리스(Greece)

디오한디(DIOHANDI)	1945-
코스타 카라하리오스(Kosta KARAHALIOS)	1923-2007

네덜란드(Netherlands)

마르크 브뤼서(Mark BRUSSE)	1937-
알폰스 프레이뮈트(Alphons FREYMUTH)	1940-
휴버트 보스(Hubert VOS)	1855-1935

노르웨이(Norway)

마리안네 헤스케(Marianne HESKE)	1946-

덴마크(Denmark)

비요른 뇌르가르(Bjorn NORGAARD)	1947-
예스퍼 유스트(Jesper JUST)	1974-
카를-헤닝 페데르센(Carl-Henning PEDERSEN)	1913-2007
폴 야누스 입센(Poul Janus IPSEN)	1936-

독일(Germany)

A. R. 펭크(A. R. PENCK)	1939-2017
게르하르트 리히터(Gerhard RICHTER)	1932-
게오르크 바젤리츠(Georg BASELITZ)	1938-
고타르트 그라우브너(Gotthard GRAUBNER)	1930-2013
귄터 위커(Gunther UECKER)	1930-
노르베르트 비스키(Norbert BISKY)	1970-
노은님(RO Eun-nim)	1946-
로레 베르트(Lore BERT)	1936-

로제마리 트로켈(Rosemarie TROCKEL)	1952-
마르쿠스 뤼페르츠(Markus LUPERTZ)	1941-
만프레트 레베(Manfred LEVE)	1936-2012
베르나르트 슐체(Bernard SCHULTZE)	1915-2005
베르너 크뤼거(Werner KRUGER)	1917-
베른트 베허+힐라 베허(Bernd BECHER+Hilla BECHER)	1931-2007 / 1934-2015
벤 빌리켄스(Ben WILLIKENS)	1939-
볼프 포스텔(Wolf VOSTELL)	1932-1998
볼프강 라이프(Wolfgang LAIB)	1950-
송현숙(SONG Hyunsook)	1952-
안젤름 키퍼(Anselm KIEFER)	1945-
얀 포스(Jan VOSS)	1936-
외르크 임멘도르프(Jorg IMMENDORFF)	1945-2007
요제프 보이스(Joseph BEUYS)	1921-1986
이미 크뇌벨(Imi KNOEBEL)	1940-
일리아 하이니히(Ilja HEINIG)	1950-
지그마르 폴케(Sigmar POLKE)	1941-2010
칸디다 회퍼(Candida HOFER)	1944-
클라우스 페터 브레머(Klaus Peter BREHMER)	1938-1997
클라우스 하이더(Klaus HEIDER)	1936-2013
키키 스미스(Kiki SMITH)	1954-
토마스 스트루스(Thomas STRUTH)	1954-
피터 클라센(Peter KLASEN)	1935-
하룬 파로키(Harun FAROCKI)	1944-2014
한스 하케(Hans HAACKE)	1936-
헤르만 클라인크네히트(Hermann KLEINKNECHT)	1943-
히토 슈타이얼(Hito STEYERL)	1966-

러시아(Russia)

마르크 샤갈(Marc CHAGALL)	1887-1985
변월룡(PEN Varlen)	1916-1990
안톤 비도클(Anton VIDOKLE)	1965-
일리아 카바코프(Ilya KABAKOV)	1933-
프란시스코 인판테-아라나(Francisco INFANTE-ARANA)	1943-

루마니아(Romania)

소린 일포베아누(Sorin ILFOVEANU)	1946-
알렉산드루 칼리네스(ALEXANDRU CALINESCU ARGHIRA)	1935-2018

벨기에(Belgium)

뤼크 페이르(Luc PEIRE)	1916-1994
얀 방리에(Jan VANRIET)	1948-
클로드 라이르(Claude RAHIR)	1937-2007

불가리아(Bulgaria)

니콜라이 마이스트로프(Nikolay MAYSTOROV)	1943-
스토얀 트자네브(Stojan TZANEV)(Stoyan Tsanev)	1946-2019
이반 칸체프(Ivan KANCHEV)	1973-
크룸 다먀노프(Krum DAMYANOV)	1937-

스웨덴(Sweden)

벤트 린드스트렘(Bengt LINDSTROM)	1925-2008
아니카 스티에른뢰프(Annica STIERNLOF)	1941-
에리크 디에트만(Erik DIETMAN)	1937-2002
카를 오토 훌텐(Karl Otto HULTEN)	1916-2015
카를 프레드릭 레우테르스베르트(Carl Fredrik REUTERSWARD)	1934-2016
알로이스 두바흐(Alois DUBACH)	1947-
알폰소 휘피(Alfonso Huppi)	1935-
올리비에 모세(Olivier MOSSET)	1944-
장 팅겔리(Jean TINGUELY)	1925-1991
피터 크나프(Peter KNAPP)	1931-

스페인(Spain)

라파엘 카노가르(Rafael CANOGAR)	1935-
발도메로 페스타나(Baldomero PESTANA)	1918-2015
살바도르 달리(Salvador DALI)	1904-1989
안토니 타피에스(Antoni TAPIES)	1923-2012
파블로 피카소(Pablo PICASSO)	1881-1973
페르난도 산 마르틴 페(Fernando San Martin PEREZ)	1930-
호세프 수비락스(Josep M. SUBIRACHS)	1927-2014
호안 미로(Joan MIRO)	1893-1983

슬로바키아(Slovakia)

알렉스 믈리나르치크(Alex MLYNARCIK)	1934-
요제프 양코비치(Jozef JANKOVIC)	1937-2017
이리 게오르그 도코우필(Jiri Georg DOKOUPIL)	1954-

슬로베니아(Slovenian)

요제 치우하(Joze CIUHA)	1924-2015

아이슬란드(Iceland)

에로(Erro)	1932-

영국(United Kingdom)

나이젤 홀(Nigel HALL)	1943-
데이비드 내시(David NASH)	1945-
데이비드 호크니(David HOCKNEY)	1937-
리처드 해밀턴(Richard HAMILTON)	1922-2011
보이드 웹(Boyd WEBB)	1947-
사이먼 놀포크(Simon NORFOLK)	1963-
앤디 골즈워시(Andy GOLDSWORTHY)	1956-
앤서니 카로(Anthony Caro)	1924-2013
존 크리스토포루(John CHRISTOFOROU)	1921-2014
토니 크랙(Tony CRAGG)	1949-
토니 햅번(Tony HEPBURN)	1942-2015
하워드 호드킨(Howard HODGKIN)	1932-2017

오스트리아(Austria)

레오 초크마이어(Leo ZOGMAYER)	1949-
아르눌프 라이너(Arnulf RAINER)	1929-

이탈리아(Italy)

마시모 비탈리(Massimo VITALI)	1944-
마우로 스타치올리(Mauro STACCIOLI)	1937-2018
미켈란젤로 피스톨레토(Michelangelo PISTOLETTO)	1933-
밈모 팔라디노(Mimmo PALADINO)	1948-
바네사 비크로프트(Vanesa BEECROFT)	1969-
아킬레 페릴리(Achille PERILLI)	1927-2021
안젤라 오키핀티(Angela OCCHIPINTI)	1938-
엔초 쿠키(Enzo CUCCHI)	1949-
윌리엄 제라(William XERRA)	1937-
잔니 베르티니(Gianni BERTINI)	1922-2010
정완규(Oan Kyu)	1953-
콘스탄티노 시에르보(Costantino CIERVO)	1961-
파비오 라탄치 안티노리(Fabio Lattanzi ANTINORI)	1971-
파올로 디 카푸아(Paolo di CAPUA)	1957-
패트릭 튜토푸오코(Patrick TUTTOFUOCO)	1974-
피에로 도라치오(Piero DORAZIO)	1927-2005

체코(Czech Republic)

아드리에나 시모토바(Adriena SIMOTOVA)	1926-2014
야로슬라프 베이체크(Jaroslav BEJCEK)	1926-1986

크로아티아(Croatia)

마트코 트레보티치(Matko TREBOTIC)	1935-
시메 불라스(Sime VULAS)	1932-2018
에도 무르티치(Edo MURTIC)	1921-2005
페르디낭 쿨머(Ferdinand KULMER)	1925-1998

키프로스(Cyprus)

마이클 마이클리디스(Michael MICHAELEDES)	1923-2015

포르투갈(Portugal)

아우구스토 바로스(Augusto BARROS)	1929-1998

폴란드(Poland)

레온 타라세비치(Leon TARASEWICZ)	1957-
마그달레나 아바카노비치(Magdalena ABAKANOWICZ)	1930-2017
크지슈토프 보디츠코(Krzysztof WODICZKO)	1943-

프랑스(France)

기 바르돈(Guy BARDONE)	1927-2015
니콜라 물랭(Nicolars MOULIN)	1970-
니키 드 생팔(Niki De SAINT PHALLE)	1930-2002
로랑 그라소(Laurent GRASSO)	1972-
루이 토폴리(Louis TOFFOLI)	1907-1999
마디 드 라 지로디에르(Mady de La Giraudiere)	1922-2018
마르셀 뒤샹(Marcel DUCHAMP)	1887-1968
마르셀 케르벨라(Marcel KERVELLA)	1930-
마르셀 크라모아장(Marcel CRAMOYSAN)	1915-2007
마크 파브레스(Marc FAVRESSE)	1938-2004
마티유 메르시에(Mathieu MERCIER)	1970-
모리스 기리옹 그린(Maurice GHIGLION-GREEN)	1913-1989
발레리 블랭(Valerie BELIN)	1964-
베르나르 뷔페(Bernard BUFFET)	1928-1999
베르나르 브네(Bernar VENET)	1941-

베르나르 샤루아(Bernard CHAROY)	1931-	
베르나르 포콩(Bernard FAUCON)	1950-	
벤 보티에(Ben VAUTIER)	1935-	
빅토르 바사렐리(Victor VASARELY)	1906-1997	
빈센트 귀로(Vincent GUIRO)	1935-	
세르주 엘레농(Serge HELENON)	1934-	
세자르 발다치니(Cesar BALDACCINI)	1921-1998	
시몬 한타이(Simon HANTAI)	1922-2008	
시프리앙 가이야르(Cyprien GAILLARD)	1980-	
알랭 본느푸와(Alain BONNEFOIT)	1937-	
알베르 우다(Albert WODA)	1955-	
알베르 자바로(Albert ZAVARO)	1925-	
알베르토 구스만(Alberto GUZMAN)	1927-	
앙드레 브라질리에(Andre BRASILIER)	1929-	
에릭 보들레르(Eric BAUDELAIRE)	1973-	
오를랑(Orlan)	1947-	
올리비에 드브레(Olivier DEBRE)	1920-1999	
이방 르 보젝(Yvan LE BOZEC)	1958-	
이브 브라이에(Yves BRAYER)	1907-1990	
자비에르 베이앙(Xavier VEILHAN)	1963-	
자크 드페르트(Jacques DEPERTHES)	1936-	
장 뒤뷔페(Jean DUBUFFET)	1901-1985	
장 메사지에(Jean MESSAGIER)	1920-1999	
장 샤를 블레(Jean-Charles BLAIS)	1956-	
장 얀셈(Jean JANSEM)	1920-2013	
장 카르주(Jean CARZOU)	1907-2000	
장 피에르 레이노(Jean-Pierre RAYNAUD)	1939-	
장 피에르 팡스망(Jean-pierre PINCEMIN)	1944-2005	
장-밥티스트 발라디에(Jean-Baptiste VALADIE)	1933-	
장-클로드 퀼리시(Jean-Claude QUILICI)	1941-	
조르주 라포르트(Georges LAPORTE)	1926-2000	
질 고리티(Gilles GORRITI)	1939-	
질 아이요(Gilles AILLAUD)	1928-2005	
카데르 아티아(Kader ATTIA)	1970-	
카미유 일레르(Camille HILAIRE)	1916-2004	
카미유 피사로(Camille PISSARRO)	1830-1903	
콘스탄틴 제나키스(Constantin XENAKIS)	1931-2020	
크리스티앙 볼탕스키(Christian BOLTANSKI)	1944-2021	
클로드 모네(Claude MONET)	1840-1923	
클로드 바이스부흐(Claude WEISBUCH)	1927-2014	
클로드 비알라(Claude VIALLAT)	1936-	
테오 토비아스(Theo TOBIASSE)	1927-2012	
토니 그랑(Toni GRAND)	1935-2005	
폴 고갱(Paul GAUGUIN)	1848-1903	
폴 기라망(Paul GUIRAMAND)	1926-2007	
폴 레베이롤(Paul REBEYROLLE)	1926-2005	
폴 아이즈피리(Paul AIZPIRI)	1919-2016	
프랑수와 스탈리(Francois STAHLY)	1911-2006	
피에르 뷔라글리오(Pierre BURAGLIO)	1939-	
피에르 술라주(Pierre SOULAGES)	1919-	
피에르 오귀스트 르누아르(Pierre-Auguste RENOIR)	1841-1919	
피에르-이브 트레모아(Pierre-Yves TREMOIS)	1921-2020	
필리프 라메트(Philippe RAMETTE)	1961-	

핀란드(Finland)

에이샤-리사 아틸라(Eija-Liisa AHTILA)	1959-
유하나 블롬슈테트(Juhana BLOMSTEDT)	1937-2010

헝가리(Hungary)

라슬로 페헤르(Laszlo FEHER)	1953-
알렉산더 톨라이(Alexander TOLNAY)	1944-
야노스 베르(Janos BER)	1937-2021
이슈트반 허러스치(Istvan HARASZTY)	1934-
죄르지 요바노비치(Gyorgy JOVANOVICS)	1939-
케세뤼 일로너(KESERU Ilona)	1933-
헨체 타머스(HENCZE Tamas)	1939-2018

MMCA 국제미술 소장품 기획전
《미술로, 세계로》

Highlights of MMCA Global Art Collection from the 1980s–1990s:
To the World through Art

발행일
2022년 1월 20일

발행처 국립현대미술관
(28501) 충청북도 청주시 청원구 상당로 314
Tel. 043-261-1400
www.mmca.go.kr

가격 32,000원
ISBN 978-89-6303-302-0 (93600)

ⓒ2022 국립현대미술관
이 책에 수록된 작품 이미지 및 글의 저작권은
국립현대미술관, 작가, 저자 및 저작권 소유자에
있습니다. 저작권법에 의해 보호를 받는 저작물이므로
무단 전재, 복제, 변형, 송신을 금합니다.

Date
January 20, 2022

Published by National Museum of Modern
and Contemporary Art, Korea
(28501) 314 Sangdang-ro, Cheongwon-gu,
Cheongju-si, Chungcheongbuk-do, Koreal
Tel. +82-43-261-1400
www.mmca.go.kr

Price 32,000 KRW
ISBN 978-89-6303-302-0 (93600)

ⓒ2022 National Museum of Modern
and Contemporary Art, Korea
All rights reserved. No part of this publication
can be reproduces in any manner without
permission in writing from the each copyright
holder: MMCA, the artist, respective authors
and other copyright holders.

발행인
윤범모

기획·편집
이효진

공동 편집
장래주

편집 보조
허동희

글
양은희, 오광수, 이효진,
정은영, 한승혜, 르네 블록

번역
김재현, 김지원, 박기덕, 박기현, 손유진,
제니스정

사진
김진현, 이현무

디자인
황석원, 전용완

인쇄
인타임

제작 진행
국립현대미술관 문화재단

Publisher
Youn Bummo

Editor
Lee Hyojin

Co-editor
Jang Raejoo

Editorial Assistant
Huh Donghee

Text by
Yang Eunhee, Oh Gwangsoo, Lee Hyojin,
Jung Eun Young, Han Seunghye, René Block

Translation
Jae Ted Kim, Ji Won Grace Kim, K. G. Brown,
Camille K. H. Park, Eugene Son, Jannice Y Chung

Photography
Kim Jinhyun, Lee Hyunmoo

Design
Hwang Seogwon, Jeon Yongwan

Printing
Intime

Published in association with
National Museum of Modern and Contemporary Art
Foundation, Korea

국립현대미술관
National Museum of
Modern and Contemporary Art, Korea